Seashore Life of Southern California

REVISED EDITION

California Natural History Guides: 26

Seashore Life of Southern California

An Introduction to the Animal Life
of California Beaches South of
Santa Barbara

REVISED EDITION

Sam Hinton

Illustrated by the Author

UNIVERSITY OF CALIFORNIA PRESS
Berkeley   Los Angeles   London

University of California Press
Berkeley and Los Angeles, California
University of California Press, Ltd.
London, England

Library of Congress Cataloging-in-Publication Data
Hinton, Sam, 1917–
    Seashore life of southern California.
    (California natural history guides ; 26)
    Bibliography: p.
    Includes index.
    1. Seashore biology—California, Southern.
2. Seashore biology—California—Pacific Coast.
I. Title.   II. Series.
QH105.C2H56   1987   591.9794′9   87-5861
ISBN 0-520-05923-9
ISBN 0-520-05924-7 (pbk.)

Printed in the United States of America
1 2 3 4 5 6 7 8 9

This is for Leslie, with endless gratitude, admiration—and love.

Contents

Preface

The dry land is one world and the wet sea is another, but the line separating them is never the same from one moment to the next. The boundaries change with every spent wave; with every rise and fall of the tide, the ocean surrenders or repossesses some of its realm. And the very sands of the beach move with the seasons, so that in some summers we may walk the beach with our feet higher than our heads would have been a few months earlier.

The dividing line between the sea and the land, then, is not really a line at all; it is an area, a zone, a dominion in its own right. Partaking in some measure of both land and water, it belongs wholly to neither. Because its upper and lower limits are defined by the extremes of the tides, we speak of it as the *intertidal zone,* or sometimes as the *littoral.* This book is an introduction to some of the features of this zone and its contiguous waters and to a selected few of the countless creatures who make it their home.

There are many reasons for becoming familiar with the marvels of the intertidal zone. The most important one is, of course, that it is fun. Human beings have probably always shared our feelings of exhilaration and wonder at the sights, sounds, and smells of the seashore. Another reason stems from the fact that the sea as a whole is so vast as to be almost beyond our comprehension. By focusing our attention down to the scale of a small part of the littoral or a tiny tidepool, however, we can gain an inkling of some of the attributes and processes of the world ocean—factors of the utmost importance to the continuance of the human race.

The aim of this book is to provide a sort of beach-walker's guide, giving a general picture—with a few added details—of the Southern California shore and its abundant life. I have not even attempted to approach completeness; fewer than 300 species are presented here, and for each of these there are probably, at a conservative estimate, a hundred others not mentioned. I hope that some readers will be led to seek further information, and to this end a list of selected references will be found at the end of the book.

It is not possible to list all the individuals who have shared with me their knowledge and their enthusiasms, but some must be mentioned with special gratitude: Walter Penn Taylor, who showed me how to observe and remember; Martin W. Johnson, who, at UCLA in 1939, introduced me to the glories of the seashore; Harald U. Sverdrup, who bravely took me on as Curator of the Aquarium-Museum of the Scripps Institution of Oceanography; Carl L. Hubbs, who taught me what I know about fishes and provided the role model of an energetic scientist whose delight in his work never flagged; Joel W. Hedgpeth, who generously shared his encyclopedic knowledge of invertebrates and the voluminous literature concerning them; and, most of all, my wife Leslie, whose wise counsel and quiet support have made possible whatever I have done— and made it all worth doing.

Sam Hinton
La Jolla, California

1 · THE SEA

Not long after my mother moved to Los Angeles, an old friend from Oklahoma came to visit. This friend had never seen the ocean, so Mom drove her to Pt. Vicente on the Palos Verdes peninsula, where she could stand at the top of the cliff and gaze out over the Pacific Ocean, from the breakers on the rocks below to the limits of a horizon surrounding her in an arc of almost 180 degrees. The visitor gazed for a few minutes, then came up with a judgment that became a byword in our family: "Well," she said, "It's not as big as I expected!"

We've never been able to figure out just what she was expecting, but as far as I know her reaction was unique. Most people are deeply impressed by the vastness of even that small portion of the sea that can be taken in by the human eye. And rightly so, for the sea is by far the largest surface feature of the Earth.

And note that we can say "the sea" as if there were in fact only one sea, which is, in a sense, true. The precise boundaries between the Arctic Ocean and the Atlantic, between the Pacific and Indian Oceans, and so on are arbitrary, and no matter how we name the oceans and seas, they all share the same water.

This vast sheet of water is not very deep when compared to the diameter of the whole Earth, forming a relatively thin skin of moisture. In relation to human perception, however, and to the habitats of many of the ocean's myriad life forms, it is deep indeed. The average depth is something on the order of 3,600 m (12,000 ft.), and no part of it is, solely by virtue of its depth,

1

without life. The volume of living space in the sea is many times greater than that on land and contains many different kinds of habitats. By far the greatest volume is taken up by the deep-sea habitats, which are almost unimaginably different from our usual ideas about places to live. Conditions there include a constant temperature close to the freezing point, pressure many times greater than that at the surface, and a total lack of light except for that produced by bioluminescent life forms.

The habitat that is the subject of this book—the intertidal zone—is relatively small but tremendously rich in the number of species living there and in the number of individuals of most of these species.

In spite of all these varied habitats, sea water is itself remarkably homogeneous, with features that affect life everywhere on Earth. For one thing, all water has the unusual quality of expanding just as it reaches the freezing point—a quality not shared by other earthly materials. Because of this, ice floats at the surface of the water; if it did not, it would sink to the bottom never to melt, and all the seas would eventually be solid ice.

Another physical feature of water is its high heat capacity. This means that it takes a lot of energy to raise its temperature, and once the temperature is raised, water holds its heat longer than any other substance. Thus ocean water warmed or cooled in one part of the world may be transported by currents over great distances, maintaining in a large degree whatever temperature it started with and having a profound effect upon the climates of our world.

The Chemistry of Sea Water

The waters of the sea, together with the waters of lakes and rivers, are part of a vast, constantly repeated process called the *hydrologic cycle*. In this process, water passes into the atmosphere as vapor then falls as rain, snow, or dew somewhere on the Earth. Eventually nearly all of this water—even if it falls on the land—returns to the sea. During its downhill seaward journey, the water picks up a load of substances dissolved from the soil and rock over which it flows. Water may seem to us the gentlest and blandest of liquids, but in reality it is the most corrosive substance on Earth, dissolving more different materials, and in greater quantity, than any other liquid. Its chemical cargo is carried to the sea and left there when the water re-evaporates once more to continue the hydrologic cycle. It is not surprising, therefore, that sea water is an extremely complex mixture, which has been aptly characterized as a "dilute solution of practically everything."

What *is* surprising is that the salts that make up the major constituents of sea water vary within quite narrow limits in total quantity and vary hardly at all in their relative proportions. The total quantities of these salts range in the open sea from about 34 to 36 parts per thousand (3.4 to 3.6 percent), but their relative proportions remain constant. The following table shows these proportions in parts per thousand parts of sea water whose total salinity is 35 parts per thousand:

Substance	*Parts per thousand*
Chlorine	19.32
Sodium	10.72
Sulphate ion	2.70
Magnesium	1.32
Calcium	0.42
Potassium	0.38
Bromine	0.07
Carbonate ion	0.07
Total:	35.00

These ratios are so constant that the chemical oceanographer need measure only the amount of chlorine (which is expressed as the chlorinity of the sea water) in order to ascertain accurately the total salinity of a sample.

This equilibrium is especially surprising when we remember that new salts are continually being brought to the sea in runoff from the land, that the proportions of salts in rivers are very different from those in the ocean, and that salts remain in the sea when water is evaporated. River water is not, of course, anywhere near as salty as sea water, but it does contain salts. If we were to analyze a given weight of river salt, we would find that carbonates constituted about 60 percent of its weight, while carbonates make up less than 0.3 percent of the weight of sea salt.

One might expect that this constant addition of different mixtures would cause the ocean water to change the proportions of its salty constituents and become saltier and saltier as time goes by. But sea water seems to remain in a steady state, which is partly accounted for by the abundant life processes constantly taking place within it. Further conditioning is provided by underwater volcanic activity, which recent research has shown to be much more prevalent than was formerly supposed.

Unlike salts, gases dissolved in the sea are subject to considerable variation, with important consequences for plant and animal life. Oxygen content, for example, may vary from zero, as at the bottoms of certain fjords, to far above the average 8.5 parts per thousand. Carbon dioxide, necessary to plant growth, also has a wide quantitative range, but is always many times more abundant than in air. There is a constant interchange of carbon dioxide between air and water, with atmospheric quantities stabilized by the tremendous reservoir of the sea. This stability is of great importance to the climate of the whole world, as small changes in atmospheric carbon dioxide can result in large changes in ground-level temperature.

Many other types of chemicals are important to life in the sea, even though they may occur only as *trace elements,* in very small quantities. Living things, both plants and animals, can extract and store certain of these trace elements with remarkable efficiency. Some tunicates (sea squirts) do this with vanadium; molluscs concentrate copper; radiolarians, strontium; and jellyfishes, tin, lead, and zinc. Iodine, in many seaweeds, is built up in a concentration several orders of magnitude greater than its concentration in sea water. Sometimes it is relatively easy to remove such substances from the tissues of these living things (as in the commercial extraction of iodine from kelp) when it is neither feasible nor profitable to extract them directly from sea water.

Complex molecules based on various combinations of carbon, oxygen, and hydrogen are known as *organic* compounds, and they are the stuff of which living tissue is made. Such molecules, in the form of suspended organic matter, are fairly abundant in most parts of the sea and are necessary to the growth of marine plants. Phosphates and nitrates—the "fertilizers"—occur in widely varying quantities, and their relative abundance is one of the chief factors determining the distribution of plants. Abundant sea life is found only where there is an adequate supply of these materials and where a cycling process returns them to the water for further use. The whole process of life in the sea (or anywhere else) may be viewed as a cycling and recycling of these trace elements to distribute a finite amount of energy among the living things that use it.

The Cycle of Life in the Sea

Living comprises a set of processes that require energy, and practically all of this life energy comes from the Sun. Animals, however, have no way of using the Sun's energy directly, so they must obtain it secondhand by eating plants. Plants use solar energy to power the wonderful process of *photosynthesis,* by means of which certain elements are combined to make organic compounds. A surplus of energy is stored in these compounds—energy that is passed on to animals that eat the plants, or eat other animals that have eaten plants, and so on through many *trophic levels.*

A fascinating and unanticipated type of community that is not based on solar energy has recently been discovered. These seafloor communities were first found living in the deep-water "hot spots" surrounding volcanic vents such as those at the edges of tectonic plates. More recently, similar aggregations have been found at saline and oil-methane seeps. Their gigantic red-tipped beardworms and other creatures, found nowhere else on Earth, base their food cycle on bacteria that exist by means of chemosynthesis rather than photosynthesis. They are therefore independent of the Sun; this is not, however, the case with our more familiar marine communities.

Take an intertidal mussel bed (Pl. 17) as an example. Here the Sun's energy is supplied to the community through floating planktonic plant and animal life, plants growing within the community, and water-suspended particles of detrital organic matter. The mussels themselves feed by passing water over their gills and straining out edible material. The many little creatures that find shelter among the firmly attached mussels feed on plankton, detritus, or the encrusting mat of algae growing on rocks and shells. This biota contains numerous scavengers, which feed on locally produced waste material or solid detritus swept in from the sea and settling among the mussels; the settling is facilitated by eddies created as the water swirls past the shells. Still another factor in such a community is a population of predators feeding on other animals and thus exerting a measure of control over the ultimate size of the population.

Eventually every animal or plant must die, and the elemental organic matter of its tissues is returned to the sea. This return is due to the work of bacteria that decompose dead bodies or waste products from living ones. Thus, the all-important fertilizer trace elements are returned to the water for further use. The roles of bacteria throughout this cycle are extremely important. They facilitate the *food web* at every level and are directly used as food by many animals.

Most marine communities are open systems, in which part of the cycle occurs outside of the community itself. In our mussel bed, the energy-bearing plankton may have drifted in from afar, and dead animals and plants may be washed away before they decompose. But somewhere in the sea the circle is closed and the chain continues. Any creature of the sea or shore is not so much an entity in itself as it is a minute portion of a continuous worldwide process.

Sea, Swell, and Surf

Next to the water itself, waves constitute the most obvious aspect of the seashore environment. They are very important to the flora and fauna of the intertidal zone, the power of their breakers playing a large part in determining where life is possible for various species. Ricketts and Calvin, in the epoch-marking first edition of *Between Pacific Tides,* used wave force as a major criterion in defining different intertidal communities. They used the terms "protected outer coast," "open

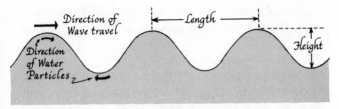

FIG. 1 Some distinguishing features of ocean waves. The vertical scale is greatly exaggerated.

coast," and "bay and estuary" (where high waves are almost unknown) as primary divisions (see Chapter 2).

Ocean waves are born in storms and travel from storm areas to the far shores of the sea. Waves breaking on Southern California shores may have traveled halfway round the globe, or they may come from nearby storms.

In the open sea, waves differ from one another in height (the vertical distance from trough to crest) and in length (the distance from one crest to the next crest, or from trough to trough.) They differ also in the speed at which they travel; this, however, is entirely a function of their length in relation to Earth's constant acceleration of gravity. A wave of a certain length can travel only at a certain speed. The longer the wave, the faster it travels. Another term often used is *wave period,* which is the time interval between successive waves; this too is controlled entirely by the length and speed. Some of these parameters are shown in Fig. 1.

Where the waves originate in a storm area, the sea surface is confused and the waves have no regular pattern. The term *sea* is used to describe this situation: some of the waves are high, some are low, and they seem to be coming from every direction.

Waves of many lengths are being produced in all this confusion, and these travel away from the storm, each wave moving at a fixed speed determined by its length and the unvarying constant of gravity. As they move away they begin sorting themselves out, the faster-moving longer waves outdistancing the slower-moving shorter ones; also, shorter waves contain less energy and therefore die out sooner. At some distance from the storm, then, the sea surface will show a regular procession of waves, collectively known as *swell*. It is in this form that the waves finally arrive at some shore.

If all the oceans were calm except for one storm somewhere, this distant pattern would be even more regular. However, we are always seeing waves from a number of sources, so the swell has a certain irregularity. Each train of waves is superimposed on other trains. When two or more crests coincide, the swell at that moment is high; conversely, when the crest of one train coincides with the trough of another, the swell at that moment is low. The periods of these wave trains do not match, so it is only occasionally that coinciding crests will produce an unusually high breaker.

An unimpeded wave moving across the open sea does not carry the water with it. The water particles move in vertical circles, going forward at the crest of a wave and backward (against the direction in which the wave is traveling) in the trough (see Fig. 1.) For water particles at the surface, the diameter of the described circle is equal to the wave height; deeper particles move in smaller circles until, at a depth of about seven times the wave length, there is virtually no motion at all. Where the water is much less than seven wave lengths deep, the circular motion of the water particles is interfered with and the wave is said to "feel the bottom." At that point it begins to behave differently: it slows down; its length decreases, bringing successive crests closer together; and it becomes steeper and taller until its top finally topples forward. The wave has then become what we call a *breaker,* and breaking waves are collectively known as *surf.* Breakers usually begin to form where the water is about one and a half times as deep as the wave is high, although where there is a bottom with a pronounced break or where there is a strong wind blowing toward the shore, breaking may occur where the water is twice the wave height.

Surfers are well aware that waves come in "sets," and much of their time in the water is spent letting the lower waves go by as they wait to catch the big ones of the series. Fishermen too make use of this, only in reverse—waiting for the low part of the series before putting their skiffs out through the surf. Various tales are told of the magic numbers by which wave height may be predicted. Some say that every seventh wave is a big one, while others insist that it is the ninth. The latter may also say that the ninth ninth is one well worth waiting for!

There is, of course, no wave cycle that consistently coincides with such numbers, but like many traditional beliefs, this one is founded on a core of truth—the fact that waves reach the shore in high groups and low groups. From a statistical point of view, over a long period of time the chances are that one wave in every 25 will be twice as high as the average during that period, while one in every 1,175 will be three times the average.

Some characteristics of waves are easy to observe from the shore, and this accessible information allows us to infer other characteristics that cannot be seen so readily. For example, we can easily measure the period of a particular wave train—the time in seconds between successive crests—and from this we can calculate the length and velocity of the waves as they were before they reached shallow water. The velocity of a wave in deep water is determined only by its length and by the unchanging constant of the acceleration of gravity on this planet; that is, a wave of a certain length can travel, in deep water, at only a certain speed. Its period, which is the measure of the time it takes the wave to pass a given point, is simply a function of this velocity. As we have seen, when a wave moves into shallow water, its velocity and length are diminished, but the period remains the same. So, if we measure a period as 7 seconds, this tells us that the wave had a length of 245 ft. and an open sea velocity of 21 knots (a little over 24 miles per hour.) This is because these relationships are constant and can be expressed by simple formulae. The velocity in knots is always three times the period in seconds ($V = 3T$, where V is the velocity and T is the period); and wave length in feet is always five times the period squared ($L = 5T^2$, where L is the wavelength and T is again the period).

Still more information may be gained if you can estimate the height of a wave, although an accurate measurement is hard to come by. The easiest way is to observe the waves

SEASON	HEIGHT	PERIOD	SOURCE
Spring	9 to 14 ft.	5 to 7 sec.	Local storms
Summer	3 to 6 ft.	6 to 9 sec.	Winds surrounding a high-pressure area to the west.
Summer	6 to 9 ft.	13 to 20 sec.	Storms in the "Roaring 40's", 40° south of the Equator.
Winter	5 to 12 ft.	7 to 10 sec.	Storm fronts approaching from the west.

FIG. 2 Sources of waves on Southern California shores as determined by their heights and periods.

against a pier piling beyond the breakers and estimate the distance between the highest and lowest points the waves reach as they pass. Physical oceanographers have been able to back-track wave trains so as to discover where they came from and have found that these sources may often be identified by using only the height and period of a wave plus the season of the year. Fig. 2 shows where certain waves originated before setting out for the Southern California shore.

Unlike the water in a wave moving across the open sea, the water in a breaker actually does move with the wave. As a result, water literally piles up on the beach. During a heavy surf, the water level right next to the beach may be several feet higher than out beyond the breakers. This water cannot remain there, of course, and must flow out to sea again. This it may do as a *rip current,* also known as a *riptide,* although it has nothing to do with the tides. Rip currents are narrow streams of water flowing rapidly seaward, and they constitute a serious danger to inexperienced bathers. At times the flow is strong enough to scour out a channel in the beach sand, so that someone wading in the shallow water may suddenly step into the deeper water of such a channel and be swept seaward.

If you should ever be caught in a rip current, it is quite easy to escape—if you don't panic and do know how to swim. Just swim at right angles to the current, parallel to the shore, and you will soon be out of it and free to turn again toward the beach.

Many beach bathers are afraid of what they call *undertow,*

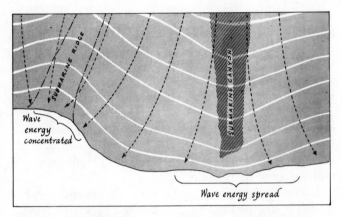

FIG. 3 Breaker height (wave energy) as affected by offshore submarine topography.

a term that connotes a strong current running seaward along the bottom, said to pull swimmers under water as it carries them away from the shore. It is not certain, however, that there is any such thing as undertow. Certainly as you wade you can feel a current pulling your feet toward the open sea, but if you'll wait just a moment or two, until the next wave, you'll feel the pull in the opposite direction. Less than 1 percent of the piled-up beach water flows back along the bottom, and undertow is mainly imaginary.

The fact that passing into shallow water causes a wave to move more slowly gives rise to all sorts of phenomena related to *refraction* (Pl. 4). For instance, when a wave approaches a shore at an angle, the portion of the wave first feeling the bottom is slowed; this swings the wave around until its crest is more nearly parallel to the shore at that point.

Where a submarine ridge extends out from the shore, the portion of the wave that overlies the ridge travels more slowly than the parts on either side, and this causes a focusing of wave energy at the landward end of the submerged ridge (see Fig. 3). Such ridges are often marked by a *headland* projecting from the shore, and seafaring people for thousands of years have wisely steered clear of such headlands, saying "headlands draw the waves."

Conversely, a marked indentation in the shore line or a submarine canyon at right angles to the shore will spread the wave energy, so that the surf at that point on the shore is lower than it is elsewhere in the vicinity (see Fig. 3). Again, seafarers are aware of this and traditionally select such locations from which to launch their skiffs through the surf.

The refractive power of the beach slope is not always enough to turn waves completely parallel to the shore, and some waves—especially those of shorter period—thus arrive at an angle. This is an important factor in the formation and maintenance of sandy beaches.

Waves of a short period are the most effective ones in moving beach sand, and most such waves in Southern California come in from the northwest. Being short, they are not as quickly affected by decreasing water depth as longer waves and strike the beach at a considerable angle. This helps set up local *longshore currents* moving south along the shore. There are temporary and limited areas of northward flow, but the net movement is southerly. The sand stirred up by these breaking waves is therefore carried toward the south.

During the winter, when appropriately short waves are coming in from the frequent northwesterly storms, which are close at hand, a lot of sand is removed from the beach to form low bars well offshore. Later, the longer waves of summer carry the sand to shore again and leave it there—but at a point considerably south of where it had been before. In some places the seasonal rise and fall of the beach sand may be more than 2 m (6 ft.), although this doesn't happen every year. (See Pls. 6 and 7.)

This southward movement is interrupted by several processes: it may be caught on the up-current side of a headland, it may be blown inland as sand dunes (which do not occur extensively in Southern California), or it may drop off into a submarine canyon. The latter process is the most common one here, and it has been estimated that, every year, more than a million cubic yards of sand are lost into submarine canyons between Oxnard and Newport Beach. Because of this, beaches on the south sides of submarine canyons in California are usually narrower than on the north.

This process of sand moving southward for some distance, then being lost in a manner that permanently removes it from the beach, takes place in a series of cells all along the coast. A great deal of the sand on our California beaches is from rivers, and the damming of these rivers causes sand to be caught above the dams rather than flowing to the ocean. Marine geologists are seriously worried about whether there will be enough sand to maintain our beaches as damming continues. The beaches would already be in more trouble than they are if it were not for the extensive dredging that has been done in building marinas, such as the one at Playa Del Rey in Los Angeles County. Sand from these operations has been added to the beaches, but this supply is ending, and the future of our beaches is uncertain.

Another interruption to the flow of sand occurs where a rip-rap or other solid artificial structure extends out at right angles to the shore. This causes the sand to build out along the northern sides of such structures, while beaches on the south sides may be denuded of their sand. Also, breakwaters built in the form of narrow islands parallel to the shore reduce the force of waves striking the beach, and less sand is scoured out. The beach line then has a tendency to bend outward toward the breakwater, and several such structures—intended to provide a safe anchorage for small boats—have ended up as peninsula tips rather than islands.

Ocean Currents

In addition to the small longshore currents and rip currents already discussed, there are ocean currents of far greater magnitude, and these are extremely important as controllers of climate and distributors of marine organisms. These currents result from the combined effects of the major atmospheric wind patterns, differential heating of the oceans in different latitudes, the presence of interruptive continents, and the rotation of the Earth. Off our coast, the most important current of this sort is the California Current, a cold mass of water some 645 km (400 mi.) wide, flowing southward at .3 to 1 km (0.2 to 0.6 mi.) per hour. Many ocean currents are larger than this one; the Gulf Stream of the Atlantic, for example, moves ten times as much water. Nevertheless, our little California Current has a quite respectable flow—carrying more than 200 times as much as the Mississippi River, or about three times as much as all Earth's rivers combined!

Some people call our main current the Japanese Current, but this is incorrect. The Japanese Current, or Kuroshio, is a warm current flowing northward on the western side of the Pacific, while the California current is a cold one and flows southward on the eastern side. Its temperature averages 2° C cooler than the surrounding water, which has a profound tempering effect on the Pacific Coast climate.

Between the shore and the near edge of the California Current there is a zone of complex and variable water movements. During the winter, for instance, this area often has a north-flowing current with a speed of up to 2.4 km (1¹/₂ mi.) per hour. At other times there is a vast eddy, often more than 160 km (100 mi.) across, rotating counterclockwise at a rate of one revolution in 20 to 40 days. Factors such as these have a direct bearing upon the distribution of such creatures as sardines, whose floating eggs are completely at the mercy of the currents.

In any movement of a large mass, such as the water in a current, the rotation of the Earth imparts what appears to be a deflective force to the right. (In the southern hemisphere it is to the left.) This is called the *Coriolis force*. In our main southbound California Current, the Coriolis force accounts for an element of movement tending away from the shore, toward the west. As surface water veers away from the shore, it is replaced by water welling up from below; close to shore, therefore, there is often an *upwelling* of cold bottom water. This is particularly obvious to the swimmer during some of the Santa Ana periods, when a hot, dry wind blows from the east and intensifies the surface flow away from the shore.

This upwelling has a number of effects. For one thing, the deep cold water is rich in the nutrients demanded by plants, and the sea off Southern California is characterized by an abundance of plants—both stationary seaweeds and microscopic planktonic forms. This floral abundance leads to a corresponding abundance of animal life, since plants are the basic energy source for all animals. The major fisheries of the temperate zone are located where upwelling is a common feature.

The colder water near the shore has another effect, this one on our weather and climate. It often happens, especially in winter, that a mass of warm, dry air moves out from the land and comes to rest several miles out to sea. The lower part of such an air column is cooled by contact with the water, and at the same time it soaks up moisture. Both of these activities increase the density of the lower air and help to form a stable inversion. This stability allows the process to continue until the air next to the water is almost as cool as the water and has soaked up all the moisture it can contain at that temperature. Finally, when sea breezes start up again and move this air toward the land, it meets the zone of colder water near shore and its temperature is lowered still further. Colder air cannot hold as much moisture as warmer air, so now the air mass holds more water than it can retain, and the excess is precipitated in the form of fog. This is the occasion of the majestic vertical walls of fog that move onto the coast on so many winter afternoons. These advancing fog banks are among the more spectacular of natural wonders and can only be described as beautiful.

The Tides

The slow rise and fall of the sea, in a complex but predictable pattern, has long appealed to the human imagination. The tidal rhythm has been explained as the result of the regular breathing of some tremendous and unknowable sea monster, or as the breathing of the living sea itself. The true explanation is perhaps even more romantic: the tides are brought about by the influence of the Sun and Moon.

Every object in the universe has a gravitational field directed toward the object's center. This field, or gravitational attraction, becomes weaker as distance from the object increases, but does not disappear completely. It can therefore be said that every object in the universe exerts a gravitational pull on every other object, the magnitude of the attraction depending on the masses of the objects and the distances between them. Our Solar System is an assemblage of such mutually attracted bodies, held together by the force of gravity, but prevented from falling into each other by the centrifugal effects of their respective orbits around the Sun. The Earth is thus prevented from flying off into space by the interaction of its gravity field with that of the Sun, while the centrifugal effect of its orbital motion keeps it and the Sun from falling together. In the same way, the relative positions of the Earth and its Moon represent a balance of these two forces.

Throughout the Earth-Moon system as a whole these effects are exactly in balance, but local variations allow one or the other of them to be felt more strongly in a given place at a given time. Three heavenly bodies—Earth, Sun, and Moon—control the tides of the Earth's seas, and many variables affect the strength of their gravitational interactions. For one thing, their respective orbits are elliptical, so the distances among them undergo constant changes. Also, the three bodies are constantly changing in their angular relations, at some times arranged in a straight line and at other times forming the points of a triangle. Still another variation arises from the fact that the surface of the Earth, where the sea lies, is some 4,000 miles closer to the Moon than is the Earth's center, toward which Earth's gravity is directed.

We must remember that it is not correct to think of the Earth as stationary while the Moon orbits around it; they actually revolve around a common center. If the two bodies were of equal mass, that common center would lie halfway between them. As it is, the Earth is many times the more massive, and the common center lies 1,000 miles beneath its surface, or 3,000 miles from its actual center (see Fig. 4). So the motion of the Earth-Moon system is around this center of orbital motion. (It should be pointed out that this has nothing to do with the day-night turning of the Earth upon its own central axis of rotation.)

The results of this motion were summed up, with apologies to Christina Rossetti, by Walter Knight, physicist and at that time Dean of the College of Letters and Science at the Berkeley campus of the University of California:

> Who has weighed the moon?
> Neither you nor I;
> But the solid earth is wobbling
> As the moon goes tumbling by.

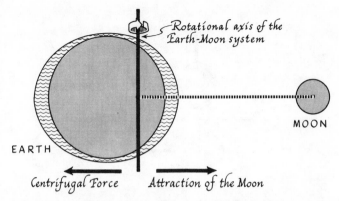

FIG. 4 Tide-producing balance of forces in the Earth-Moon system.

This Earth-wobble is of great importance to the variations in the tide-producing forces. At a point directly under the Moon, the Moon's gravitational attraction is felt more strongly than the centrifugal force; at the point on the opposite side of the Earth, the reverse is true, and the centrifugal force is the stronger. In both places, the basic result is the same: an element of the balanced system is directed outward, away from the Earth's center. This outward force is only one nine-millionth as great as the Earth's gravity, but it is nevertheless enough to cause the water to bulge out at these two points, creating two zones of high tide on opposite sides of the globe.

Between the two high tide points there is a band where low tides prevail, from which the water has in a sense been pulled to create the high tide bulge. This distribution may be considered, in a simplistic way, as an envelope within which the Earth rotates on its axis. Thus any given spot on the Earth will pass through two high tide points and two low tide zones with every complete rotation. This timing is complicated by the fact that the Moon is moving in its orbit in the same direction as the Earth's rotation, and the tidal bulge follows the Moon. Therefore, when a spot on the Earth has made a 24-hour revolution, the Moon and the tidal bulge have progressed a little, and it takes that given spot about 50 minutes to catch up. So in each period of about 24 hours and 50 minutes, there are two high tides and two low tides. The time from one high

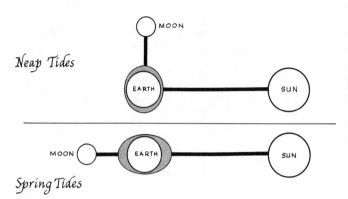

FIG. 5 Spatial arrangements of Earth, Sun, and Moon at neap tides and spring tides. The point of view is directly above one of the Earth's poles.

tide to the next (or from low to low) is around 12 hours and 25 minutes.

The Sun creates tides of its own in our seas, although these are much smaller than those of the Moon. This difference occurs because, although the Sun's gravitational attraction is much greater than the Moon's, it is more nearly equal on every part of the Earth's surface; it is the differing strengths of attraction that create the tides. So the most visible effect of the Sun's tide-producing force is an augmentation or diminution of the Moon's effect. When the Sun-tide coincides with the Moon-tide, their respective high tide bulges are "piled up" on one another, and the high tides are greater than usual. At the same time, the low-tide zones also coincide, and the low tides are lower. So, when the Earth, Moon, and Sun all lie in an approximately straight line and are thus working together, the difference between high and low tides is greatest; that is, the *tidal range* is increased. But when the high tide bulge of the Sun coincides with the low area of the Moon-tide, the total range is decreased, and the difference between the height of the low and high tides is not as marked (see Fig. 5).

By observing the Moon's phases, it is easy to tell whether Sun and Moon are working together or opposing one another. When the three bodies are more or less effectively lined up, we

The Tides / 19

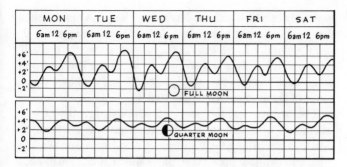

FIG. 6 Six summer days during a typical spring tide series (upper) and a typical neap tide series (lower). Note that the low low tides of summer occur in the very early morning; in winter, they are in the afternoon.

have either a new Moon or a full Moon, and the tide-producing forces are working together. At these times the high tides are higher than usual and the low tides lower, and we speak of the *spring tides*—referring not to a season of the year but to a word in Old English meaning, among other things, "to grow or swell."

When the Moon is in its quarters—when we see it as a half Moon—the three heavenly bodies are not in line, but form a triangle, and the separate effects of the Sun and Moon partially cancel one another. That is, the low tide of one is reducing the high tide of the other, so the high tides are not very high, and the lows not very low. These are *neap tides*. This word too is from an Old English root meaning "scarce." (See Fig. 6.)

Tides are strongly affected by the phenomenon of resonance. Every mass of water has its own natural period of oscillation, and even in the open sea the water has a tendency to divide itself into various complex bodies, each body wanting to vibrate at its own rate. This propensity is emphasized in partially enclosed bodies of water. If the natural oscillatory period of such a body coincides with the rhythmically repeated gravitational pull of the Sun or Moon, the oscillation will be magnified. The water in the Bay of Fundy, for example, is of a volume and shape that give it a natural oscillatory period that is in phase with the periodic attraction of the Sun; the result is that the tides there may rise and fall more than 18 m (60 ft.), with only one high and one low tide each day. A similar situation is found at the head of the Gulf of California, where the one daily high may be 7 m (23 ft.) or more above the one daily low—and this only a few score miles from the Pacific Coast, where each day sees two highs and two lows, with a maximum range of rarely more than 3 m (10 ft.).

The astronomical factors of gravitational attraction plus local factors of resonance and reflection give us our complex tidal picture. Along the California Coast, there are two high tides and two low tides every day—although there will occasionally be only three tides in a calendar day, with the fourth coming just after midnight. (This, as we have seen, is due to the tidal day's being longer than 24 hours.) One of these highs is usually quite a bit higher than the other, and one of the lows is lower. Thus we have "higher high water," "lower high water," "higher low water," and "lower low water."

To provide a frame of reference for mariners who must maneuver their vessels into and out of shallow harbors, an arbitrary sea level known as *tide zero* has been selected. On this coast, it developed that the most useful place for zero was at *mean lower low water;* that is, all of the lower low tides over a long period of time are averaged and their mean level is designated tide zero. On the Atlantic coast of North America, both of the daily lows are at about the same level, and zero there is the mean of *all* the low waters. On both coasts, tide heights are always expressed as so many feet and tenths of feet above or below zero.

The observer of tidepool life waits for those tides that are expressed as being "below zero." These *minus tides* expose parts of the shore that are usually covered with water and provide a fine opportunity to observe seashore inhabitants that are inaccessible at other times. In Southern California the tide situation is such that the minus tides of midwinter occur in the middle of the afternoon, while those of midsummer come in the wee hours before dawn. This makes a great deal of difference in planning field trips!

The heights and times of the tides are predictable, but the schedule is different in every locality. Daily and weekly local predictions are given in the newspapers of most seacoast towns. Tide booklets for the entire year may often be obtained without cost from marine hardware stores, shops selling fishing equipment, and service stations that cater to the boat trade. Bookstores have for the last several years been stocking excellent annual tide calendars showing the tidal picture for every day of the year in graphic form. These are available for a number of Pacific and Atlantic locations. (See, for example, Tidelines, Inc., for the current year.) All of these predictions are taken from tide tables published annually by the National Oceanic and Atmospheric Administration (NOAA) of the U.S. Department of Commerce. These tables may be purchased from agencies dealing in government publications; the useful one in our area is that for the West Coast of North and South America. It not only shows the tide picture for all major reference localities, but also gives correction factors for the spots in between.

2 · THE INTERTIDAL ZONE

The Intertidal Zone As a Habitat

The narrow zone between the normal limits of the tide, following thousands of miles of convoluted coastline, is one of the Earth's most densely populated areas. The millions of creatures living there have had to solve a number of problems in order to survive in a place that is neither sea nor land and is never quite the same from one moment to the next.

Numerous factors affect where a particular organism can live. Biologists, in an effort to understand the complexities of zoological and botanical distribution, have developed several systems of classifying intertidal environments. The following list shows some of these classifications according to different parameters. Most of this information is adapted from a book that is basic to an understanding of the Pacific Coast littoral: *Between Pacific Tides,* by Edward F. Ricketts, Jack Calvin, and Joel W. Hedgpeth (1985).

Environments According to Wave Exposure

1. Protected Outer Coast. Semisheltered coast, protected by the shape of the coastline (open bay entrance or other concave shape), offshore reef or kelp bed, and so on.

2. Open Coast. Entirely unprotected outer coast, often of convex shape, such as headlands or gently bulging stretches.

3. Bay and Estuary. Enclosed bays and sloughs without appreciable surf; often with muddy substrate.

Environments According to Substrate

1. Rocky Shores
   a. Exposed rock
      (1) Absorbent, moisture-retaining rock
      (2) Nonabsorbent, water-shedding rock
   b. Protected rock and seaweed
   c. Under-rock
   d. Tidepools
   e. Cobbles
2. Sandy Shores
3. Muddy Shores
4. Wharf Piling and other structures

Environments According to Tidal Exposure

Zone 1. Splash Zone (Pl. 15). From uppermost reach of storm waves and spray down to mean high water. Usually above + 5 ft.

Zone 2. High Tide Zone (Pl. 16). From mean high water down to mean higher low water: from + 5 to about + 2½ ft.

Zone 3. Middle Tide Zone (Pl. 17). From mean higher low water down to mean lower low water: from + 2½ to tide zero.

Zone 4. Low Tide Zone (Pl. 18). Below lower low water; from tide zero down to extreme lower low water. The minus tide zone.

Sublittoral Zone. This zone is never exposed to the atmosphere and is beyond the scope of this book—except that a number of sublittoral and *pelagic* (open sea) species are often found washed up on our beaches and are therefore considered here.

Among the problems faced by intertidal animals is that of wave shock. The intertidal zone is the chief focus of the surf, which brings tons of water crashing repeatedly against sand or rock. Well-attested accounts tell us something of the power in these breaking waves. In one instance a rock weighing 80 tons was moved 21 m (70 ft.) across a rocky beach; and the windows of the lighthouse at Dunnet Head, 88 m (290 ft.) above mean sea level on the northern tip of Scotland, have repeatedly been broken by wave-hurled stones. Where waves of this magnitude are frequent, the shore may be scoured to barrenness; but where the forces are only a little less violent, there are many living things fully capable of withstanding them.

One of the simplest solutions to the problem of the waves is simply to hide from them, and this is what hundreds of intertidal animals do. When the waves are dangerous, they crawl under or between stable rocks, letting the rocks bear the brunt of the surf. Many animals spend their entire adult lives in such rocky retreats, often attached immovably and never emerging even in periods of calm.

Sandy beaches are deficient in rocky hiding places, but the sand itself offers protection to burrowing animals. Such creatures as the Pismo Clam (no. 68), the Bean Clam (no. 78), and the Wedge Clam (no. 79) live in this way, and if necessary they can carry out all their life processes without ever emerging fully from the sand. Sand Crabs (no. 196) are also burrowers, but they emerge from the sand after the main shock of each wave has passed and swim to a new locality. When the surf is dangerously high, however, they retreat deeper into the sand and stay there.

A beach covered with rounded cobbles offers very little shelter (see Pl. 11). The cobbles roll and grind against each other in the waves (which is how irregular rocks are made into smooth round cobbles), and such beaches are relatively barren of visible life. The microscope, however, reveals the usual intertidal fecundity.

Starfish, limpets, and a number of other forms move about on the rocks and in the tidepools when they are not immediately threatened by pounding waves; when the risk of being swept away increases, they stop moving and hang on tightly to their substrate. Most of these have low, rounded, streamlined bodies or shells presenting minimum resistance to the sweeping water.

Still other animals attach themselves permanently to the rocks. Barnacles glue themselves down when still in their larval form and spend the rest of their lives in that one spot. Mussels attach themselves by *byssus* threads, each of which has its free end firmly attached to the substrate. These methods are so successful that the attached animals provide a haven for smaller creatures that live among them. A mussel bed, for example, is a whole community of many different species.

Seaweeds, too, are firmly anchored, and, like mussel beds, they provide a refuge for a whole fauna. Dr. John Colman, studying the seaweed habitat on English shores, estimated that a stand of the common Tufted Lichen, *Lichina pygmaea,* contained among its tufts an animal population approaching one million inhabitants for each square meter of rock surface.

Permanent attachments of this sort are a defining feature of what is known as the *sessile* way of life. This way of living would not work on land, where an attached animal could not get enough food. The moving waters of the sea, however, carry a rich cargo of nourishing materials, and sessile animals have evolved many efficient methods of collecting it. Barnacles, for example, sweep their feathery legs rhythmically through the water to strain out food particles. Mussels also use a sort of net, but they do not move it through the water: rather, they pump the water through the net. Their gills act as the net, thus serving the double functions of respiration and food gathering. A large California Mussel (*Mytilus californianus,* no. 52) may filter as much as 16 gallons of water every day.

Certain burrowing forms, such as the Innkeeper (*Urechis caupo,* no. 158) and the Parchment Tube Worm (*Chaetopterus variopedatus,* no. 163), spin a fine mucous net across their tunnels, then cause a current of water to flow through it. Later, the loaded nets and their contents are devoured. The Scaly Tube Snail (*Serpulorbis squamigerus,* no. 106) also uses a net of mucus, but this one floats up in the water; a colony of these animals produces a community net, which is allowed to wave about in the water before being pulled down and eaten by the whole colony.

Selective digestion is used by the Red Worm (*Euzonus mucronata,* no. 164) and numerous other forms. In the manner of the familiar earthworm, the Red Worm swallows large quantities of sand; edible materials among the sand grains are digested, while the indigestible sand passes on through. The Lugworm (*Arenicola brasiliensis,* no. 165) feeds in much the same manner, pushing aside about one-third of the sand in its path and swallowing the other two-thirds. If it is not hungry, the Lugworm can continue digging without swallowing any sand at all.

Beneath quiet waters, the ocean bottom is often covered with a film of organic debris that provides food for a good many creatures. The Bent-Nosed Clam (*Macoma nasuta,* no. 75) buries itself in the sediments of shallow quiet bays and extends its long, flexible incurrent siphon to a point above the sedimentary surface; the siphon then bends down until its tip just touches the food film, which it takes up like a vacuum cleaner. Other animals have other methods of obtaining this detritus.

Seaweeds provide nourishment for those relatively few animals that are capable of digesting them. Certain limpets feed on the Sea Lettuce (*Ulva*) and other green algae growing on the rocks. Each limpet maintains its own personal grazing ground like a well-kept lawn. Sea hares, abalones, and sea urchins eat just about any kind of seaweed.

Predation is a frequent means of procuring food. The octopus, for example, is a skillful and active hunter, and even some of the sessile (permanently attached) animals are predacious. Sea anemones, for example, have tentacles armed with thousands of microscopic, venomous stinging cysts, with which they are able to capture and subdue any small creatures that blunder into them.

Active feeding of this sort usually goes on when the tide is high, so that both predator and prey are covered with water. During low tides, when the habitat is exposed to the air, the fauna is generally quiescent. At these times, the animals are faced with the twin problems of asphyxiation and desiccation, but again, many solutions have evolved. Limpets and periwinkles attach themselves tightly to their rocky substrate, their impermeable shells slowing down evaporative drying. Having no means of extracting oxygen from the air, they must hold their breaths until the tide comes in.

The Aggregate Anemones (*Anthopleura elegantissima,* no. 28) retain their moisture by means of a well-known geometric principle: a large mass has proportionally less surface area than a small mass of the same shape. This has a profound effect on water retention, for the larger the surface, the greater the rate of evaporation. A single anemone would have a very large surface area in relation to its mass, but a whole host of them, crowded tightly together, act in some ways as a single, larger mass, with a correspondingly smaller ratio of exposed evaporative surface. These anemones often occur in concentrations of almost 3,000 individuals per square meter of rock surface, and they can survive in zones that undergo more air exposure than can be tolerated by the solitary anemones.

Animals that live under rocks, among mussels or seaweeds, or in other permanently damp environments have little trouble in maintaining their moisture. The seaweeds themselves are protected by their own numbers and their ability to sacrifice a few exposed individual plants in order to protect the whole colony. The outer layers protect the inner ones, and while the former may be damaged or killed by the sun and dry air, a reservoir of repair materials survives in the lower strata.

Barnacles and mussels simply close their shells tightly to prevent evaporation, retaining a large amount of water inside.

The reproduction of sessile animals (and of many mobile ones as well) is most often accomplished by *external fertilization*, which means that eggs and sperm are discharged separately into the water. This is a wasteful method, for many of the eggs are not fertilized, and those that are have no protection against being eaten. Thus most of the eggs never succeed in growing up, and survival is assured only by the production of tremendous numbers of eggs. For instance, each Common Oyster (*Crassostrea virginica*) of the East Coast is known to produce some 500 million eggs every year. Only one of these eggs during the entire life of each parent must attain maturity in order to perpetuate the species.

High numbers of this sort are required by swimming organisms as well as by sessile ones, provided their eggs and sperm are deposited separately into the water. Where internal fertilization occurs or where there is some parental guarding of eggs and the very young, not as many eggs are required. A small Pacific coast fish known as the Sarcastic Fringehead (*Neoclinus blanchardi*) illustrates this. The female lays only 300 or so eggs inside an empty shell or an old bottle, and the male, after fertilizing them, zealously stands guard until they hatch. Among the surfperches (family Embiotocidae), fertilization is internal, and the young are born alive. These young are quite large and can take fairly good care of themselves, so each adult female has to produce only 10 to 25 offspring each year.

Where to See Intertidal Animals

Just about any place where the sea and the land come together is worth a visit, and we are fortunate to live in a state that encourages such visiting. About 42 percent of the California shoreline is publicly owned and accessible. Of the remaining 58 percent, a small portion is held by various governmental agencies, which are legally entitled to forbid access. Most of this 58 percent, however, is privately owned—but only down to the mean high tide line. Beyond that imaginary line, the public has free access. Article X, Section 4 of the Constitution of the State of California provides "that navigable waters of this State shall always be attainable for the people thereof." Thus the state holds all lands seaward of the mean high tide line, and the public is entitled to visit these lands. The precise line is hard to determine, but as a general rule of thumb, no private agency can deny your right to walk along the beach on the wet sand.

Furthermore, the law requires that reasonable access to these state-owned lands be maintained, even if such access crosses private property. The state has undertaken a program of erecting directional signs (see Pl. 5), but these access routes are still not always easy to find. Fortunately, an inexpensive book is of inestimable value in this connection. It is the *California Coastal Access Guide* by the California Coastal Commission (1983). In its expanded edition of 1983, it is published by the University of California Press. This book is gratefully acknowledged as the source of much of the information in these paragraphs. Another useful book, especially for finding out something about the physical nature of specific coastal areas, is Griggs and Savoy (1985).

Figure 7 is a map of Southern California showing a few spots of interest. These have been selected primarily for their

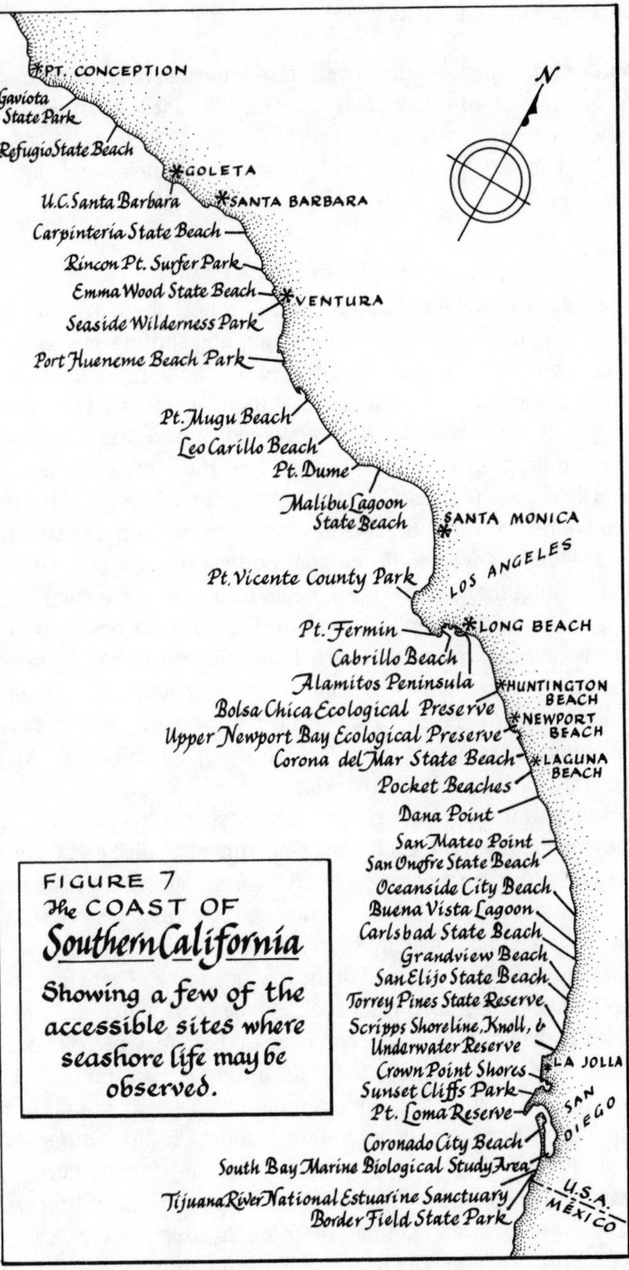

PT. CONCEPTION

Gaviota
State Park

Refugio State Beach

GOLETA

*SANTA BARBARA

U.C. Santa Barbara
Carpinteria State Beach
Rincon Pt. Surfer Park
Emma Wood State Beach
Seaside Wilderness Park
Port Hueneme Beach Park

*VENTURA

N

Pt. Mugu Beach
Leo Carillo Beach
Pt. Dume
Malibu Lagoon
State Beach

SANTA MONICA

LOS ANGELES

Pt. Vicente County Park

Pt. Fermin
Cabrillo Beach
Alamitos Peninsula
Bolsa Chica Ecological Preserve
Upper Newport Bay Ecological Preserve
Corona del Mar State Beach
Pocket Beaches
Dana Point
San Mateo Point
San Onofre State Beach
Oceanside City Beach
Buena Vista Lagoon
Carlsbad State Beach
Grandview Beach
San Elijo State Beach
Torrey Pines State Reserve
Scripps Shoreline, Knoll, &
Underwater Reserve
Crown Point Shores
Sunset Cliffs Park
Pt. Loma Reserve
Coronado City Beach
South Bay Marine Biological Study Area
Tijuana River National Estuarine Sanctuary
Border Field State Park

*LONG BEACH

*HUNTINGTON
BEACH
*NEWPORT
BEACH
*LAGUNA
BEACH

LA JOLLA

SAN
DIEGO

U.S.A.
MEXICO

FIGURE 7
The COAST OF
Southern California

Showing a few of the
accessible sites where
seashore life may be
observed.

value in having more than one sort of intertidal habitat, such as a combination of rocky areas and sandy beaches. Most but not all of these are listed in the *California Coastal Access Guide*, with many details of location, access routes, and local facilities.

Conservation

The intertidal habitat, adapted though it is to the harsh conditions of pounding waves, burning sun, and shifting sands, is a fragile environment and can all too easily be upset or even destroyed. Part of the problem is that there are simply too many people in the world. Most of us wouldn't purposely do anything to harm this environment, but our mere presence in the intertidal zone is stressful. It is therefore absolutely necessary that we behave so as to have the least possible inimical effect.

This means we should look at the tops of the rocks rather than turning them over—or, if we do turn over one or two, we must be careful to replace them in their original positions. It means just looking at the starfish and the sea hares, without picking them up, and most emphatically without carrying them or any form of sea life away from the shore. It even means watching where we place our feet, so as not to tread on the Aggregate Anemones or periwinkles.

Much of this is just plain good manners, but it also involves obeying the law. The California Department of Fish and Game has enacted a number of protective rules concerning invertebrates in the intertidal zone. Basically, these rules simply state that you must not take any invertebrates between the high tide mark and 1,000 ft. seaward of the low tide mark. There are exceptions applying to certain species, many of which are protected by bag or size limits, and none of these may be collected unless you have a valid California fishing license plus whatever type of measuring device is required where size limits are applicable. For more detailed information, see the *California Sport Fishing Regulations* (summary edition) for the current year, published by the Fish and Game Commission, California Division of Fish and Game, 1416 Ninth Street, Sacramento, CA 95814. This booklet may be obtained free of charge direct from the Commission or at most sporting-goods and bait stores.

All in all, the best thing is to impinge on the intertidal zone as little as possible. Sitting quietly beside a tidepool and watching all its undisturbed activities is far more rewarding than tramping and splashing about, sending the mobile members of the littoral community into hiding.

3 · THE CLASSIFICATION
OF ANIMALS

Humanity seems always to have felt the necessity of bestowing a name on every living thing. This was the first job assigned to Adam while he was living, still Eveless, in the Garden. If Mark Twain's researches into the diaries of both Adam and Eve are correct, Eve later took over the job, and her method depended on the appropriateness of certain sounds. She would say, in effect, "Well, it just *looks* like a dodo, and that's what I'm going to call it!" And many names do come to possess a certain appropriateness—witness Gracie Allen's remark at the circus: "No wonder they call them 'elephants'—they're so *big!*"

Unfortunately, the children of Adam have not been very consistent in their naming. The same kind of animal has quite different names in various parts of the world, and the same name may be used for several different—and unrelated—creatures. Further, vernacular names do not usually convey any sense of relationship, and when they do the sense is apt to be wrong. For scientific purposes a classification scheme must provide for both the orderly arrangement of information and the making of logical changes as the information improves. The system of scientific nomenclature was invented to meet these needs, among others.

Scientific names are bestowed only after a great deal of study, and the process has to follow many complex rules. For example, no two animals may have identical names, so there must be a thorough search to make sure a new name has not been used before. The first name correctly proposed is the official one. As the scientific name is the same in every country, it must be couched in a non-nationalistic amalgam of Latin and Greek according to certain official grammatical customs. These and many other rules are set forth in three codes of nomenclature, one each for botany, zoology, and bacteriology. Each code is brought up to date at irregular intervals by an international congress of scientists; together they constitute perhaps the oldest still-active instrument of international agreement. (See the three entries under *International Code of . . .* in the Selected References at the end of this book.)

This discussion of scientific names is necessary because most marine creatures have no agreed-on common names; indeed, many of them have no common names at all. Where this is the case, I have tried to provide names, but it must be understood that these may not be found in other publications. So please don't be discouraged by these long, unpronounceable scientific names; they are important, and they are unavoidable.

The technical name of an animal species consists of at least two basic words. The first, always spelled with a capital initial, is the *generic* name, specifying the genus of the animal in question. A genus may be divided into a number of species, and the second word—the *specific* name—identifies the species in that genus. The specific name of an animal never begins with a capital letter, although botanists are permitted, if they wish, to capitalize a plant's specific name when it is derived from a proper noun.

A species in nature is a population or group of populations within which breeding is carried on or is at least potentially possible. This population must be reproductively isolated from others. Although the genus usually contains several species, there are many *monotypic* genera in which only one species has been named. (Note that the word "species" is both singular and plural: the terminal "s" is never dropped.)

A third name—the subspecies—may also form part of the scientific name. This indicates a population different from neighboring groups, but with the differences usually showing a gradual intergradation. Two different subspecies of the same species could probably breed with one another but are usually geographically separated.

A subgenus is also used when necessary for clarity. This comes in parentheses between the genus and species, thus:

Idotea (Pentidotea) resecata

All these terms are customarily written in italics. In technical literature, they are followed by the authority, not in italics; this is the name of the person who proposed the name of the animal, or, as biologists usually put it, "described" the species. Thus the full name of the California Blind Goby is technically written:

Typhlogobius californiensis Steindacher

If subsequent research indicates the need to move a species into another genus, the name of the original author is still cited, but in parentheses. Thus the Grunion is labeled:

Leuresthes tenuis (Ayres)

This book, however, is not intended as a technical reference work, and space is saved by leaving out the authorities.

There is more to the describing of a new creature than merely giving it a name. It must be properly placed in a hierarchy of classificatory groups that, although not part of the name itself, must be made known. The genus must be placed in the proper family, the family in an order, the order in a class, the class in a phylum, and the phylum in a kingdom. Additional categories such as suborder, superfamily, and so on may be placed between these major ones where necessary. In some groups these additional terms are very important.

This scientific nomenclature is, of course, artificial and not a part of nature; but ideally an animal's full taxonomic position can tell us something about its evolutionary background. Our knowledge of these backgrounds is far from complete, but it is constantly being improved by research. This improvement often means that classifications have to be changed; the scientific name is not a fixed, immovable entity. Taxonomists are in some ways like the first explorers in a strange land, who use whatever knowledge they have at the moment in naming geographical features. When later explorations show that two different names have been given to different stretches of the same winding river, confusion will exist until everyone agrees to drop one of the names. So don't be disturbed if the scientific names in one book are not exactly the same as those in another. Remember that while name changes may be confusing, they are necessary for precise classification.

As an example of desirable change, consider our ways of regarding the two largest taxonomic categories—kingdoms and phyla. For a long time we tried to get along with only two kingdoms—Plantae and Animalia—and with procrustean effort, every organism was assigned to one or another of these whether it fitted or not. Many of the unicellular organisms plainly *didn't* fit, and several scientists proposed a separate kingdom for the bacteria. There wasn't much agreement about this until the last 20 years or so, since the late R. H. Whittaker set up a beautiful system with no fewer than five kingdoms.

Whittaker recognized cell type as the most basic division. *Prokaryotic* cells, or *prokaryotes,* have no nucleus and no chromosomes, the genetic material DNA not being bound within a membrane. *Eukaryotic* cells, or *eukaryotes,* do have a nucleus, bound by a nuclear membrane, containing chromosomes that hold the DNA. It appears that eukaryotes evolved through symbiotic combinations of prokaryotes. Prokaryotes do not develop multicellular tissues; practically all of them exist as single cells. They constitute the kingdom Monera, the bacteria.

Eukaryotes may exist as single cells or as multicellular organisms. The single-celled eukaryotes and some multicellular kinds such as the algae are put into the kingdom Protoctista. Three primary nutritive strategies are used in this kingdom: production, absorption, and ingestion. Each of these strategies led to the development of multicellular organisms now recognized as kingdoms: Plantae, which are producers, living mainly by photosynthesis; Fungi, which obtain their nutrients by absorption; and Animalia, which ingest their food. Thus the five kingdoms.

All of these kingdoms are well represented in the sea, but in this book we are concerned almost entirely with Animalia. Treatment of the kingdom Protoctista is limited here to two species. For a presentation of the algal seaweeds, which also belong to this kingdom, see Dawson and Foster (1982).

The same sort of change has been necessary among phyla as

well as kingdoms. Only four animal phyla had been recognized by the middle of the nineteenth century. Gradually this number has been increased to around 40; the total number in all five kingdoms is around 100.

I have tried to be consistent with regard to vernacular names, and where several different names are appropriate, I have tried to choose the one doing the least violence to taxonomic relationships. But where a vernacular name has become firmly established in our language, there has been no attempt to call it wrong and change it: starfishes are called starfishes, even though they are in no way related to fishes—nor, for that matter, to stars.

It is a great temptation to try to invest common names with more meaning than they actually carry. For instance, the question is often asked: "Are these so-called lobsters in California really lobsters? Aren't they really crayfish?" Because there are no widely accepted rules in vernacular naming, this question has no clear-cut answer. If enough people choose to call an animal a lobster, then lobster it is, even though it is only very distantly related to the clawed Northern Lobster, *Homarus americanus*. About all you can say is that in some parts of the world these spiny lobsters are called crayfish. But it should be pointed out that they are not at all closely related to the freshwater crustaceans for which the term "crayfish" is widely accepted, and that the term is not intrinsically better for one group than for the other. Etymology doesn't help much, either: "crayfish" probably derives from the French *écrevisse,* pertaining to something living in a crevice, and in this sense it could just as logically be applied to the clawed Northern Lobster of the Atlantic. A name should evoke the proper picture in the mind of a listener. To do this in Florida, it's best to call the animal a crayfish; in California, lobster (or among certain snorkeling hunters, bug); where Spanish or French is spoken, langosta or langouste. And if a restaurant demands that you order by number, and broiled California Spiny Lobster is number 7 on the menu, the correct name is "number 7."

The least confusing approach is to become familiar with the scientific name (which is *Panulirus interruptus* for the California Spiny Lobster) and its position in the hierarchy of scientific nomenclature.

4 · SPECIES ACCOUNTS

KINGDOM PROTOCTISTA

Phylum Dinoflagellata

Although the many kinds of one-celled organisms are of basic importance in all marine communities, individual specimens cannot be seen without the aid of a microscope. Certain forms, however, do at times become so numerous as to be clearly observable en masse to the human eye—and all too often to the human nose as well. Chief among these are several members of the phylum Dinoflagellata, which are responsible for periodic displays of *red tide*.

In the older taxonomy, with only two kingdoms, every organism had to be designated either plant or animal. But it was difficult to assign the dinoflagellates to one or the other of those kingdoms, for they exhibit many characteristics of both: they move about like animals and often feed at least partly by ingesting food particles. But they also practice the wonderful process of photosynthesis, using the Sun's energy to power the conversion of inorganic matter to organic matter. As far as the overall processes of the sea are concerned, it is this plantlike activity that matters the most, for the dinoflagellates, in their incalculable numbers, are among the most important of the ocean's primary food producers.

The term "dinoflagellate" comes from two roots: the Latin *flagellum*, meaning "a little whip," in reference to the two whiplike locomotory organs, and the Greek *dineo*, meaning "to spin," referring to the dinoflagellates' spiraling progress through the water.

These organisms are nearly always present in any sample of ocean water, but at certain times a "bloom" occurs, during which they become so numerous as to turn the water the color of weak tomato soup. This phenomenon is referred to as "red tide" or simply "red water."

Many species of dinoflagellates are brilliantly *bioluminescent;* that is, they have the ability to produce light and do so when they are disturbed. When such bioluminescent species constitute the bulk of a red-water visitation, the surf on a moonless night presents a fireworks display that is unforgettable. A fish swimming through this water will leave a bright cometlike trail in its wake. Tuna fishermen used to find their live bait during red water by watching for the telltale glow set up by the movements of a school of anchovies. Even after being cast up on the beach, these tiny organisms continue their light-producing reaction to any disturbance; the feet of a beach-walker produce flashes each time they hit the sand, leaving a trail of slowly dimming footprints.

We don't know what purposes may be served by these light flashes, and those dinoflagellates that do not produce them seem to get along as well as those that do. The chemical processes are somewhat better understood, but even here, a lot of work remains to be done. In nearly all bioluminescent life forms, light is produced by the interaction of two chemicals called luciferin and luciferase. These compounds are present in the dinoflagellates, but the way they work is complicated by the presence of tiny crystalline particles called scintillons. A change in the acidity of fluids surrounding the scintillons appears to be a triggering event, and it is still not certain how luciferin and luciferase enter the picture.

A remarkable periodicity in the intensity of the luminescence was discovered some years ago. Dinoflagellates produce brighter light during the night hours than during the day, and this is the case even when they are kept in the laboratory under conditions of unchanging light. The brightest flashes occur at about 1:00 A.M., while the least light is produced around noon.

A common term for life-produced light is *phosphorescence,* which is all right as long as one understands it in the original sense of the Greek words meaning "to bear light." It has no connection, however, with the chemical element phosphorus. Further, phosphorescence in technical language may refer to the re-emitting of stored light, which is not the same as the actual production of light. Biologists prefer the less confusing term "bioluminescence" for light that is produced biologically.

1. Common Red-Water Dinoflagellate, *Gonyaulax polyedra*. This is one of our most abundant dinoflagellates, sometimes occurring in concentrations of 7 million cells per gallon of sea water. Such concentrations, or blooms, are most likely to come about during the warm months of late summer and early fall, although a fairly heavy population has been known to persist for the better part of a year. This species is not, under ordinary circumstances, a toxic one, but may on occasion constitute a danger to other forms of marine life. This happens when a large concentration is moved into shallow near-shore water and is further concentrated by being squeezed between the surface and the bottom. There are then more cells than the volume of water can support, and after using up all the available oxygen, the dinoflagellates die by the billions. Decay sets in and the water becomes heavily contaminated with bacteria, thus becoming unfit for the support of fishes and other marine organisms. At such times, dead fish may be washed ashore in windrows. It used to be that the term "red tide" was reserved for this sort of catastrophic occasion, while the term "red water" was used for the harmless visible concentrations.

Other dinoflagellates differ in that they contain toxins in their living bodies and may pollute the water even while alive. One of these is *Ptychodiscus brevis,* which periodically brings about destructive red tides on the southern Atlantic and Gulf of Mexico coasts in the United States and Mexico.

2. Mussel-Poison Dinoflagellate, *Gonyaulax catenella.* This Pacific Coast species does not seem to produce any wholesale destruction of marine life but is quite capable of poisoning human beings. When this occurs it is not because the afflicted humans have ingested the poison directly from the water. If you were to swim in even the very heaviest concentration, you would have to swallow many gallons of sea water in order to take in enough cells to do harm. But if you were to filter the

cells out in some way and swallow the concentrate, you could become very ill, with a good chance of dying. This is exactly what can happen if you eat mussels during a period of this dangerous red water.

Mussels are filter feeders (see nos. 52 and 53), and whoever eats a mussel will be eating everything that the mussel filtered from the water during the preceding several hours. The danger is not only from undigested dinoflagellates in the mussel's system, but also from the toxic materials that seem to be concentrated in certain parts of the mussel's tissues. The mussel itself is not harmed by this infestation.

Mussel poisoning is better known to the medical profession as paralytic shellfish poisoning and has been known since ancient times. Indians of the Pacific Coast were well aware of it long before contact with Europeans, and, according to Rachel Carson (1951), they sometimes posted sentinels at the shore to warn uninstructed visitors from inland. The association of the disease with red water has been noticed in many parts of the world, but it was not until 1937 that Hermann Sommer of the University of California pinpointed *Gonyaulax catenella* as the culprit.

Bruce Halstead (1965), in his monumental *Poisonous and Venomous Marine Animals* (vol. 1, pp. 185–187), summarizes all the cases of paralytic shellfish poisoning reported in the medical literature up to 1962. These total 957 cases, with 222 fatalities—a death rate of about 23 percent. This includes the tragedy that befell the party headed by the Russian fur trader Aleksander Baranov, in which over 100 Aleuts, half of Baranov's work force, perished as the result of a single meal of mussels; this was in 1799, at the well-named Peril Strait, Alaska. Cases have been very rare in Southern California. In Halstead's list, only four cases, with two deaths, occurred south of Point Conception.

Even though mussel poisoning is so uncommon in Southern California, the barest possibility is a matter of great concern, and you should never eat mussels anywhere along the Pacific Coast if there is the slightest chance of their having been exposed to any kind of red water. Quarantine notices set up by state and county health departments prohibit the collecting of mussels and other shellfish from May 1 to October 31, and these strictures are to be scrupulously obeyed. Mussels are good to eat, but not good enough to risk your life for.

Cooking, by the way, does not destroy the toxin, and there is no easy way to discern its presence.

Clams are somewhat less dangerous than mussels, partly because we customarily discard the dark portions containing the digestive organs; nevertheless, they too can be dangerous, and should not be eaten when the quarantine is in effect. Abalones (see nos. 86–88), on the other hand, are grazers, not filter feeders, and may be eaten safely at any time—subject, of course, to the game laws.

KINGDOM ANIMALIA

Phylum Porifera
(Sponges)

Unlike the dinoflagellates and many other protoctists, the sponges are composed of many cells. But unlike the so-called higher animals, their cells are assembled in a rather loose aggregation, and under some circumstances each individual cell can carry on by itself for a time if separated from the others. A classic experiment has shown it possible to dissociate the cells of a sponge by squeezing it gently through a piece of fine silk and have the separated cells not only survive but eventually reassemble in the original sponge form. It is hard to decide whether a sponge should be considered an individual or a colony.

The word "Porifera" means "pore-bearing" and refers to the numerous tiny openings scattered all over the sponge's body. These are *incurrent* openings, through which sea water flows inward, often into elaborately branched internal canals. This flow is created by the beating of thousands of hairlike flagella belonging to the specialized *collar cells* that line the inside of the body. Outgoing water from which food and oxygen have been obtained is channeled through different openings, the *oscula,* which are larger and fewer in number. In many species there is only one of these excurrent openings. Water passing out takes away waste metabolic products, and, in the proper season, sperm cells. In some species eggs also are carried out, but most sponges retain these in the body, relying for fertilization on sperm cells brought in through the incurrent pores.

All sponges have a "skeleton" of intertwined microscopic spicules, often of bizarre shapes. The materials composing these spicules provide a primary criterion in sponge classification. In the class Calcarea they are composed of calcium carbonate in the form of calcite; in the class Hyalospongiae (also known as Hexactinellida, or glass sponges) the spicules are made of opaline silica and are usually of a six-rayed shape; among the Demospongia, the spicules are made either of glass (in other than the six-rayed form) or of a unique horny material called spongin. The familiar bath sponge belongs to the Demospongia; the useful part of this organism consists of the spongin skeleton with flesh removed. A fourth class has recently been described: the Sclerospongiae, all living in the deep sea, with spicules of both silica and calcium carbonate, the latter in the form of aragonite.

There are probably 50 or more species of sponges on the Southern California coast. Those living intertidally are found only at the lowest tide level. Their accurate identification is a matter for a specialist with a microscope and lots of time. Even the primary identification of a specimen merely as a sponge is not always easy; most are irregular and inconsistent in size, shape, and color, and some of them closely resemble other kinds of unrelated animals. One general identifying mark is the presence of the hundreds of tiny incurrent pores, which may not be noticed except on close examination with a hand lens. Another feature is that most sponges have a gritty texture in contrast to the slickness of some of the other superficially similar animals, such as the compound ascidians.

Class Calcarea

3. White Fan Sponge, *Clathrina blanca*. Mainly subtidal, but occasionally seen under overhanging rocks at the lowest low tides. It stands (or hangs) about 2.5 cm (1 in.) high, and its color is white or light tan. Its known range is from Los Angeles County to the middle of Baja California.

4. Urn Sponge, *Leucilla nuttingi*. Symmetrical, urn-shaped, growing in clusters suspended from crevice walls and overhanging rocks in the lowest tide zone. Each little pale gray urn grows to a length of 5 cm (2 in.) or so. The urn shape is a common one among the sponges, seen in different species from all over the world.

5. Macaroni Sponge, *Leucetta losangelensis.* An encrusting sponge with a thickness of about 3 cm (1¼ in.), thicker than most of our encrusting forms. Diameter of the colony up to around 15 cm (6 in.). The surface is covered with numerous oscula (excurrent openings) of 12 mm (½ in.) in diameter; these, with the white color and tangled appearance of the colony, prompted one child to say that this sponge looked like a plate of macaroni, and that seems as good a vernacular name as any. Fairly common in the lowest low-tide zone on rocks and pier pilings.

Class Demospongia

6. Sulphur Sponge, *Aplysina fistularis.* The term "sulphur" is appropriate to both the color and the smell of this organism. It forms a fairly thick encrusting mat on the undersides of rocks composed of a number of "individual" sponges. A raised osculum is seen in every 3 or 4 square inches of surface.

7. Red Sponge, *Plocamia karykina* (Pl. 21). Color bright red. Forms mats of up to 2 cm (¾ in.) thick in the low tide zone. The oscula are scattered irregularly over the surface. When irritated, this sponge releases copious quantities of gelatinous mucus. This species is one of several that go by the common name "red sponge."

8. Free-Living Sponge, *Tetilla mutabilis.* Color dull brown. Most sponges are firmly attached to some sort of substrate, but not this one; it lives unattached on insubstantial mud flats. Young individuals are anchored to the mud by means of a holdfast of fibrous spicules, but when they have grown to more than 5 cm (2 in.) across they can apparently dispense with this security and are moved about by tides and currents.

9. Crumb-of-Bread Sponge, *Halichondria panicea* (not illustrated). There are several species of *Halichondria* in our area, all of them difficult to identify in the field. The encrusting colonies of this species are rarely more than 2.5 cm (1 in.) in diameter and only about 6 mm (¹/₄ in.) thick. The color may be orange, yellow, or green. It is found on the undersides of rocks in the low low tide zone. While not abundant in Southern California, this is a cosmopolitan species found in cool and temperate seas around the world. It was the subject of microscopic observation by the Scottish physician R. E. Grant, who in 1825 observed the water currents flowing out of the oscula. Up to that time, naturalists had not agreed as to whether sponges were plants or animals, although Aristotle had guessed at their animal nature long before. The matter was settled by Grant's observations, and the sponges were universally accepted as animals.

10. Purple Sponge, *Haliclona* sp. (Note: the letters "sp." in place of a specific name indicate that the specific name is not known to the author, or that perhaps this species has not yet been fully described.) Similar to the Sulphur Sponge (no. 6), but usually of a purple color, with the oscula distributed in a regular pattern.

11. Yellow Sponge, *Mycale macginitiei* (see Pl. 22). Forms thin yellow encrusting mats on the undersides of rocks, especially in quiet waters. In exception to the general rule about sponge surface texture, this sponge is slick—almost slimy—to the touch, although the presence of stiffening spicules is obvious. Named in honor of the pioneer California invertebrate zoologists, George E. and Nettie MacGinitie.

12. Pacific Loggerhead Sponge, *Spheciospongia confoederata* (not illustrated). The largest of our sponges, attaining the diameter of a bowling ball. Found only at the extreme low tide level. It is not common, although perhaps more abundant than seems to be the case, for it can easily escape notice because of its resemblance to a round gray rock.

13. Orange Sponge, *Tethya aurantia.* Round when viewed from the top, this sponge varies in profile from a slightly humped disk to a sphere. Diameter to 7.5 cm (3 in.), with a granular, lumpy orange surface. It attaches itself to rocks, often in crevices, at the lowest tide level and is fairly common. This is one of the sponges with a great geographical and eco-

Phylum DINOFLAGELLATA

(HIGHLY MAGNIFIED)

1.
Gonyaulax polyedra

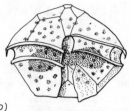

2. *Gonyaulax catenella*

Phylum PORIFERA

1"

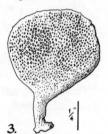

¼"

3.
Clathrina blanca

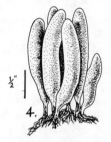

½"

Leucilla nuttingi

5.
Leucetta losangelensis

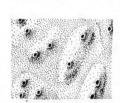

NOT ILLUSTRATED:
NO'S 6, 9, 11, 12, & 14

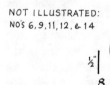

½"

8.
Tetilla mutabilis

7. *Plocamia karykina*

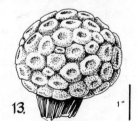

1"

10. *Haliclona* sp.

13.
Tethya aurantia

logical range, as it is found in most seas from shallow shore waters to the depths. It is an important part of the fauna attached to the walls of Californian submarine canyons.

14. Vanilla Sponge, *Xestospongia vanilla* (not illustrated). Found all along the Pacific Coast. Forms a thin, smooth, hard encrustation that looks like cake icing.

Phylum Cnidaria
(Jellyfishes and Their Relatives)

At first glance, the 6,000 or so species that make up this phylum present an assemblage of bewilderingly different forms, but close examination shows them all to be relatively superficial variations on a theme.

The basic plan of cnidarians is a radial one, with a circle of tentacles surrounding a central mouth. The mouth, which serves both for the ingestion of food and the egestion of wastes, opens directly into the body cavity. There is no digestive tube; digestion takes place within the body cavity itself. The body is formed of two layers of cells, between which is sandwiched a gelatinous material called *mesoglea.*

There are two forms in cnidarian bodies: the polyp and the medusa. The *polyp* is cylindrical, most often firmly attached to a substrate with tentacles and mouth facing upward. The *medusa* is shaped like an umbrella or sometimes a square box and is usually free-swimming; the tentacles, which may be very long, hang downward. Some cnidarians go through life as medusae, others as polyps, and still others alternate between the two forms in successive generations.

Another characteristic of this phylum is the presence of tiny stinging structures known as *nematocysts.* These may occur on any part of the body but are most concentrated in the tentacles. They consist of tiny capsules containing a coiled line. A triggering mechanism operated by either mechanical or chemical stimuli brings about a sudden increase of pressure within the capsule, which violently ejects the free end of the line. Some nematocysts use an entangling sticky thread, while others have sharp, penetrating harpoonlike tips. Recent exploration with the electron microscope shows that the line in the latter type is hollow and is turned inside out as it is ejected. The line exits with a twirling motion that bores the harpoon tip into whatever it is thrown against, carrying with it a small dose of a potent toxin. All cnidarians are carnivorous, and these nematocysts serve as a means of capturing prey as well as a defense against predators.

Most of these barbed nematocysts are too short to penetrate human skin, but this is not universally true. Some members of the phylum can inflict painful or even deadly stings. The Portuguese Man-of-War, a hydrozoan that does not occur in our waters, is one of the most potent stingers. Its medical effects have been studied in detail; for example, the first systematic study of the immunological phenomenon known as anaphylaxis was undertaken by Richet and Portier in Monaco using the toxins from this species. Other species, such as the sea-wasps of tropical waters, are even more virulent.

The exploding action of these stinging organs is automatic and independent of any act of will on the part of the animal. For this reason, a dead jellyfish can sting as badly as a live one, and fishermen trolling with hand lines have often been stung by the lines after they were dragged through a school of jellyfish, picking up some detached nematocysts on the way. Each nematocyst operates only once and must then be replaced.

The phylum Cnidaria is divided into three classes, all of which are well represented in the area covered by this book: Hydrozoa (hydroids and related forms), Scyphozoa ("true" jellyfishes), and Anthozoa (sea anemones, corals, sea pens, and related forms).

Class Hydrozoa

Many of our local hydroids are colonial, forming "bushes" of branching tubes that carry many small polyps. These colonies grow by an asexual *budding* from the first polyp that settled in a given spot. At intervals, the colony produces medusae. In some species these medusae detach from the colony and swim off on their own, while in others they remain attached to the hydroid stage. In either case the medusae reproduce sexually, producing *planula* larvae that settle down to start new colonies. The result is a life history in which each individual is like its grandparents and grandchildren but different from its parent(s) and children. This process is known as *alternation of generation.*

Some hydroids are very small, with colonies seen only as an indistinct fuzz on the surface of a rock or bit of seaweed. Others form quite visible bushy clumps. Probably the largest is a solitary (noncolonial) form, *Branchiocerianthus,* a fragile animal living in the quiet waters at depths of 4,550 m (15,000 ft.) or more; it stands 2.4 m (8 ft.) tall.

There are many kinds of hydroids in our area, some of them probably as yet undescribed by science. Only a very few can be considered here.

15. Oaten-Pipe Hydroid, *Tubularia crocea.* Stems are up to 13 cm (5 in.) long and are rarely branched. Grows in large clumps attached to pier pilings and other structures in quiet waters at the lowest tide level. Some of the stalks are longer than the others and extend beyond the bulk of the clump, giving a pin-cushion effect. Each stalk bears a pinkish polyp at its tip. The polyps have two circlets of tentacles, between which lie grapelike clusters of medusoids, the medusa stage of the species. Medusae are not set free, but remain attached to the polyp.

Because of their ability to regenerate lost parts, the hydroids have been the subject of much study. The various species of *Tubularia* (there are more than a dozen, with worldwide distribution) have received the greatest share of attention. In this genus, the hydranths sometimes drop off at a moment's notice, as when the water grows stale or warm; when conditions improve, new heads are regenerated on the old stalks, and under some circumstances a discarded hydranth will grow a new stalk.

16. Solitary Hydroid, *Corymorpha palma.* Length to 10 cm (4 in.). Color yellowish, almost transparent. Resembles an elongated sea anemone. Found on mud flats from the middle low tide zone downward. While under water this hydroid stands upright, with the rootlike processes at the lower end of the stalk firmly imbedded in the mud. At low tide, when the animal is exposed to the air, it collapses, lying flaccid at the surface. It has two techniques for obtaining food while under water. One of these is used when a current is flowing, bringing food particles to the motionless upright hydroid. The other method is used when there is no current, and the animal makes repeated bowing motions in different directions, bending down and brushing its tentacles across the surface of the mud to pick up detrital food.

This solitary hydroid is common wherever you can find a good mudflat; such spots are, however, increasingly rare, and this habitat is in grave danger of disappearing beneath the avalanche of seaside "improvement." California once had at least 382,000 estuarine acres, but more than 256,000 acres (67 percent of the total) have been destroyed. It is to be hoped that legislation, together with the efforts of organizations like the Nature Conservancy and the University of California Land and Water Reserve System, can preserve some of this habitat in perpetuity.

17. Clam Hydroid, *Clytia bakeri*. Length to 13 mm ($^1/_2$ in.). This little hydroid grows attached to living shells, especially the Pismo Clam, *Tivela stultorum* (no. 68), and the bean clams of the genus *Donax* (nos. 78 and 79). It always attaches itself to the posterior end of the clam shell, and as the clam buries itself in the sand with its head downward, *Clytia* stays on top, extending into the water just above the surface of the sand. As Haderlie, Hand, and Gladfelter (Morris, Abbott, and Haderlie, 1980, p. 46) point out, this is an excellent adaptation to living in an intertidal environment of loose sand; attachment to a solid object, such as a stone or a dead shell, would result in the hydroid's being completely buried or completely exposed as the sand level rose and fell with the seasons. The living clams, however, adjust themselves to remain always just under the surface of the sand, whatever its level. Because of this habit, *Clytia* is able to make its home on sandy beaches. It is the only local hydroid that can do so.

There are about 27 species of *Clytia* in North America.

18. Branched Obelia, *Obelia dichotoma*. Length to 25 cm ($9^3/_4$ in.), sometimes growing as an inch-thick mat, but most often in bushy clumps. Common on pier pilings in quiet waters. *Obelia* belongs to the group of sheathed hydroids, each feeding polyp growing in a transparent cup into which the whole polyp may be retracted. Reproductive polyps are borne in urn-shaped cups set at the angles of the branches. The urns release tiny medusae 1 mm (¹/₃₂ in.) in diameter. These medusae, which constitute the sexual stage in the life cycle, swim away and produce larvae that settle down to grow up as the fixed stage. In a related species the process of alternating generations from one medusa stage through the fixed stage to the next medusa stage has been observed to take place in only one month.

The genus *Obelia* enjoys almost worldwide distribution, and at least three species are known to live on Southern California shores.

19. Furry Hydroid, *Sertularia furcata.* Length to about 1 cm (³/₈ in.). Forms a furry growth on blades of Surfgrass (*Phyllospadix*) and occasionally other seaweeds. In this species, medusae are not set free to swim away, but complete their development within the sessile cups of the fixed stage. The medusae produce eggs and sperm, the former kept within the cups and the latter released into the water to enter another cup and fertilize its eggs.

20. Fern Hydroid, *Abietinaria greenei.* Length 2–5 cm (³/₄–2 in.). Fronds fernlike, colorless. This is one of the most widespread of our hydroids, found from the Queen Charlotte Islands south to Bahía San Quintín in Baja California. It is found most often attached to rocks in the lowest tide zone and has been observed by divers at depths of up to 61 m (200 ft.). The transparent polyps are contained in cups set directly on the branches, without the slender connecting stem that is typical of other hydroids such as *Obelia.*

There is still much taxonomic work to be done on this hydroid, as on many others, and our *Abietinaria* may turn out not to be *greenei* after all.

21. Ostrich-Plume Hydroid, *Aglaophenia struthionides.* Length 10–13 cm (4–5 in.). Color usually dark brown. Much like a feather in shape. This species grows attached to a rock

Phylum CNIDARIA

15.

Tubularia crocea

16.

1"

Corymorpha palma

½"

17.

Clytia bakeri

ACTUAL SIZE

18.

Obelia dichotoma

ACTUAL SIZE

19.

Sertularia furcata

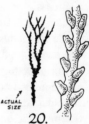

ACTUAL SIZE

20.

Abietinaria greenei

ACTUAL SIZE →

22.

Plumularia setacea

1"

21.

Aglaophenia struthionides

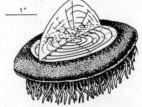

1"

23. *Velella velella*

or other solid substrate, often in clusters of a score or more of the feathery branches; its size, however, makes it vulnerable to displacement by waves, and unattached specimens are often found washed up on the beach.

Some of the branchlets of the "feather" appear thicker than others; these are known as *corbulae* and contain the sexual generation. The sexual medusae stay within the corbulae until they produce eggs and sperm. These, in turn, result in tiny ciliated larvae, which are set free to settle down nearby and grow up into the ostrich-plume form.

22. Glassy Plume Hydroid, *Plumularia setacea.* Length about 13 mm (¹/₂ in.). Transparent and, in ordinary light, almost invisible. Found on many substrates, but easiest to see in our area on the stipes and bulbs of cast-up kelp.

Like the Ostrich-Plume Hydroid, this species does not release its medusae, but retains them in a sac until they produce larvae ready to assume the hydroid form. This method of reproduction is common among hydroids living in wave-pounded coastal areas and apparently constitutes a positive adaptation to this rugged environment. Delicate free-swimming medusae would be battered to bits before reaching a quiet spot.

23. By-the-Wind Sailer, *Velella velella.* Longest diameter about 10 cm (4 in.). In beached specimens, the color is usually purple-blue on the edges of the flat, elliptical float, clear and transparent at the center and in the sail. This is a high-seas species that does not belong on the beach, and its occasional presence there in vast numbers is the result of some form of hydrographic accident.

In the open sea, living *Velella* often cover acres of the surface. Every few years, some quirk of winds or currents or both drives them ashore to their death. The process invariably damages them, rubbing away much of the delicate purple "skin" that covers the entire body of the healthy animal.

A conspicuous feature of *Velella* is the little sail that gives it its Latin name. The sail is made of what appears to be clear plastic sheeting and is set obliquely across the elliptical float.

Plate 1. High tide early on a fall morning.

Plate 2. Low tide, seven hours later on the same day.

Plate 3. Even on a relatively calm day, waves crashing against the shore pose problems for intertidal life.

Plate 4. Refraction bends waves to the shape of underwater contour lines.

Plate 5. California law requires that access to the beach be allowed and marked.

Plate 6 (left). The level of sand on the beach changes with the seasons. Here is a typical winter situation with low sand level.

Plate 7 (right). There is more sand on the beach during most summers, as shown by the higher surface of the sand in relation to the mussel colony on the pier piling.

Plate 8. The sand beach, like other intertidal habitats, has its own typical fauna.

Plate 9. A shore with some firmly fixed rocks and boulders is the richest of the intertidal habitats.

Plate 10. Surge channels on many rocky shelves provide an observable aqueous environment at low tide.

Plate 11. A cobble beach is inhospitable to most intertidal animals, and the fauna here is relatively sparse.

Plate 12. Wetlands, where the land meets the sea in a gradual transition, are an endangered habitat in California.

Plate 13. Mudflats can occur only in the absence of surf. They often host a limited number of species with a great profusion of individuals.

Plate 14. A special environment is found where fresh water, even in small quantities, flows into the sea.

Plate 15. The splash zone, here represented by pools that are filled only by flying spray, is above the reach of the highest tides.

Plate 16. The high tide zone is exposed to air more than to water. A typical plant of this zone is the mossy green alga shown here, *Enteromorpha.*

Plate 17. The middle tide zone, typified by the presence of the California Mussel (no. 52), is exposed to air and water for approximately equal periods of time.

Plate 18. The low tide zone is under water more often than it is exposed to air. The green Surfgrass, *Phyllospadix,* is typical of this zone.

Plate 19. Tidepools are small bodies of water trapped as the tide goes out; they are rich in flora and fauna. People who like to observe seashore life often refer to their activities as *tidepooling.*

Plate 20. Seaweeds of various kinds, such as the Rockweed *Pelvetia,* provide protection for hundreds of species of intertidal animals.

Plate 21. Encrusting red algae and various species of red sponges often provide bright colors in the low tide zone.

Plate 22. A yellow sponge (possibly the Yellow Sponge, *Mycale macginitiei,* no. 11) grows under overhanging rock ledges in the extreme low tide zone.

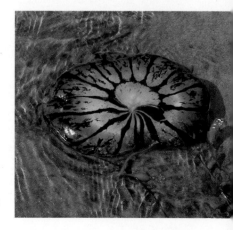

Plate 23. Forms that live in the open sea are often cast up on the beach. This is a small specimen of the Purple-Striped Jellyfish, *Pelagia colorata* (no. 24).

Plate 24. The Solitary Green Anemone, *Anthopleura xanthogrammica* (no. 27), owes its green color to the presence of symbiotic unicellular organisms in its tissues.

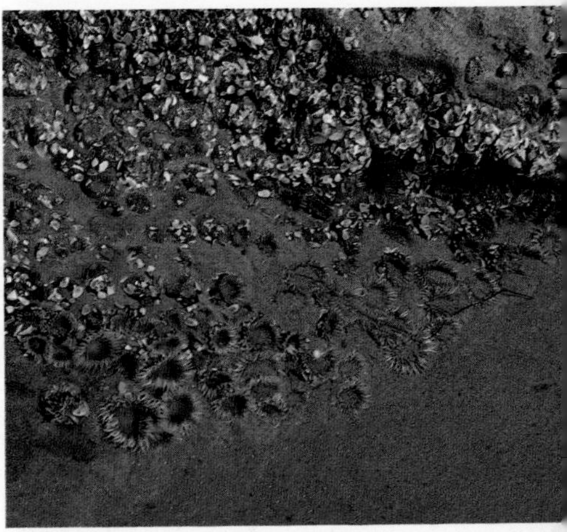

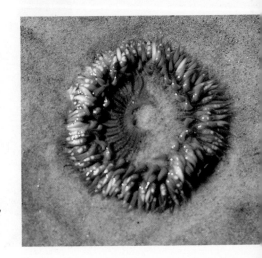

Plate 25. The Aggregate Anemone, *Anthopleura elegantissima* (no. 28), opens flowerlike in the water, but retracts into a debris-covered huddled mass when in the air.

Plate 26. The Beach Sand Anemone, *Anthopleura artemisia* (no. 29), must have its foot anchored to a solid object beneath the sand.

Plate 27. Each of the elliptical pits in the rock contains a Troglodyte Chiton, *Nuttallina fluxa* (no. 48), which remains there throughout its long life.

Plate 28. The California Mussel, *Mytilus californianus* (no. 52), forms large beds in the middle tide zone.

Plate 29. Interior of the shell of a Green Abalone, *Haliotis fulgens* (no. 88).

Plate 30. The Giant Keyhole Limpet, *Megathura crenulata* (no. 89).

Plate 31. The Smooth Brown Turban, *Norissia norissi* (no. 99), is usually found in association with the brown seaweed *Eisenia*.

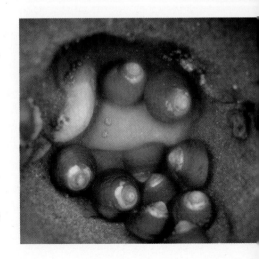

Plate 32. The Black Turban, *Tegula funebralis* (no. 101), is often found in clusters.

Plate 33. The tiny Flat-Bottomed Periwinkle, *Littorina planaxis* (no. 104), lives on rocks high in the splash zone.

Plate 34. The Little Tube Snail, *Petaloconchus montereyensis* (no. 107), is an inhabitant of the low tide zone in rocky areas.

Plate 35. A mudflat provides a rigorous environment, but the California Horn Shell, *Cerithidea californica* (no. 108), does very well there and occurs in great numbers. Each dark spot in the picture is a living California Horn Shell.

Plate 36. The shell-less snails called nudibranchs are among the most brilliantly colored creatures in the sea. This is the Purple Fan Nudibranch, *Flabellinopsis iodinea* (no. 146).

Plate 37. The Sand Castle Worm, *Phragmatopoma californica* (no. 166), builds colonial dwellings of sand attached to rock.

Plate 38. The shape of the Sand Castle Worm's compartments gives rise to another common name—Honeycomb Worm.

Plate 39. One of the most numerous inhabitants of rocks at the middle tide level is the Leaf Barnacle, *Pollicipes polymerus* (no. 169).

Plate 40. Leaf Barnacles belong to the stalked barnacle group and are permanently attached to the substrate by a fleshy stalk.

Plate 41. Thatched Barnacles, *Tetraclita rubescens* (no. 170), are acorn barnacles, which have no fleshy stalk. The shells attach directly to the substrate.

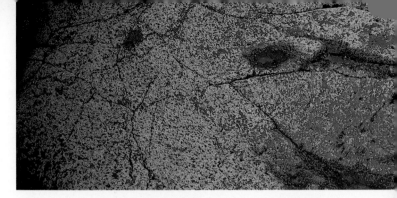

Plate 42. Tiny acorn barnacles cover the rocks in some high tide and splash zones. Shown here are Brown Buckshot Barnacles, *Chthamalus fissus* (no. 171), and White Buckshot Barnacles, *Balanus glandula* (no. 172).

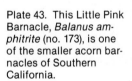

Plate 43. This Little Pink Barnacle, *Balanus amphitrite* (no. 173), is one of the smaller acorn barnacles of Southern California.

Plate 44. The numbers of Webbed Starfish, *Patiria miniata* (no. 230), have suffered an unexplained (and, it is hoped, temporary) decline in recent years.

Plate 45. The Ochre Starfish, *Pisaster ochraceus* (no. 233), is the most common echinoderm on California's surf-swept rocky shores. It is most often found in close proximity to the beds of California Mussels (no. 233).

Plate 46. The Knobby Starfish, *Pisaster giganteus* (no. 234), is not as common in Southern California as the Ochre Starfish.

Plate 47. The Purple Sea Urchin, *Strongylocentrotus purpuratus* (no. 235), is often found firmly imbedded in deep pits in the bedrock.

The drag of the tentacles below the water acts as a keel, and the oblique setting of the sail causes the animal to sail "by-the-wind" instead of following a straight downwind course. The sail and float, made of gas-filled tubes bent into concentric rings, are more resistant to decay than the rest of the body and may remain on the beach long after all the purple portions have disappeared. They are so light in weight that the wind sometimes carries them several miles inland.

Velella is well equipped with nematocysts, and some humans have reportedly been mildly stung by them; but I have handled thousands of By-the-Wind Sailers without feeling the slightest tingle.

Although this species was formerly described as a cooperating colony of many polyps with varied form and function, recent studies have demonstrated that it is an individual polyp, similar to such solitary forms as *Corymorpha* (no. 16). It is thus now placed in the order Chondrophora, rather than among the Siphonophores as formerly.

Class Scyphozoa ("True" Jellyfishes)

24. Purple-Striped Jellyfish, *Pelagia colorata* (Pl. 23). Diameter of the bell to at least 1.5 m (5 ft.), with tentacles up to 7 m (23 ft.) long. Such giants are not at all common, however, and most specimens washed ashore are about 30 cm (1 ft.) across.

Like *Velella* (no. 23), this is a creature of the open seas, but beached specimens are quite common during the summer months. It is very fragile, and all the cast-up specimens have been severely damaged by their journey through the surf.

The nematocysts of *Pelagia* are quite capable of penetrating human skin, and it is one of California's most potent stingers. Even small pieces of the dead animal retain their stinging capacity, and handling or stepping on fragments may produce a temporary burning rash. The most serious stings are those incurred by bathers who get tangled in the long, almost invisible, trailing tentacles. Some people are allergically sensitive to the poison injected by the nematocysts and have a strong reaction necessitating medical aid. This is not common, however, and the sting is usually nothing to worry about for more than the first few irritating minutes. The pain can be lessened by washing the afflicted area with an ammonia solution.

Many large jellyfish species are accompanied by small fishes and crabs that make their home among the stinging tentacles with immunity. *Pelagia* is no exception. Its consorts in Southern California are often juvenile Yellowfin or Spotfin Croakers, both of which have a habit of congregating around or under almost any kind of floating object or material. These fishes cover their bodies with slime from the jellyfish, and this keeps the nematocysts from exploding on contact—although how the fishes get that first slime coating without being stung to death in the process is still a mystery. Young crabs, especially *Cancer gracilis,* are also common associates. "Foreign" creatures that accidentally brush against the jellyfish's tentacles are immediately stung, and they form a staple portion of *Pelagia*'s diet.

Class Anthozoa (Sea Anemones, Corals, and Their Relatives)

25. Slender Sea Pen, *Stylatula elongata*. Length to 46 cm (18 in.), although most shallow-water specimens are much smaller. This is a delicate animal requiring quiet waters. It may be seen at low tide in the shallows of protected bays, while off the open sandy coasts it lives only at depths of 15 m (50 ft.) or more, below the reach of violent wave action.

The Slender Sea Pen has a stiff axial rod of shell-like material, around which is clustered a number of polyp-bearing "leaves," giving the appearance of a pale green or tan three-dimensional feather. The whole animal (or is it a colony?) is attached to a bulb buried in the muddy or sandy substrate; at low tide, or when otherwise disturbed, the soft parts slide down the axis and huddle in the mud, leaving an inch or two of the central stalk sticking out. When the tide is in, or when danger is past, the stalk is pushed up so that most of its length is in the water, and the soft parts expand to cover it. The hundreds of tiny eight-armed polyps are equipped with nematocysts and are quite effective in capturing small floating animals and other food particles.

Like some other anthozoans, the sea pens are noted for their bioluminescence. Flashes of light are produced when the polyps are prodded or otherwise disturbed, especially if the animal has been kept in the dark for a few hours. If the body is touched at midpoint, waves of light will travel in both directions away from the point of stimulation. A stimulus at one end produces a wave in only one direction, while prodding both ends at once causes two waves of light to move toward each other; where they overlap, the light is brighter. These waves are the result of passing the reaction to the stimulus from one polyp to another, the reaction growing less intense and the light getting dimmer as distance from the stimulus increases.

There are many kinds of sea pens, but most of the others are confined to deep waters.

26. Sea Pansy, *Renilla kollikeri*. Diameter about 6.5 cm (2¹/₂ in.). Color amethyst purple. Most likely to be seen in the extreme low tide zone in muddy or sandy bays, although it is also abundant on sandy open coasts in the sublittoral zone just beyond the breakers. The purple disk-shaped body is usually buried horizontally in the substrate, with the polyps protruding upward into the water. The tail-like stalk on the underside turns downward into the substrate, its expanded tip serving as an anchor.

The exposed polyps have two methods of procuring food. Their stinging tentacles, like those of the Slender Sea Pen (no. 25), collect small animals and other edible particles. They also secrete a mucus net that is held up by the polyps; when it becomes full of entrapped particles, the net is swallowed by the colony as a whole.

The Sea Pansy is, under certain conditions, brilliantly luminescent in much the same manner as the Slender Sea Pen.

The bay habitat of this species is rapidly disappearing, and intertidal specimens are increasingly difficult to find. People who can dive to 20 or 30 feet, however, can count on seeing plenty of them off sandy beaches.

27. Solitary Green Anemone, *Anthopleura xanthogrammica* (Pl. 24). Diameter, including the spread tentacles, to 25 cm (10 in.), although about half that is more usual. Color variable; in individuals exposed to the light, usually brilliant green. This green coloring is due in part to actual pigments and in part to the presence of symbiotic microscopic organisms in the anemone's transparent tissues. These symbionts may be unicellular green algae known as zoochlorellae, or these algae in combination with dinoflagellates called zooxanthellae. These tiny organisms cannot thrive in the absence of sunlight, so anemones in shaded places do not show the bright green color.

This anemone is common in rocky areas in the lower tide zones and at higher levels in tidepools that retain their water even when the tide is low.

Although firmly anchored to one spot, the Solitary Green Anemone must be considered a predator. Any small animal brushing against the tentacles is instantly transfixed by scores of nematocysts, which not only inject a paralyzing venom but also hold the prey immobile. The tentacles are then curved so as to point toward the central mouth, while rhythmic movements of microscopic cilia move the object along until it drops into the mouth. Digestion is very rapid, and indigestible portions such as shells are ejected in an amazingly short time.

MacGinitie and MacGinitie (1968) have described how this anemone is capable of learning in a diffuse manner. They placed an indigestible pebble on the tentacles of a Solitary Green Anemone and watched it turn the tentacles and swallow the stone, which was quickly found useless and ejected. When the process was repeated over and over, in the same position on the animal, those particular tentacles learned that the pebble was no good and simply curved toward the outside, dropping the stone without swallowing it. But other tentacles around the disk knew nothing of this, and the whole lesson had to be repeated when the pebble was placed on the opposite side of the anemone. This shows, of course, the effects of an uncentralized nervous system—a "scatterbrained" way of thinking.

The nematocysts are too short to penetrate human skin, and a finger may touch them without being stung. The skin of the human tongue is thinner, and some daring experimenters have reported that licking the tentacles produces a definite stinging sensation. I have not tried this.

If they can be removed from their substrate without injury to the base, these anemones will live very well in an aquarium. Several of them thrived for more than 30 years in the public aquarium at the Scripps Institution of Oceanography, and a related species in Scotland is reported to have lived in a home aquarium for more than 70 years.

28. Aggregate Anemone, *Anthopleura elegantissima* (Pl. 25). Like the Solitary Green Anemone (no. 27) in general appearance but much smaller, the aggregate form rarely exceeding an expanded diameter of 7 cm (2³/₄ in.). (Much larger solitary individuals have been reported from the Pacific Northwest; see McConnaughey and McConnaughey, 1985.) It is an abundant inhabitant of the upper parts of the middle tide zone, forming a dense mat that completely covers large areas of rock and pier pilings. The species is especially abundant on steep rock slopes facing the sea. When the tide is out, each anemone folds in on itself, forming a flat spheroid; since the surface of the column is covered with bits of shell and gravel, these retracted colonies look like the rock itself. Many beach visitors have been dismayed to discover that they are stepping not on solid stone but on the yielding bodies of hundreds of Aggregate Anemones.

A major means of reproduction in this species is by *fission*—a longitudinal splitting of the body into two halves, each of which generates a full set of tentacles and other parts. This process produces two individuals of the same sex. Within a given area, the members of an aggregation will thus be either all male or all female, all in that neighborhood being clones of a single individual. Aggregate Anemones are well equipped with nematocysts, but these stinging structures are not activated by contact with another member of the same clone group.

Where two individuals settle on a rock and start colonies, the populations will spread toward one another but will not merge. Indeed, as they approach closely the peripheral members exhibit what are, for an anemone, very warlike activities, deliberately thrusting toward one another those portions of their bodies that carry the heaviest armament of nematocysts.

Contact made in this manner usually injures both combatants, and they die or withdraw; thus there is a narrow neutral zone, bare of anemones, between the two populations.

The Aggregate Anemone also reproduces sexually by releasing sperm and eggs into the water. The resultant microscopic larvae drift away to start new colonies.

When a colony is under water, as in a tidepool, the individuals are seen in the expanded state. The delicate precision of their radial shape and the varicolored bands on the tentacles present a beautiful sight indeed, and the name *elegantissima* (meaning "most elegant") seems an apt one.

29. Beach Sand Anemone, *Anthopleura artemisia* (Pl. 26). Usually intermediate in size between the smaller Aggregate Anemones and the larger Solitary Green Anemones. Tentacles gray or tan in color. Quite common in our area in the upper low tide zone. Usually found where beach sand fills the spaces between rocks; the anemones have their bases firmly attached to the rocks beneath the sand, stretching upward as much as 30 cm (1 ft.) to bring their crowns of tentacles up into the water. When the tide is low, the anemone retracts into the damp sand to wait out the dry period. Often, however, there will be a water-retaining depression in the sand at the junction of the rock face, and as long as its water stays reasonably cool, the anemone will remain at the surface.

30. Burrowing Bay Anemone, *Zaolutus actius*. A small anemone with a tentacle spread of not more than 28 mm (1 1/8 in.). Lives in the lower low tide zone and below, in quiet bays on sandy or muddy bottoms, or well below the lowest tide level in the relatively quiet waters beyond the breakers off open sandy shores; the largest populations are in these subtidal areas. This is a burrowing form, with its base attached to a piece of shell or stone that may be buried in the mud or sand to a depth of more than 20 cm (8 in.). When the animal is undisturbed and covered with water, the tentacular crown is exposed at the surface of the substrate; when disturbed, it does not usually retract entirely, but does fold in the tentacles. Its color is a uniform cream, gray, or gray-green; the tentacles are marked with opaque gray tips, sometimes with lighter bands. It feeds

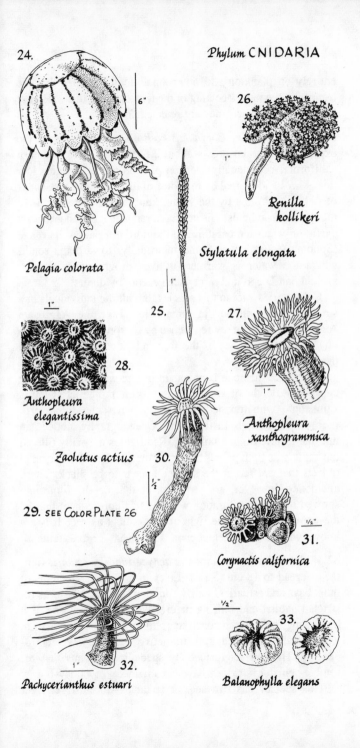

Phylum CNIDARIA

24.

Pelagia colorata

26.

Renilla
kollikeri

Stylatula elongata

25.

27.

Anthopleura
elegantissima

28.

Zaolutus actius

30.

Anthopleura
xanthogrammica

29. SEE COLOR PLATE 26

31.

Corynactis californica

32.

Pachycerianthus estuari

33.

Balanophylla elegans

entirely on plankton and other small food partlcles that are trapped in the mucus coating of the tentacles and disk; if larger bits come in contact, they are rejected.

31. Pink Anemone, *Corynactis californica.* Diameter of the expanded tentacular crown about 2.5 cm (1 in.). In Southern California, occasionally seen on pier pilings at extreme low tide. May be identified by the color of its body (various shades of red or pink) and by the white, knob-ended tentacles. Like many marine animals, this one has a range that depends at least partly on water temperature; in the northern part of its range (Sonoma County) it is found intertidally; toward the south, where the water is warmer, it lives progressively deeper; around San Diego it is rarely seen except by divers.

Color varies a lot in this species, but all the individuals in a single colony will be the same color. Like the Aggregate Anemone (no. 28), they reproduce by fission, and a given colony consists of clones of the first individual to have settled there.

The Pink Anemone is abundant on the walls of submarine canyons at depths of around 30 m (100 ft.). The late Conrad Limbaugh, who founded the well-known scuba-diving program at the Scripps Institution of Oceanography, noticed an unusual feature of their coloring. Red light is normally filtered out rapidly as light passes through water, and at 30 m or more objects that are red at the surface appear to be black. These anemones, however, are red even at that depth. Limbaugh showed that their coloration was due to fluorescence: that is, the animals receive blue light and re-emit it as red. It is not known whether this phenomenon is of advantage to the animal.

32. Tube-Building Anemone, *Pachycerianthus estuari.* Tentacle spread to 13 cm (5 in.). Lives in the muddy bottoms of quiet bays and estuaries. Fairly common, but because of its restricted habitat and retiring nature, not often seen. This is a burrowing form, and it constructs a tunnel lined with mucus in which many detached but still-active nematocysts are imbedded. The tube is formed by specialized organs that resemble nematocysts; they have been named "ptychocysts."

This species has two sets of tentacles—a short set right

around the mouth and a long, slender set located peripherally. The long tentacles expand outward around the mouth of the burrow, and when the animal retracts its body into the tube they drag across the mud, leaving a characteristic star-shaped track.

There are several species of these cerianthids in California waters. The term "anemone" is used because of a superficial resemblance, but it is not really accurate; the cerianthids constitute a separate order that is quite different from anemones.

33. Orange Cup Coral, *Balanophyllia elegans*. The deposition of lime in sufficient quantities to form a coral reef requires water warmer than ours, and there are no reef-forming corals on the California coast. There are, however, several kinds of solitary corals, this being the only one found intertidally. Its cup-shaped "skeleton," up to 2.5 cm (1 in.) in diameter, may be seen at low tide under overhanging rocks and low-level tidepools. Its orange-colored, anemonelike body may be almost completely retracted into the stony cup. The radiating walls or *septa* of this cup are typical of the stony corals.

Phylum Ctenophora
(Comb Jellies)

The ctenophores have the consistency and transparency of jellyfish but are quite different in shape, most of them being either spherical (not umbrella-shaped) or flattened into a ribbon. Their swimming is accomplished by means of eight columns of comblike bristles ("ctenophore" means "comb-bearing") whose rhythmic waving motions propel the animal. There are only two tentacles, and these are retractable into a sheath. Most kinds are brilliantly luminescent.

34. Sea Gooseberry, *Pleurobrachia bachei*. Diameter about 13 mm (½ in.). These little clear spheres are sometimes found on the beach after a storm. Their native habitat is the open sea, where their transparency makes them almost invisible. Sometimes the beach-stranded specimens are relatively unharmed and will begin swimming about if placed in a jar of clean sea water. The beating of the tiny combs then causes a beautiful play of iridescent colors over the surface of the animal.

Phylum Platyhelminthes
(Flatworms)

There are three classes in this phylum. Two of these, the flukes (Trematoda) and the tapeworms (Cestoda), are parasitic and will not be considered here. The third class, Turbellaria, has a few parasites among its 3,000 species, but most are free-living and many of these are marine.

In the animals considered up to this point, the basic plan of symmetry, if any, has been a radial one, symmetrical around a center point. The flatworms, however, and most of the groups to be mentioned later (except for the starfishes) are bilaterally symmetrical, with a right side and a left side that are mirror images of each other. Flatworms, unlike jellyfishes, have layers of tissue between the two dermal layers, and these inner parts may consist of muscle, reproductive organs, and connective tissue. Some species do not possess a digestive tract, but when such a tract is present it has only one opening, which serves as both mouth and anus.

The free-living turbellarians have microscopic cilia covering the entire surface of the body. The beating of these cilia creates a disturbance—a turbulence—in the water, which is where the class gets its name. All are carnivorous, and all obtain their food through a process of turning the throat inside out through the mouth, which is located near the center of the body's lower surface.

The members of this class are retiring in habit, living under rocks and among seaweeds. The largest are no more than about 10 cm (4 in.) in length. The turbellarian fauna of California has not been studied in detail, and some of our forms have not been named; precise identification should thus not be expected at this point.

35. Common Flatworm, *Notoplana acticola*. Length about 13 mm (½ in.), color gray or tan—but somewhat translucent, tending to take on the color of the substrate. It also may take on the color of the food it eats, as when those dining on the Red Sponge Nudibranch, *Rostanga pulchra* (no. 143), turn a rosy pink.

This species is quite common on the undersides of rocks in the middle and low tide zones. When a sheltering rock is turned over, these flatworms will be seen oozing along "much as a drop of glycerine flows down the side of a glass dish," in the words of Edward F. Ricketts (Ricketts, Calvin, and Hedgpeth, 1985, p. 44).

36. Fuzzy Flatworm, *Thysanozoon sandiegense.* Length to 4 cm (1½ in.), usually dark gray in color. The back is covered with small brown or gray papillae that look like coarse fur. Occasionally seen in the middle and low tide zones in rocky areas. Usually found crawling on rock. If removed and set free in the water, this flatworm swims gracefully and well, with a characteristic undulating motion of the edges of its flat body. Much firmer in texture than the preceding species.

37. White Flatworm, *Pseudoceros luteus* (not illustrated). Length about 5 cm (2 in.); color white, with a black stripe down the center of the body. Common in our area, usually under rocks in middle and low tide zones. Like the preceding species, this one is a good swimmer. The deep undulations along the sides of the flat body are rhythmically waved when swimming and are obvious even when the flatworm is at rest or crawling about on the bottom. Like some of the nudibranchs (such as the Rose Nudibranch, no. 145), it sometimes crawls upside down at the surface of a still tidepool, suspended from the water's surface tension.

Phylum Nemertea
(Ribbon Worms or Proboscis Worms)

This is another group whose retiring habits make its members almost unknown to most of us. This is surprising in light of the size attained by some of its species; at least one is reliably reported to reach a length of 19 m (62 ft.)! They are extremely flexible and ductile and can thicken the body and shorten it to a fraction of its extended length.

Ribbon worms possess an eversible *proboscis*—a "nose" that can be extended by turning inside out. This organ lies in a sort of sheath above the mouth. In some species its tip is armed with hooked stylets, but in most kinds it is covered with a sticky mucus. In both cases the proboscis is used for the capture of food. Most nemerteans are burrowers, spending their active hours crawling through tunnels either of their own devising or made by other creatures. Their long proboscises, which may be as long as the body, are sent scouting along the burrows ahead of the main body, ready to subdue and retrieve annelid worms or other prey.

Collection of certain kinds of ribbon worms in an unbroken state is practically impossible, for they very readily *autotomize*—that is, they break themselves into fragments if disturbed. Each piece thus produced may regenerate the parts necessary to become a whole ribbon worm. The late Wesley R. Coe found that any piece of *Lineus vegetus* (no. 39) with a length at least one-half its diameter would regenerate and become a whole animal in three or four weeks. He speculated that this might be a major mode of reproduction in this and other nemertean species.

38. Pink Nemertean, *Procephalothryx major.* Length (rarely) to 1.2 m (4 ft.); diameter of body to about 1.5 mm ($^1/_{16}$ in.). Color ranges from light straw to deep pink, with anterior portions of the body usually darker than the posterior. Lives in sand or clay under rocks in the low tide zone; the threadlike body is usually snarled into tangled knots or spiraled in coils.

39. Banded Nemertean, *Lineus vegetus.* Length to 15 cm (6 in.). Color olive or red-brown, lighter underneath; body usually encircled by up to 20 narrow, lighter bands. Fairly common beneath stones, in crevices, and among coralline seaweeds in the middle tide zone. It is also occasionally seen in quiet muddy bays.

40. Fragile Nemertean, *Cerebratulus californiensis.* Length to 24 cm (9$^1/_2$ in.). Variable in color, with the head often darker than the hind portions of the body. The front part of the body is usually round in cross section, but the posterior is flattened into a ribbon shape; when swimming, it progresses by vertical undulations of this flattened portion. Living in muddy or sandy bottoms in quiet waters, this is one of our most common nemerteans.

41. Green Nemertean, *Emplectonema gracile.* Length occasionally to 50 cm (20 in.), but usually much less; diameter about 1.5 mm ($^1/_{16}$ in.). Color green, lighter below. Common

Phylum CTENOPHORA

34.

Pleurobrachia bachei

Phylum PLATYHELMINTHES

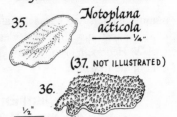

35.
Notoplana acticola
¼"

(37. NOT ILLUSTRATED)

36.
½"
Thysanozoon sandiegense

Phylum NEMERTEA

½"
38.
Procephalothryx major

39.
½"
Lineus vegetus

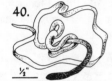

40.
½"
Cerebratulus californiensis

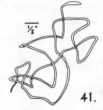

½"
41.
Emplectonema gracile

Phyla ENTOPROCTA and ECTOPROCTA

42.

Barentsia gracilis

43.
×1
Bugula californica

44. (MAGNIFIED)
Membranipora tuberculata

among mussels and barnacles and sometimes under stones on muddy substrates. The best identifying description is that by Joel W. Hedgpeth (1962); it looks like "sticky bootlaces strung among the mussels."

Phylum Entoprocta
(Entoproct Moss Animals)

This and the next-listed phylum (Ectoprocta) are superficially quite similar. It was only recently that taxonomists learned enough about them to realize not only that they constitute two phyla, but that the two are not even very closely related. We are here considering them contiguously, however, and are using the vernacular term "moss animal" to apply to both. (The old name of the phylum in which they were placed together is Bryozoa, which means "moss animals.") There are about 60 known species of entoprocts in the world, all of them small: no individual exceeds a length of 1.5 mm (1/16 in.). However, they live in mosslike colonies containing thousands of individuals, forming mats of considerable size.

Each animal is crowned with a circlet of ciliated tentacles, within which lies the mouth. Also within this ring is the anal opening, a fact to which the term "entoproct" refers.

42. Felt Moss Animal, *Barentsia gracilis.* Forms a thin, felt-like brown crust on pier pilings, rocks, seaweeds, and other objects. A hand lens will reveal a typical entoproct structure, with the body of the animal borne in a *calyx* at the end of a slender stalk. The attachment of the calyx allows it to move in a manner that has caused this genus to be called "nodding heads" in Europe.

Phylum Ectoprocta
(Ectoproct Moss Animals)

One of the features setting this phylum apart from the ento-procts is that the anus is located outside the circlet of tentacles; hence the word "ectoproct."

The ectoprocts are colonial, and not all individuals in the colony have identical structure. A few are modified to the form known as *aviculariae,* which, when seen under a microscope, resemble nothing so much as living skulls of birds of prey, with vicious-looking snapping beaks. The snapping is apparently automatic, but is coordinated, and the aviculariae must present a fearful obstacle to any little barnacle larvae that might start to settle on an ectoproct colony.

There are about 5,000 species in this phylum, and all, with the exception of about 50 freshwater forms, live in the sea. Several dozen of these can be found in our area.

43. California Moss Animal, *Bugula californica.* Grows in mosslike clumps, 4 to 6 cm (1¹/₂ to 2¹/₄ in.) high and of a brown or purplish color. Found at low tide level; the best place to look for it is under overhanging ledges in tidepools. The avicularia are very active, as can easily be seen with a hand lens; they not only play a defensive role, but also help secure food for the colony.

44. Jackfrost Moss Animal, *Membranipora tuberculata.* This is a thin, white, encrusting form, and one may find its frosty pattern on almost any sort of surface that has been immersed in sea water. Brown seaweeds are perhaps the most usual substrate. Each zooid lives in a separate little limy coffin-shaped "house" about 0.5 mm (¹/₃₂ in.) long, into which it retracts its ten-tentacled head when disturbed. It is the walls of these compartments that form the delicate pattern. There are no avicularia.

Phylum Phoronida
(Phoronid Worms)

This is a small phylum, with only two genera and about 16 species. Their wormlike bodies are encased in tubes, most of them buried vertically in the substrate with their tentacled heads extended up into the water. The tentacles grow from an organ known as the *lophophore,* and often follow its spiral or horseshoe shape. A few phoronids are solitary, but most occur in dense colonies.

45. Twining Phoronid, *Phoronis vancouverensis.* The horizontally intertwining tubes of this species contrast with the vertical orientation of most phoronids. The Twining Phoronid occurs in dense clusters with the tentacular crowns of yellowish or gray extended up into the water. Spottily abundant, usually on some hard substrate such as pier pilings or, in quiet waters, rocks. Individual tubes are about 4 cm (1½ in.) long and are not encrusted with sand as are most other phoronids.

Phylum Mollusca
(Molluscs)

The molluscs constitute a populous, widespread, ancient, and well-known phylum. Molluscs live in the sea, in fresh water, and on the land in practically every part of the world. The group has existed at least since the Cambrian period, 500 million years ago, and there are probably 50,000 or more species living today.

Members of the phylum come in a tremendous array of sizes, from smaller than a sand grain to 20 m (65 ft.), the length of the giant squid.

The Latin word *mollis,* meaning "soft," gives us the name and describes the soft, unsegmented body that is characteristic of the group. Another uniquely molluscan feature is the *radula,* an organ shaped like a flexible ribbon of sandpaper. In some species this is used as a scraper to rasp plant growth from the substrate; in others it is used for boring, often through the shells of other molluscs, which are then devoured.

Other typical mollusc structures include a broad muscular foot and a fleshy *mantle,* which secretes the limy shell. This shell, whether external or hidden within the soft parts of the animal, is the most familiar characteristic of the phylum. The hard shells of molluscs are durable, resisting dissolution for some time after their inhabitants have died. This increases the probability of mineralization, so molluscs are well represented in the fossil record. The soft parts of the body, however, decay rapidly and do not lend themselves to these processes. Consequently, our knowledge of the internal anatomy of the more ancient forms has been a matter of comparison, inference, and speculation. Biologists were accordingly enthusiastically interested when, in 1952, a "new" kind of shellfish was discovered. It represented a group of molluscs thought to have been extinct for 30 million years or so and known only from imperfect fossils. The soft parts of this freshly preserved animal provided all sorts of information about the evolution of the phylum. Some of its anatomical features had been postulated as theoretically necessary, but here they were in the flesh! The animal was christened *Neopilina galatheae* and placed in the class Monoplacophora. Until then, all living molluscs had been placed in six other classes: (1) Aplacophora, the deep-sea solenogasters; (2) Polyplacophora (or Amphineura), the chitons; (3) Pelecypoda (or Bivalvia), the clams and oysters; (4) Gastropoda, the snails; (5) Scaphopoda, the tusk shells; and (6) Cephalopoda, the squids, octopuses, and cuttlefishes. Five of the seven molluscan classes—all but the Monoplacophora and the Aplacophora—are well represented on the California coast.

Class Polyplacophora (Chitons or Sea Cradles)

Chitons (pronounced KITE-'ns) are molluscs with armadillo-like jointed shells. These shells are composed of eight separate plates (also known as *valves*), the outer edges of which are imbedded in a tough fleshy mantle; this mantle extends beyond the ends of the valves, forming a peripheral band known as the *girdle*. Chitons also possess a broad muscular foot, which they use to creep along or cling tenaciously to the substrate. Most are vegetarians or scavengers, using their radulae to rasp food particles from rock, seaweed, or other substrate. The teeth on their radulae are specially hardened with magnetite, an iron mineral the chitons synthesize themselves. This discovery only a few years ago by researchers such as Townsend and Lowenstam ushered in a new scientific specialty known as biomineralization.

The lateral ends of the eight transverse plates are partially buried in the girdle, which in some species has a mossy or wooly appearance. In the Gumboot Chiton, *Cryptochiton*, this girdle is expanded to cover the plates completely. This species, by the way, is a cold-water form not now occurring in Southern California, but shell fragments in the kitchen middens left by our early Indian predecessors attest to the fact that it was once common here. The chiton's former distribution indicates something of the fluctuations in the sea's average temperature. A great deal of paleoclimatology has been revealed through the study of the middens left by California Indians.

46. Tan Chiton, *Leptochitona rugatus*. Length 1.3 cm (1/2 in.). This is our smallest chiton and is not common. Rocks half-buried in a sandy substrate at the low tide levels constitute its most favored habitat. It is a neat little animal, the divisions between its plates precisely marked. The plates themselves are tan or orange in color, while the foot is purplish brown.

47. Hartweg's Chiton, *Cyanoplax hartwegii*. Length to 5 cm (2 in.), body wider in relation to its length than most of our chitons. Lives in the upper middle tide zone and is especially common in the shelter of the stiff brown kelp *Pelvetia*. It is active at night, roaming about to graze on algae, but returns to its permanent home spot for the day. The color is generally brown or olive, with the mantle darker than the valves.

48. Troglodyte Chiton, *Nuttallina fluxa* (Pl. 27). Length to 3.5 cm (1 1/4 in.), width about one-third of the length. Color variable, from dark brown to light yellow-brown; valves and girdle usually obscured by algal growth. The valves show a pattern of tiny raised granules. There is a slight ridge down the middle of the back with a shallow groove on each side. In Southern California these chitons are most often found living in shallow depressions on the near-horizontal tops and sides of sandstone rocks in the middle and high tide zones. These depressions are often more than 1.3 cm (1/2 in.) deep and are used by generation after generation of chitons. The pits not only protect the animals from waves and most predators, but help feed them as well; they cause turbulent riffles as the water swirls past them, which in turn causes the settling of bits of seaweed and other debris on which the chitons live. The Troglodyte Chiton usually grows so as to fit the bottom of its pit exactly, and may never move away during its long life of 20 years or more.

49. Mossy Chiton, *Mopalia muscosa*. Length to 6 cm (2 1/2 in.). Color usually dark brown; the plates are often obscured by plant growth. The fleshy girdle is covered with stiff "hairs" that look like a fringe of moss. Like *Nuttallina,* this chiton often inhabits a shallow depression on the nearly horizontal surface of a rock in the middle and high tide zones, but it regularly leaves its habitation, when darkness coincides with a sufficiently high tide, to graze nearby; it comes home with the advent of daylight or low tide.

50. Mertens' Chiton, *Lepidozona mertensii.* Length occasionally to 5 cm (2 in.), but usually much smaller. Color variable, most often some shade of red-brown or orange-brown, often with white spots. The valves are quite heavily granulated, and the girdle is scaly. This is one of several species in the genus *Lepidozona,* all of which are quite similar in appearance.

51. Conspicuous Chiton, *Stenoplax conspicua.* Length to 15.4 cm (6 in.); color gray, green, and brown, usually with pink in the centers of the valves. This is our largest local chiton. It is found most often on the undersides of small, rounded rocks half-buried in sand in the middle and low tide zones. When such a rock is turned over, the Conspicuous Chitons attached to its underside will crawl away from the light with surprising speed.

Class Pelecypoda (Clams, Mussels, Oysters, and Their Relatives)

The term "Pelecypoda" means "hatchet-foot," and the muscular foot in some species may indeed remotely resemble a hatchet. Although "Pelecypoda" is not very descriptive of the class, I prefer it to the term "Bivalvia," which has come into recent use. One reason is that many of the other classes of molluscs are named for some feature of their feet, and there is a pleasant euphony to "Gastropoda, Pelecypoda, Scaphopoda, Cephalopoda," and so on. Another reason is that "Bivalvia" means "two shells," and while it is generally appropriate, we now know that some snails (gastropods) such as *Berthelina* also have two valves, so the term loses its distinctiveness.

In any event, the characteristic members of the class Pelecypoda have two shells, or valves—a right one and a left one—that most often fit closely together. They are opened and closed by means of powerful connecting muscles.

52. California Mussel, *Mytilus californianus* (Pls. 17 and 28). Length to 18 cm (7 in.) occasionally, but most individuals in the intertidal zone of our area are less than 12 cm (5 in.) long. Abundant in the upper middle tide zone in areas exposed to surf, attached to rocks or pier pilings. The *periostracum,* or outer covering of the shell, is dark brown, but is usually worn away near the beaks of the shell, revealing the blue-gray layer beneath. The shell usually shows strong radiating ribs, especially around the unworn outer edges.

The great colonies—"mussel beds"—in surf-swept areas are made possible by the mussels' effective means of attachment to the substrate and to each other using *byssus* threads. While settling down in its permanent home, the young mussel slightly parts its two valves and sticks out a special part of its orange foot between them. This touches the substrate then withdraws, leaving behind a yellowish thread that quickly hardens. A number of these, glued firmly over several square centimeters of the substrate with their other ends converging into the mussel's shell, provide an excellent anchorage not only to the rock or pier piling but to already attached mussels. Thus a mussel bed consists of a thick series of layers among which many other kinds of animals find a relatively safe refuge from the surf. MacGinitie and MacGinitie (1968) once counted 625 California Mussels in an area about 25 cm (10 in.) square, and among them they found 4,096 other creatures of 22 different species.

Mussels feed by using ciliary action to create a flow of water through their siphons and over their gills, where sheets of mucus move food particles—after an automatic sorting process—to the digestive tract. A large mussel may process as much as 60 liters (16 gallons) of sea water in a full day of feeding, and the quantities of water turned over by a large mussel bed have a powerful influence on the nature of the surrounding water.

Mussel beds are primarily associated with the upper parts of the middle tide zone. An interesting feature of their distribution is that while the number of mussels gradually decreases toward the upper limits of the bed, the lower limit is marked by a sharp cutoff; this is especially noticeable in exposed areas.

Phylum PHORONIDA

45.
Phoronis vancouverensis
¼"

Phylum MOLLUSCA

¼"

46.
Leptochitona rugatus

½"

47.
Cyanoplax hartwegii

½"

48.
Nuttallina fluxa

Lepidozona mertensii

50.
½"

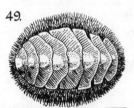

49.
Mopalia muscosa   ½"

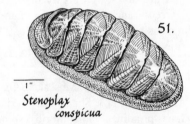

51.
Stenoplax conspicua   1"

52.
Mytilus californianus

53.
Mytilus edulis

54.
Septifer bifurcatus

(ALL TO SAME SCALE)
1"

The orange flesh of this mussel makes fine fish bait and is also excellent as human food, although perhaps not quite as tasty as the Bay Mussel (no. 53). Both species may at times contain dangerous levels of the toxic dinoflagellate *Gonyaulax catenella* (no. 2) and should be eaten only after due consideration of the season and the quarantine rules.

Two other conspicuous species are commonly associated with the California Mussel beds, to the extent that Ricketts, Calvin, and Hedgpeth (1985) have referred to them as "the Big Three of the wave-swept outer coast." These are the Ochre Starfish, *Pisaster ochraceous* (no. 233), and the Leaf Barnacle, *Pollicipes polymerus* (no. 169).

53. Bay Mussel, *Mytilus edulis*. Length to 10 cm (4 in.). Color blue-black; often called the Blue Mussel. Surface smooth, without the radiating ribs of the preceding species. Sometimes found on rocky outer coasts at a lower level than the California Mussel; more common in bays. The anchor lines of mooring and marking buoys often accumulate great bunches of these blue mussels. This is a widespread species, and in Europe it is highly prized as the "moules" of multi-starred French restaurants. Rather surprisingly, however, it is not eaten extensively in California. If you wish to be an exception, be sure to observe the months of quarantine. (See the discussion of *Gonyaulax catenella*, no. 2.)

54. Branch-Ribbed Mussel, *Septifer bifurcatus*. Length to 4.5 cm (1³/₄ in.). Shape almost triangular; color light brown. It has prominent radiating ribs, some of which branch. The inside of the shell has a little covered "deck" near the small end. Common in the middle and low tide zones. In the middle zone, it occurs among California Mussels but does not form beds of its own; those in the lower tide zone occur singly.

55. Fat Horse Mussel, *Modiolus capax*. Length usually about 12.5 cm (5 in.). Similar to the California Mussel but broader in relation to its length, with the sharp end of the brown shell extending beyond the hinge. The periostracum is thick and in places extended into a "beard" of stiff filaments. This is the most common mussel of protected bays and lagoons and may be found either singly or in small clusters. In some places it may be associated with beds of California or Bay Mussels.

56. Date Mussel, *Lithophaga plumula.* Length to 5 cm (2 in.), in shape much like a large date seed. The name *Lithophaga* means "rock-eating" and is appropriate in a metaphorical way, for this gray-brown mussel drives its neat round tunnels into shale, clay, and other shells. It does not actually eat the rock, but drills through it with a combination of mechanical rasping and chemical dissolution. In certain kinds of shale its tunnels may be lined with a substance harder than the surrounding rock, so that weathering away of the parent rock often leaves short tubes projecting from its surface. Fairly common in the low tide zone.

57. Native Oyster, *Ostrea lurida.* Diameter to about 6 cm (2³/₈ in.). Shells thin, fairly flat, irregularly round; the two valves are of equal size and usually show coarse concentric growth rings. The color on the outside varies from gray-white to purple-black, occasionally with maroon or purple bands. The interior of the shell is moderately shiny, ranging from gray to green, often with a metallic sheen. Common in sheltered waters attached to practically any kind of solid object or substrate.

This oyster is native to the Pacific coast and is appreciated as a gastronomic delicacy. Its abundance in Indian kitchen middens shows that this appreciation has a long and unbroken history. Efforts at cultivation have been made in the Pacific Northwest (where it is usually referred to as the Olympia Oyster) and are meeting with increasing success.

Breeding habits of the Native Oyster involve a series of successive alternations of sex, each individual changing from male to female and back again several times during its lifetime. Some of those in the process of changing may be fully functioning hermaphrodites, operating for a short time as both male and female.

58. Speckled Scallop, *Argopecten aequisulcatus.* Diameter to 9 cm (3¹/₂ in.). Color variable, usually some shade of light brown with darker (often purplish) irregular markings. Both valves are deeply convex, each with 19 to 22 prominent ribs, which are somewhat rounded in cross section. The Speckled Scallop was formerly abundant in bays and estuaries, but human predation coupled with the diminution of its estuarine habitat have so depleted its numbers that legal control has become necessary. At this time there is *no* open season and possession of this species is expressly forbidden by the game laws of California.

The scallops in general are the most alert and "intelligent" of the pelecypods. Their nervous system is the most complex in the class, and many species have highly developed eyes, which appear as bright little blue buttons between the tentacles that fringe the mantle. Scallops are quite active as swimmers, a characteristic that helps them escape from slow-moving predatory starfishes. They swim by rapidly and repeatedly opening and clapping together the valves like a pair of self-powered castanets. With each closing of the valves, a jet of water forced out between them through openings at the hinge propels the animal forward. Movement is toward the open side of the shells, with the hinge as the trailing edge, and proceeds in a zigzag manner.

Scallops are among the most delectable of seafoods and fetch a high price in the marketplace. Unscrupulous merchants have been known to manufacture fake scallops by cutting scallop-sized disks from the cheek muscles of the relatively inexpensive Northern Halibut and other fishes and selling them at full scallop prices. Such scallop scalping is, needless to say, frowned upon by the law.

59. Kelp Scallop, *Leptopecten monotimerus.* Diameter about 2.5 cm (1 in.). Valves fairly flat, very thin and fragile. Color yellow, brown, or orange, usually with white zigzag cross stripes. The size of the population is subject to tremendous variation. In most years the Kelp Scallop is an uncommon, rare, or even absent species—then suddenly there will be millions of them attached to seaweeds, especially the Elk Kelp, *Pelagophycus porra.* These scallop-laden seaweeds do not grow in the intertidal zone, but detached plants are frequently cast up on the beach.

Phylum MOLLUSCA

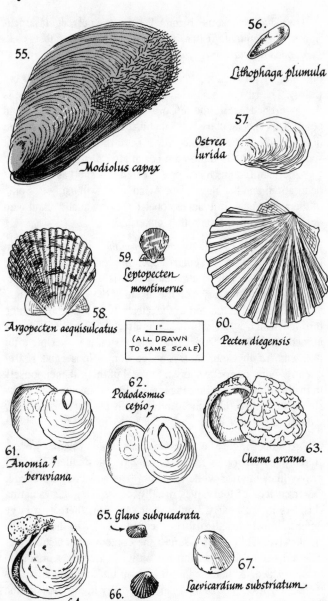

55. *Modiolus capax*

56. *Lithophaga plumula*

57. *Ostrea lurida*

58. *Argopecten aequisulcatus*

59. *Leptopecten monotimerus*

60. *Pecten diegensis*

1"
(ALL DRAWN
TO SAME SCALE)

61. *Anomia ♂ peruviana*

62. *Pododesmus cepio*

63. *Chama arcana*

64. *Pseudochama exogyra*

65. *Glans subquadrata*

66. *Americardia biangulata*

67. *Laevicardium substriatum*

There has been some argument about the correct classification of this animal. It has often been listed as a subspecies, *Leptopecten latiauratus monotimeris.*

60. San Diego Scallop, *Pecten diegensis.* Diameter to 13 cm (5 in.). The ribs are square in cross section. The right valve is deeply arched, while the left one is flat and usually darker in color. This spectacular shell inhabits deep waters offshore and does not live in the intertidal zone; nevertheless, an occasional specimen may be found on the beach after a storm.

American Indians have long favored this shell as a base for decoration, and the Navajos of Arizona are still using it. Some of their most beautiful pieces consist of entire shells inlaid with designs of turquoise and other materials.

61. Pearly Jingle Shell, *Anomia peruviana.* Diameter to 5 cm (2 in.). Shape very irregular, depending on the nature of the substrate to which it is attached. Color is usually a pale blue-green with a pearly luster on the inside of the valves. The right valve is flat and cemented to the substrate; it has a large notch through which byssus threads are attached. The left valve is arched, with three distinct muscle scars on the interior; after the death of the animal, this valve comes loose and is frequently found on rocky shores. Several of them shaken loosely in the hand produce a jingling sound. Found on exposed rocky shores in the low tide zone. Living shells are not often seen by the casual beach visitor.

62. Abalone Jingle Shell, *Pododesmus cepio.* Diameter occasionally 10 cm (4 in.), but usually much smaller. Exterior gray-white, interior white to green. The soft body is orange. Outer surface of the valves usually shows irregular radiating ribs. As in the Pearly Jingle Shell (no. 61), there is a large notch, almost closed to form a circular hole, in the attached right valve. This valve assumes the contours of its substrate. The left valve is arched and has only two muscle scars on its inner surface. Abundant in our area in the low tide zone, attached to rocks, pier pilings, and especially to the shells of the Red Abalone, *Haliotis rufescens* (no. 86).

63. Agate Chama, *Chama arcana.* Diameter to 7 cm (2³/4 in.). Color white, sometimes (especially in young individuals) with a red tinge. Young specimens have concentric rows of square-tipped translucent frills. Attaches to the substrate by the left valve, which, unlike the attached valves of the jingle shell, is arched. The upper (left) valve is smaller than the lower, fitting into it like the lid of a cunningly contrived jewel box. This upper valve spirals inward in a clockwise direction. This is an abundant species on the undersides of rocks from the middle tide zone downward and on more exposed substrates in quiet waters. It is also frequently found on floating objects, in which case the square-tipped frills are not usually eroded or broken.

64. Reversed Chama, *Pseudochama exogyra.* Similar in size, shape, and color to the Agate Chama (no. 63) except that it attaches to the substrate by the right valve. The inward-coiling structure of the upper left valve is counterclockwise, as opposed to the clockwise spiral of the Agate Chama. The two species are often found together.

65. Little Heart Shell, *Glans subquadrata.* Length 15 mm ($^5/_8$ in.). Color brown or tan outside, usually green or purple on the inside of the valves. The heavy ribs, squarish outline, and small size will distinguish this clam from any other in our region. It has been listed under several names, including *Glans carpenteri, Glans minuscula,* and *Cardita subquadrata.* Often found under rocks below the middle tide zone.

66. Stout Heart Shell, *Americardia biangulata.* Length about 3 cm ($1^3/_{16}$ in.). Shape circular. The *beaks* (projections of the shells above the hinge) are prominent. About 27 sharply defined radiating ribs are square in cross section. A velvety brown periostracum covers the shells of living specimens, but these are not found intertidally in our area. Dead shells, however, of a flat white color, are often abundant where offshore sand has been dredged up for extension and repair of the beach.

67. Common Eggshell Cockle, *Laevicardium substriatum.* Length to 3.5 cm ($1^3/_8$ in.). The rounded valves are smooth, of a whitish or light brown color, usually with fine interrupted radial markings. The interior of each valve is yellow with purple blotches. Abundant in bays and estuaries.

The word "cockle," by the way, is generally used for members of the family Cardiidae, but this restriction is fairly recent. The ancient Indo-European root was *konkho-,* which could mean any kind of shellfish. (Our word "conch" comes from this same root.). The Greek *konkhe* means "mussel," while the French *coquille* can be used for any kind of shell—as well as for a typographical error!

68. Pismo Clam, *Tivela stultorum.* Length to at least 15 cm (6 in.). The valves are thick and strong, covered with a glossy varnishlike periostracum. Radial dark brown or purplish lines fan out from the beaks, which are located about in the middle of the hinged edge. The hinge ligament holding the two valves together is large and has the appearance of horn. Formerly common on broad, sandy beaches, where it buries itself vertically in the sand, sometimes to a depth equal to its own length. When undisturbed, however, the posterior tip of the shell is just barely beneath the sand's surface. Thus the incurrent siphon reaches just above the sand to take in water for respiration and filter feeding. This water may then be jetted out of the excurrent siphon, which points down and helps the clam penetrate dense beach sand. A medium-sized Pismo Clam processes as much as 60 liters (almost 16 gallons) of water per day.

The clam takes its name from the area of Pismo Beach, rather than the other way around. "Pismo" is from an Indian word for "tar," but no one is quite certain exactly how this applies to Pismo Beach. There are offshore sources of oil in that area, and that particular beach may have been a good place for gathering up gobs of tar from natural seepage to use in the waterproof caulking of baskets. This derivation of the place name, however, is undocumented.

The Pismo Clam is one of the noblest of seafoods, and it has been hunted all along the California coast to the verge of extinction. In the record year 1918, 350,000 were collected at Pismo Beach and Morro Bay; in 1973, only 21 legal-sized specimens were taken at Pismo Beach, and fewer than that at Morro Bay (Morris, Abbot, and Haderlie, 1980, p. 373). The fact that human predation was primarily responsible for this decrease was demonstrated when, during World War II, the whole coast around Pismo Beach was closed, resulting in the total cessation of human clam digging. When the area was opened again in 1949, the clams had had a chance to multiply, and clam-hungry hunters took thousands of clams every day for two and a half months, at which time the population was once more depleted. Today no clam digger is allowed to possess more than 10 Pismo Clams at one time, all of which (in Southern California) must be at least 11.5 cm (4½ in.) long.

In preparing Pismo Clams for the table, some people are surprised to find in the flesh a pencil-shaped object that looks like clear plastic, and are suspicious of it as an unnatural foreign intruder. It is quite natural, however, being common to many pelecypods and gastropods; called the crystalline style, it contains a storehouse of the enzyme *amylase,* without which the animal cannot digest starch. The crystalline style is largest when the clam has been fasting.

69. White Venus, *Amiantis callosa.* Length occasionally to 10 cm (4 in.). Color white. The shell is heavy, with bold concentric rounded ridges; there are no radiating lines. This is another species that lives beyond the lowest tides whose dead shells are frequently found on the shore.

70. Wavy Chione, *Chione undatella.* Length to 6 cm (2³/₈ in.). Fairly prominent radial ribs, although these are somewhat obscured by the closely spaced continuous concentric ridges that cross them. The color is gray or white, sometimes with purplish blotches. Abundant in sandy bays and lagoons as well as in deeper waters off sandy beaches. The dead shells are bleached white and are especially abundant on filled beaches.

71. Smooth Chione, *Chione fluctifraga.* Quite similar in size and shape to the Wavy Chione (no. 70), but its radial ridges are more prominent than its concentric ridges, and the ridges are not raised into vanes. Shells of living specimens are yellowish, usually with a purple-brown blotch at the hinge. Fairly common on mud and sand flats in quiet bays.

72. Common Littleneck, *Protothaca staminea.* Length to 7 cm (2³/₄ in.). Oval in shape. Valves with many fine but prominent radiating ribs, crossed by less prominent irregularly spaced concentric ridges. Lives in sand and coarse sandy mud in bays and estuaries, usually buried several centimeters deep. The color is variable: usually a uniform gray or brown in sheltered waters, while those living on more exposed beaches are lighter, with geometric zigzag brown markings. Highly edible and much sought after.

73. California Mactra, *Mactra californica*. Length to 6 cm (2³/₈ in.). Oval in shape. The shell is white, but usually partially covered with a fibrous brown periostracum that may form concentric wrinkles, giving the valve a ridged appearance. Fairly common in sand or sandy mud of bays and estuaries, especially near the entrances, usually buried at depths up to 15 cm (6 in.); also common below the low tide levels off sandy beaches, and fairly often cast ashore there.

74. Gaper Clam, *Tresus nuttalli*. Length to 20 cm (8 in.). One of our largest bivalves, attaining a weight of at least 1.8 kg (4 lbs.). The whitish valves are thin and covered with a thick brown periostracum, which is usually eroded away in spots. This clam has a wide range, from the high tide mark out to depths of at least 30 m (100 ft.). It buries itself to a depth of 1 m (more than 3 ft.) in sand or sandy mud in estuaries and on protected outer beaches. In intertidal areas the siphons are sometimes exposed at the surface. When disturbed the Gaper retracts its large siphons in a way that creates a spurt of water; clam diggers on mud flats locate their prey by watching for these squirts. The Gaper Clam provides one of the finest seafoods of the Pacific Coast.

Like several other clams in our area, the gaper is frequently infested with larval tapeworms, whose life cycle requires eventual transfer from the clam to the Bat Stingray, *Myliobatus*. This species of tapeworm is completely harmless to man, and all vestiges of the larvae are destroyed by cooking.

75. Bent-Nosed Clam, *Macoma nasuta*. Length to 5 cm (2 in.). Shell fragile, white, covered with a thin gray periostracum. The posterior end is elongated and bent to the right. This clam habitually buries itself in sand or mud, lying in a horizontal position with the bent "nose" pointing upward. The siphons protrude from this tip, the incurrent siphon reaching into the water above the substrate; it then bends downward until its tip just touches the surface. This mud-water interface is covered with a thin film of organic detritus, which is drawn into the siphon as water is pumped through. When the clam has cleared all the surface it can reach, it moves to another location.

76. White Sand Clam, *Macoma secta.* Length to 9 cm (3½ in.). Rather similar to the Bent-Nosed Clam (no. 75) but larger and without the bent tip; also, the thin periostracum tends toward an olive color. Fairly common in sand or sandy mud of bays and estuaries. Its feeding habits are identical to those of the Bent-Nosed Clam, and the lack of the bent nose does not seem to inhibit food gathering. It does, however, take in quite a lot of sand with the incurrent water, and the sand-packed gut makes it less palatable for human consumption.

77. Yellow Metis, *Leporimetis obesa.* Length to 8 cm (3⅛ in.) or more. The yellow-brown valves are oval, asymmetrical, and covered with an irregular thin gray periostracum. A wide, shallow groove runs from the beak to the outer edge, marking off the posterior slope of the shell. The inside of the shell is glossy white, suffused near the center with clear yellow or peach; this color fades soon after the death of the animal. Fairly common in coarse sand or fine gravel in quiet waters and buried in sand among rocks on the outer beaches.

78. Bean Clam, *Donax gouldii.* Length to about 2.5 cm (1 in.). The valves are strong, with beaks set near the posterior end. Color is very variable, from light buff to chocolate brown or deep blue-gray, sometimes yellow, orange, or purplish. Many individuals show a pattern of darker or lighter bands, either concentric or radial. Dead shells, before the two valves become completely separated, often gape widely, and in this position have been called Sea Butterflies.

Living Bean Clams maintain a constant position relative to the tide level, usually well above the tide at any given moment, and moving with the waves just far enough to remain at that level. They dig into the sand in a vertical position with the posterior end up. This end of the shell often bears a tuft of the

Clam Hydroid, *Clytia bakeri* (no. 17), which extends above the sand surface even when the clam is buried.

The numbers of this clam are as variable as its colors. In some years, portions of a given beach may be covered with a solid pavement of Bean Clams lying several layers thick; in other years, not one can be found. The late Wesley Coe of the Scripps Institution of Oceanography once made a public offer of one dollar for the first live Bean Clam found on the beach, and several years went by before the reward was claimed. The years of abundance do not appear to form any sort of predictable cycle or pattern. There were especially memorable resurgences of the La Jolla population in 1910, 1915 (when canneries were set up to prepare Bean Clam broth on a commercial scale), 1932, 1938, 1951 (the year that Wesley Coe's reward was claimed), and 1963. The 1932 bloom is still remembered by some La Jolla old-timers who say that the clams appeared like manna, furnishing a free dietary staple during lean times, and still refer to them as Depression Clams.

When the clam population is in the midst of one of these explosions, there is no room for individuals to assume the proper feeding position and not enough food to go around; consequently, the death rate is high at first.

To prepare Bean Clam broth, first make sure that all your clams are alive. Then wash them in running fresh water for several hours, drain, and add a pint of water for each quart of clams. Steam until the shells are wide open. Pour off the broth, add butter and lemon juice to it, and wish for more!

79. Wedge Clam, *Donax californicus*. Similar to the Bean Clam (no. 78), but usually a little larger, with the beaks nearer the center of the edge. It is not as skillful a digger as the Bean Clam, and populations are apt to lie on or close to the sand surface; thus they are not well adapted to shores exposed to high surf and are usually found on more protected beaches. The population shows the same sort of variation as that of the Bean Clam, but the cycles of the two species do not necessarily coincide.

80. Sunset Shell, *Gari californica*. Length to 10 cm (3⁷/₈ in.). Base color creamy white; there is a thin brown periostra-

Phylum MOLLUSCA

1"

68.
Tivela stultorum

69.
Amiantis callosa

70.
1"
Chione
undatella

71.
Chione fluctifraga
1"

72.
Protothaca
staminea

73.
1"
Mactra
californica

74.
Tresus nuttalli
1"

75.
Macoma nasuta
1"

78. 1"
Donax gouldii

76.
Macoma secta
1"

77.
Leporimetis obesa
1"

79. 1"
Donax
californicus

80.
1"
Gari californica

81.
Nuttallia nuttallii
1"

cum, but most of this is worn away except on the edges. Radiating rays of pink expand outward from the beaks, much as in a typical calendar-art sunset. The valves do not completely close, leaving a thin gap at the posterior edge. Common at low tide levels in sand and gravel near rocky areas and on sand flats in bays and estuaries; most often seen as dead shells.

81. Purple Clam, *Nuttallia nuttallii*. Length to 9 cm (3¹/₂ in.). Shells thin and rather flat, with the right valve more flattened than the left. The surface is covered with a smooth, varnishlike, reddish-brown periostracum. The interior of the shell is purple. The Purple Clam lives in bays on low tide level mud and sand flats and buries itself deeply, stretching its long narrow siphons up to the surface.

82. California Jack-Knife Clam, *Tagelus californianus*. Length to 11 cm (4¹/₄ in.). The valves are thin and flat, with the umbo (beak) located near the middle and the long sides almost parallel to one another. The shell is gray-white, covered with a thin brown periostracum. This species lives in the muddy parts of protected waters and constructs permanent burrows as much as 50 cm (20 in.) deep. When feeding, it moves up near the mouth of its burrow; when disturbed, it quickly moves to the bottom. This common species is quite edible, but in our area it is more often used as fish bait.

83. Rosy Razor Clam, *Solen rosaceus*. Length to 7.5 cm (3 in.). Shells thin, elongate, nearly round in cross section, with the umbo located near the blunted anterior end. The two valves do not close completely, and part of the dark-colored foot usually protrudes at the posterior end. The valves are covered with a glossy periostracum that is thin enough to allow the rosy color of the shell to show through, especially near the umbo. Found in sandy mud in sheltered areas at the low tide level, living in permanent burrows 10 to 30 cm (4 to 12 in.) deep. Not common.

84. Rough Piddock, *Zirfaea pilsbryi*. Length to 13 cm (5 in.). Shells thin but sturdy, gray-white in color. The two valves do not fit together when closed, leaving wide gaps at both ends. Long sides of the shells are almost parallel. The anterior half is covered with a concentric arrangement of file-like teeth; this roughened area is set apart from the smooth posterior portion by a shallow diagonal groove. This piddock lives in smooth round tunnels that it bores into clay, heavy mud, or soft rock in or below the low tide zone. The boring is accomplished by movements of the shell, the roughened part abrading the substrate. The shell itself is worn away by this process but grows at a rate as fast as its abrading. Chemical action may also help soften the substrate. Fairly common.

85. Scale-Sided Piddock, *Parapholas californica.* Length to 15 cm (6 in.). Rather similar to the preceding species, except that the long sides of the shell are not parallel, so the shells are more pear-shaped; also, the rough and smooth sections of the shell are separated not by a groove, but by an open area showing concentric growth rings. Bores into hard clay, shale, sandstone, and other soft rocks at the low tide level and below on open coasts and at bay entrances. It is common in the low tide zone but is most abundant in subtidal waters; its burrows on the walls of the Scripps Submarine Canyon off La Jolla are so numerous as to be an important cause of erosion on the canyon's rim.

Class Gastropoda (Snails)

The snails constitute one of the more numerous groups of animals, about 40,000 species having been recognized; the vast majority live in the sea. They are sometimes referred to as univalves, as a single shell is the general rule of construction. These shells in every case begin their lives in a spiral form, but in some groups, such as the limpets, the spiral growth pattern is not discernible in the adults.

There are at least 300 kinds of gastropods in the area covered by this book, and merely listing them, let alone identifying them accurately, would require space and detail not possible here. Some groups have not received taxonomic study in recent years, and much work remains to be done in the classification of their relationships. Work is proceeding, however, and some hitherto confusing groups, such as our local limpets, have recently been effectively organized. (See, for example, McLean, 1978.)

The gastropods we are most likely to regard as typical are those with a single shell coiled around a central axis. In most, this coiling spirals outward in a clockwise direction when the shell is viewed from the top or apex, but there are a few "left-handed" species. There is also very rarely a counterclockwise "sport" in a normally dextral (right-handed) group. The opening in the large end of the shell is equipped, in many species, with a sort of protective trapdoor called an *operculum*.

The shells of gastropods come in a fantastic array of sizes, shapes, and colors, and are accordingly very popular among collectors. Tropical species especially are often very beautiful, and the existence of a good many species may well be threatened by the activities of collectors who sell to shell dealers all over the world.

Some gastropods are herbivorous, some carnivorous, and still others omnivorous. Their style of feeding is governed to a large extent by the shape of the radula, which is important in precise classification. In this book, however, the descriptions apply primarily to the shells and to other attributes that do not require laboratory dissection.

Subclass Prosobranchia

Order Archaeogastropoda

The Abalones

The coast of California is famous for its abalones; unfortunately, this fame, coupled with the state's burgeoning population, has decimated the abalones in the intertidal zone, and beach-goers are not likely to see any legal-sized specimens unless they dive to 10 m (30 ft.) or so.

In its general shape, an abalone resembles a clam shell, and innocent collectors have been known to search vainly for the other half of what they took to be a bivalve. It really is a snail, though, and has a single shell that, on close examination, clearly shows the spiral structure so typical of the gastropods.

The aperture has become as large as the shell itself and is completely filled, in the living animal, by a tremendous muscular foot. This foot is used by the abalone for locomotion and for clinging tightly to rocks, and by humans for abalone steaks. The foot is ringed by the edge of the mantle, which extends into numerous short sensory tentacles.

There is a row of holes across the top of the shell, and a widespread belief holds that their number denotes the age of the abalone. This is not true. The number of holes for each kind of abalone has a restricted range, and the number will remain within this range throughout the animal's long life. A close look at an empty shell will show that the holes at the inner end of the spiral—those that were formed first—have been closed off, while new holes are opened at the outer end. Quite frequently, the outermost hole will be in the process of forming and will show as a notch at the edge of the shell.

The function of these openings illustrates a basic tenet of the conditions of life: namely, no animal can live in its own waste products. In the evolutionary process known as torsion, which is peculiar to the gastropods, the anal opening has been brought close to the head, and every snail has had to find some way to keep from ingesting or breathing its own waste. The holes in the abalone shell constitute a method, developed quite early in gastropod evolution, of separating incoming and outgoing water, allowing waste material to be carried away without polluting the fresh supply. Water passes in under the edges of the shell, goes across the gills, picks up waste, and is discharged through the openings on the top of the shell.

This flow of water may provide a small amount of food in the form of suspended particles, but the abalone's chief mode of sustenance is browsing on seaweeds. The type of food eaten has a direct bearing upon the color of new shell growth, and David Leighton (1961), when he was a graduate student at the Scripps Institution of Oceanography, raised a number of "rainbow" abalones among which periodic changes of diet produced successive concentric growth areas in strikingly different colors.

Some kinds of abalones rarely roam about in search of food; rather, they remain attached to their home spot on a rock, with the front edge of the foot raised and ready to pounce on strands of seaweed that drift their way.

The inner suface of the shell is highly iridescent (see Pl. 29), and the abalone has long been valued from the artistic point of view as well as the gastronomic. American Indians were great shell traders, and Pacific Coast abalones were carried at least as far as the Mississippi a thousand years before Columbus.

It is interesting to note that an observant amateur naturalist used the distribution of the Black Abalone (no. 87) to prove that Baja California, then thought to be a tremendous island, was in fact a peninsula. The naturalist was Padre Eusebio Kino. A Jesuit missionary, he was sent to Baja California in 1681, and he soon noticed that while abalones were plentiful on the Pacific shores, they were not found in the Gulf of California. A Mohave Indian friend presented him with some "blue shells" near what is now Yuma, Arizona, saying that they had been obtained from the ocean straight to the west and that his collecting trip had not required the crossing of any water. The Padre realized then that there must be land around the head of the Gulf and that Baja California must therefore be a peninsula. With characteristic zeal, he set out to test this notion and in 1702 reached a point from which he and his ill companion (who died shortly thereafter) saw the sun *rise* across the Gulf of California, giving dramatic proof that they had rounded the Gulf and were now on its western shore. Kino thereupon produced a map of the area, and it was to be 200 years before anybody made a better one.

The collecting and possession of abalone is strictly governed by the game laws, and the would-be collector must obtain a fishing license and follow all the rules of season, size, and bag limits. In recent years, there have been a number of successful attempts to raise abalones in hatcheries, giving rise to an important new industry.

Pearls of several shapes and types are not uncommon in abalones. Many of these are quite lovely, but they have no commercial value.

86. Red Abalone, *Haliotis rufescens*. Length to 28 cm (11 in.), the largest of our abalones. Three or four open holes, with their edges raised into short tubular projections. The inside of the shell is iridescent, with a distinctive central muscle scar of concentric lines, crossed in the middle by a set of much finer parallel "flow lines." The outside of the shell is brick

Phylum MOLLUSCA

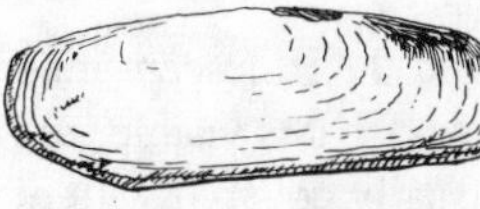

1"

82. *Tagelus californianus*

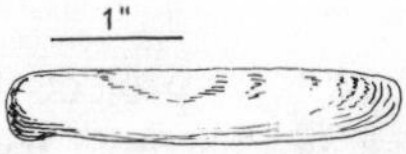

83. *Solen rosaceus*

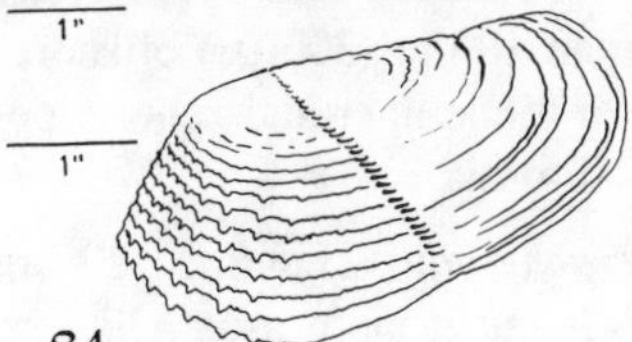

1"

84.
Zirfaea pilsbryi

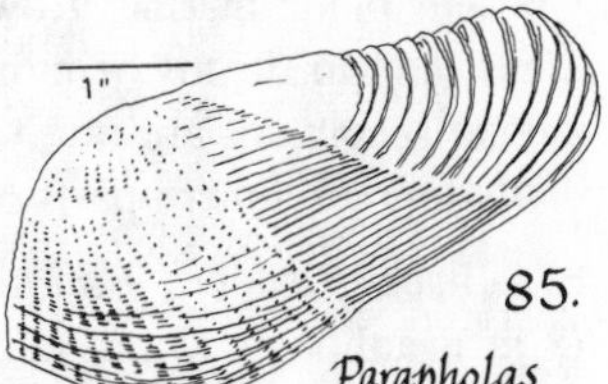

85.
*Parapholas
californica*

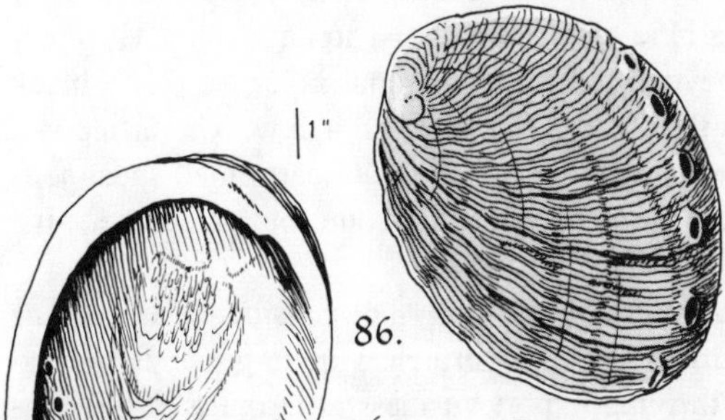

1"

86.
Haliotis rufescens

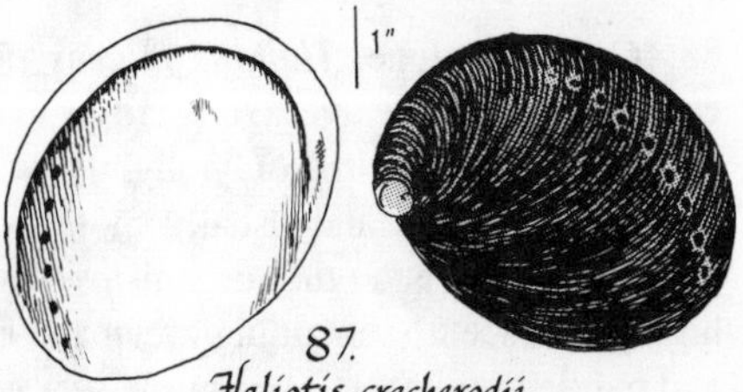

1"

87.
Haliotis cracherodii

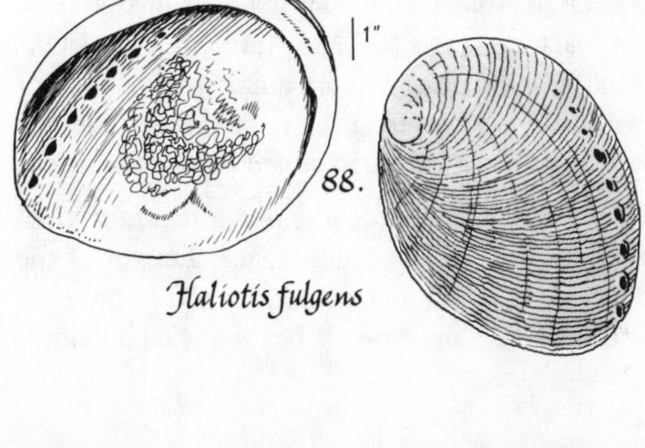

1"

88.

Haliotis fulgens

red; the red layer projects a little beyond the iridescent inner layer, making a narrow peripheral red band that is visible from the underside. The top of the shell is usually covered with algae and other marine growths. Found in surf-swept rocky areas, and to depths of more than 100 m (300 ft.) offshore. Living specimens are rarely seen in the intertidal zone, especially in the southern parts of California.

87. Black Abalone, *Haliotis cracherodii.* Length to 20 cm (8 in.), although 13 cm (5 in.) is much more usual. Five to nine open holes, flush with the shell, the edges not raised into short tubes. The shell is smooth, usually free of marine growth, and is blue-black in color. The dark outer layer extends a little beyond the inner nacreous layer, so that a black border around the shell is visible from below. The inside is a pearly iridescent white, with no muscle scar. Small specimens are fairly common in the intertidal zone, but remember—it's against the law to take them!

The Black Abalone is generally not considered as tasty as the Red and Green but is nevertheless quite good. It formed the basis of a thriving export business at the turn of the century, when abalone were plentiful, and has been found in Indian kitchen middens dating to 7,000 years before the present.

88. Green Abalone, *Haliotis fulgens* (Pl. 29). Length to 26 cm (10 in.), but the average is closer to 20 cm (8 in.). Five to seven open holes, rims only slightly raised. Outer surface of the shell is rough and usually more or less covered with a growth of algae and other organisms. The inside of the shell is highly iridescent, containing green and blue patches with pink and purple highlights. The muscle scar is prominent. This species resembles the Red Abalone but does not have the red band around the inner margin of the shell. Now rarely seen at depths of less than 10 m (30 ft.). It is sad to remember that only 40 or so years ago we could wade among the rocks at low tide and choose the specimens whose size best suited our dinner plans.

89. Giant Keyhole Limpet, *Megathura crenulata* (Pl. 30). Fairly common in rocky low tide zones. Length of the shell up to 10 cm (4 in.); the animal itself is too large to fit completely within its shell and extends beyond it on all sides.

The shell is oval, light tan in color, with a rough texture formed by fine radiating ribs. There is a single large opening at the apex. The mantle may be gray with stripes and spots of brown or darker gray, or it may be black—in which case the black pigment can rub off on the hands of a collector. This mantle extends beyond the edges of the shell and curves back so as nearly to cover the shell's upper surface. The large muscular foot is bright yellow.

The single opening in the top of the shell helps separate outgoing wastewater from incoming clean water, as does the line of holes on the abalones' shells. (See the introductory section on abalones preceding no. 85.) This "primitive" method of separating incoming from outgoing water is shared by the following species and other keyhole limpets.

90. Volcano Limpet, *Fissurella volcano.* Length to 2.5 cm (1 in.). Shell elliptical, with a single oval opening at the apex. Color usually reddish or purplish, with irregular radiating streaks of darker color. Abundant in the middle and lower tide zones in rocky areas.

The "True" Limpets (Family Acmaeidae)

These are snails whose shells are of a simple shield or plate shape, showing none of the usual spiral construction; in fact, some families have gone so far in discarding the coiled pattern that it is hardly discernible even in the earliest stages of development. Limpets make their homes on rocks, seaweeds, pier pilings, and other sorts of solid substrate, and all are entirely herbivorous. Recent research has required a number of name changes among the limpets; for example, many that appeared under the genus *Acmaea* in older works (including the first edition of this one) are now placed in the genus *Collisella.*

91. Shield Limpet, *Collisella pelta.* Diameter to 2.5 cm (1 in.). Shape elliptical, in profile a flat cone with slightly rounded slopes; the apex of the cone is off center, toward the front. Color variable, from cream to gray, greenish, brown, or nearly black; occasionally there are darker radiating stripes or white checkered markings, and there is often a checkered border around the shell on the upper side. The inside of the shell is white, usually with a border of light and dark bars. Common in rocky areas in the middle and lower tide zones.

92. Fingered Limpet, *Collisella digitalis*. Length to about 2.5 cm (1 in.), usually less. The apex is near the anterior margin, sometimes hooked forward. Raised radial ribs, all on the rounded posterior slope of the shell, extend to the finely scalloped edge. Color gray, mottled with areas of fine white dots and darker gray lines and streaks. Common in rocky areas, at middle and low tide levels. Most likely to be found on near-vertical rock faces, while the Shield Limpet (no. 91) prefers horizontal or gently sloping surfaces.

93. Rough Limpet, *Collisella scabra*. Length to 3 cm (1³/₈ in.). Basic color usually mottled brown or green, white where eroded. Shell oval, with rather low apex placed well forward. Strong ribs radiate from the apex in every direction, their ends imparting a scalloped edge to the shell. Abundant at high tide level and in the splash zone.

94. File Limpet, *Collisella limatula*. Length to 4.5 cm (1³/₄ in.). The shell is a rounded oval, fairly flat, colored brown or almost black on the outside; on the inside, it is bluish white with a dark blotch at the apex. The margin is also dark. The shell bears radial ribs with a toothed, file-like texture. The muscular foot is black along the sides, white on the bottom. Common on rocks and other hard substrates in the middle and lower tide levels.

95. Black Limpet, *Collisella asmi*. Length to 11 mm (⁷/₁₆ in.), height about 8 mm (⁵/₁₆ in.). Color dark brown or black outside, brown inside. This is one limpet that is easy to identify, for it is always found clinging to the shell of a Black Turban (no. 101) or Speckled Turban (no. 102). It feeds by rasping microscopic algae from the larger snail's shell, and moves to another individual when its first host is all cleaned.

96. Kelp Limpet, *Notoacmaea insessa*. Length to 2 cm (³/₄ in.). Elliptical, narrow, with the long sides parallel. The shell is higher than wide, and all slopes are convex. Color light red-brown, surface smooth. May be immediately identified by its habitat, which is the straplike center stipe of the Feather-Boa

Phylum MOLLUSCA

90.
Fissurella
volcano

89.
Megathura crenulata

91.
Collisella
pelta

92.
Collisella
digitalis

93.
Collisella
scabra

94.
Collisella
limatula

95.
Collisella
asmi

Notoacmaea
paleacea
97.

96.
Notoacmaea insessa

98.
Lottia gigantea

Kelp, *Egregia laevigata.* The limpet eats its way into the kelp, making a depression into which its shell just fits; this pit is not deep enough to bury the shell past its apex, but it does damage the host plant. A single limpet may make a succession of pits along the stipe, which eventually weaken that portion of the plant and cause it to break off. On just about any piece of *Egregia* you will find a series of these pits, even if there is no living Kelp Limpet.

97. Surfgrass Limpet, *Notoacmea paleacea.* Length to 1 cm (³/₈ in.). This is our smallest limpet. It is very narrow and not as high as the preceding species; the apex is well forward of the center and usually hooked toward the front. There are very fine radiating grooves on the brown shell, which is bluish white on the inside. Lives exclusively on the narrow blades of green Surfgrass, *Phyllospadix,* in the low intertidal zone of open coasts. Unlike the Kelp Limpet, the Surfgrass Limpet does no harm to its host plant, feeding only on the micro-algae that grow on the Surfgrass.

98. Owl Limpet, *Lottia gigantea.* Length to more than 7.5 cm (3 in.), making this the largest of our true limpets. Shape oval, with low, rounded profile. Outside brown and black in irregular patterns, usually with some eroded areas of dull white. Common in the high tide zone and even into the splash zone, although the larger individuals live lower down. A large chestnut-brown area at the apex of the inner surface of the shell somewhat resembles the silhouette of a horned owl with its "ear" tufts extended straight out.

The Owl Limpet spends its daylight hours clamped motionless to the rock, some individuals residing in a rock "scar" that exactly fits the shell; at night, it wanders out to graze on its own jealously guarded patch of *Ulva* or similar seaweed. Other grazing animals, including other Owl Limpets, are driven away in fierce battles that resemble dueling bulldozers in extreme slow motion. Settling barnacle larvae and other tiny squatters are rasped away with the radula. The territory of each Owl Limpet covers about 1,000 square centimeters (156 square inches), and within it, the algal growth is clipped short, like a well-kept lawn.

99. Smooth Brown Turban, *Norrisia norrisi* (Pl. 31). Diameter to 5.5 cm (2¹/8 in.). Color rich red-brown, with a deep, bright green *umbilicus,* a depression near the center of the whorl on the underside of the shell. The flesh is bright orangered. In the intertidal zone, most often seen crawling about on the flat stipes and blades of *Eisenia arborea,* the Southern Palm Kelp; below the low tide level, it lives on other kinds of kelp. A species of slipper shell, *Crepidula norrisiarum* (no. 112), is often attached to the shell of this turban, and has been given the common name Turban Slipper Shell.

100. Gilded Turban, *Tegula aureotincta.* Diameter to about 4 cm (1¹/2 in.); color gray-brown. The surface of the shell is rough, quite unlike the smooth brown of the preceding species. It has a deep umbilicus with a golden-orange center, often surrounded by a pale blue band. Moderately common in the middle tide zone.

101. Black Turban, *Tegula funebralis* (Pl. 32). Diameter to 4 cm (1¹/2 in.). Shell heavy, blue-black in color; the dark covering on parts of the spire is usually worn away, revealing the pearly layer beneath. Abundant at times in the middle tide zone, often in congregations filling protected crevices and hollows on the sides of rocks; in each such cluster, the individuals, which may number in the hundreds, are all very close to the same size. The food of this snail consists of relatively soft seaweeds; it does not rasp tiny algae from the rock as the chitons do.

102. Speckled Turban, *Tegula gallina.* Diameter to 3 cm (1¹/8 in.). The shell is dark, finely mottled with lighter spots, usually arranged in slanted vertical stripes. Very common in the middle tide zone, but not as abundant in our area as the Black Turban (no. 101).

103. Wavy Top-Shell, *Astraea undosa.* Diameter to 11 cm (4¹/4 in.). Shell heavy, the bottom side flat and showing distinct spiral lines. A fuzzy brown periostracum covers the upper parts of the shell; in dead specimens, this is often abraded away, showing an especially attractive pearly layer beneath. Numerous strong angled vertical ridges on the upper part of the shell are crossed by less distinct parallel spiral ridges. Like many snails, this one has an operculum—a door attached to the soft body parts, so arranged as to close the aperture when the animal withdraws into its shell. This operculum is thick and strong, with a smooth brown spiraled surface on the inside and strong toothed ribs on the outside. Fairly common in the low tide zone, but most abundant—and averaging larger in size—in the kelp beds offshore.

Order Mesogastropoda

104. Flat-Bottomed Periwinkle, *Littorina planaxis* (Pl. 33). Length occasionally to 19 mm (³/₄ in.), but usually less. Color variable, usually a light gray or brown, sometimes with light spots or faint bands. The shape of the *columella,* the central axis of the shell on the lower surface, is flattened—a feature that is diagnostic of this species. Very abundant in the splash zone; lives higher in the tide range than any other mollusc. This periwinkle can stand long periods of dryness, fastening its shell to the face of the rock with a sort of mucous glue, and retaining the necessary moisture inside the shell. When conditions are right, with some moisture available from the wave spray, it moves about the rock—usually following the slime trail left by fellow periwinkles—and uses its radula to rasp microscopic diatoms and other small plant material from the substrate.

The periwinkles (family Littorinidae) are an important group, found in almost every rocky intertidal zone throughout the temperate and tropical parts of the world. The family contains some 20 genera; in the genus *Littorina,* close to 100 species have been recognized.

105. Checkered Periwinkle, *Littorina scutulata.* Shell up to 13 mm (¹/₂ in.) high, usually smaller. Color often a dingy gray, but sometimes a faint pattern of minute darker spots is visible. The inside of the aperture is purplish. Lives high on the rocks in the splash zone, although not quite as high as the preceding species.

106. Scaly Tube Snail, *Serpulorbis squamigerus.* This is a sessile snail with a long, tubular shell attached firmly to the substrate. The tubes, at the open end, are about 12 mm (¹/₂ in.)

in diameter and up to 13 cm (5 in.) long—although this length is hard to measure, as the snail habitually lives in clusters with the tubes irregularly coiled and intertwined. The tubes of young Scaly Tube Snails exhibit the typical spiral pattern of the gastropods, but when they settle down in their permanent home, the growing tube follows the substrate or other tube snails windingly, with the last couple of centimeters extended at right angles. The tube is marked with longitudinal ridges and has a somewhat scaly appearance. There is no operculum. The feeding of this snail by means of a community net of mucus has been described earlier in Chapter 2.

107. Little Tube Snail, *Petaloconchus montereyensis* (Pl. 34). Tubes about 2 mm (5/64 in.) in diameter, and up to 3 cm (1 1/4 in.) long; except for its much smaller size, this looks very much like the Scaly Tube Snail (no. 106) and has quite similar habits. It is locally common, usually on the undersurfaces of rocks, in the low tide zone, but more abundant subtidally. Unlike the Scaly Tube Snail, it does have an operculum, colored brown, set a little way down in the tube, which it does not quite fill. The portions of the tube that were grown first are usually marked with diagonal wrinkles, while more recent growth is smoother.

108. California Horn Shell, *Cerithidea californica* (Pl. 35). Shell turret-shaped, about 4.5 cm (1 3/4 in.) high. Color brown or gray. Distinct longitudinal ridges, with less distinct spiral markings; whorls are rounded, and the operculum is smooth and brown. Abundant on protected mudflats at high tide from Central California to the tip of Baja California. It is a biological axiom that when a species is adapted to living in an environment in which few other species can survive, the successful one can occur in tremendous numbers. So it is with the California Horn Shell; in its oxygen-poor, muddy environment, it may often be seen at low tide lying on the surface of the mud in numbers of 20 or more per square foot.

109. Common Violet Sea Snail, *Janthina janthina.* Diameter to about 2.5 cm (1 in.). The shell is fragile, violet in color; the color is deepest at the big end, fading almost to white at the tip of the spire. This is not an inhabitant of our intertidal zone, but makes its home in the open sea; nevertheless, shells are occasionally found washed up on shore. In its home territory, the violet snail lives at the surface of the water, keeping itself afloat by means of a self-constructed raft of foamy bubbles, from which it hangs spire-downward. This bubble-raft is also the repository for the snail's eggs. The coloring of the shell is such that the lighter area is turned away from the light in an application of the universal principle of *countershading,* which reduces an animal's visibility. The violet-and-white coloring is typical of creatures living at the surface or at shallow depths out on the high seas.

110. Tinted Wentletrap, *Epitonium tinctum.* Length to 16 mm (5/8 in.), color white. Each whorl has 12 ridges raised into flat vanes. This animal is found around the bases of sea anemones, upon which it feeds. Other species of *Epitonium* live on sandy bottoms well offshore.

The name "wentletrap" comes from the Dutch or German and means "winding staircase." One Indo-European species, the Precious Wentletrap (*Epitonium scalare*), has long been prized by shell collectors, and in the days before scuba diving, was so rarely collected that it fetched a very high price. According to a story that may be apocryphal but is nonetheless worth repeating, an enterprising Asian artist learned to *make* wentletrap shells of rice flour paste. This he did so skillfully as to fool several shell collectors into buying them for a great deal of money. The swindle was discovered when one buyer attempted to wash his purchase in water, only to see it dissolve. Today, improvements in collecting methods and access to collecting grounds have lowered the monetary value of the genuine shells, while the forgeries are said to have become extremely valuable as works of art!

111. Hoof Shell, *Hipponix cranioides.* Diameter to 2.5 cm (1 in.). The shell is not spiraled, but resembles a gray-white limpet with a concentrically wrinkled surface; the rounded apex is near the posterior end of the shell. Fairly common on the undersides of rocks and in protected crevices in the low tide zone, sometimes occurring in clusters, and occasionally attached to other shells.

99.
Norrisia norrisi

100.
Tegula aureotincta

101.
Tegula funebralis

102.
Tegula gallina

Astraea undosa
103.

104.
Littorina planaxis

105.
Littorina scutulata

106.
Serpulorbis squamigerus

107.

Petaloconchus montereyensis

108.

Cerithidea californica

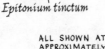

110.
Epitonium tinctum

ALL SHOWN AT APPROXIMATELY NATURAL SIZE.

111.
Hipponix cranioides

109.
Janthina janthina

112.
Crepidula norrisiarum

113.
Crepidula onyx

Crucibulum spinosum
114.

Quarter-Deck Snails and Their Relatives

Members of this superfamily (Calyptraeacea) superficially resemble the limpets when viewed from above. When they are
seen from below, however, an obvious difference is the presence of a sort of shelf or "quarter deck" that supports certain
internal organs and gives the group another name—slipper
shells. In the cup-and-saucer shells, this shelf is central and is
curved into a cuplike shape. On the Pacific coast, there are
five families with many species.

112. Turban Slipper Shell, *Crepidula norrisiarum.* Length to
1.5 cm (⅝ in.). Smooth, brown; apex near the posterior end—
even overhanging. The inner shelf is white, rounded forward
at its ends. Quite common; most frequently seen attached to
the shell of the Smooth Brown Turban, *Norrisia norrisi* (no.
99). The slipper shells are *protandrous hermaphrodites,* meaning that they start adult life as males, then change to females as
they grow older.

113. Onyx Slipper Shell, *Crepidula onyx.* Length to 7 cm
(2¾ in.). Color red-brown, occasionally with faint lighter
rays. Apex at posterior end, but only slightly (if at all) hooked.
Interior of shell variable, often glossy brown—but the shelf is
always white and notched at the ends rather than curved forward, as in the Turban Slipper Shell (no. 112). Most abundant
attached to pilings, rocks, larger shells, or even each other, at
low tide levels in quiet bay waters; also found in the low tide
and subtidal zones on protected outer rocky shores.

114. Spiny Cup-and-Saucer Shell, *Crucibulum spinosum.*
Length to 3 cm (1⅛ in.), shape nearly circular. Outer surface
of shell covered with small prickly spines except for the
smooth apex, which is sharp and often twisted. Color brownish outside, glossy red-brown inside, with the small white
"cup" just off-center. From Los Angeles southward, common
from the middle tide zone down to a depth of at least 55 m (180
ft.) attached to shells and other objects.

115. Lewis's Moon Snail, *Polinices lewisii.* Diameter to 13
cm (5 in.), one of our largest snails. Globular, with low spire,

rather heavy. Umbilicus deep and narrow, not covered by a shell callus. Color light brown, with a high polish resulting from the body's enveloping the shell when the animal is active.

Moon Snails are carnivorous, preying mainly on clams, which they kill and eat by drilling through the clam's shell with a file-like radula, aided by softening secretions from the accessory boring organ. Moon snails have a large, soft body, which at first glance appears totally incapable of retraction into the shell, since its volume may be four times greater than the shell's. The body contains a great deal of water, however, stored in special connective-tissue containers opening to the outside, much like the ballast tanks of a submarine. When the excess water is expelled, the body can be completely withdrawn and the aperture closed with a thin brown operculum.

These snails are found primarily on sandy bottoms of quiet bays. Under water, they crawl through rather than over the sand, with only the shell protruding up into the water. They lay their eggs in rubbery "collars" consisting of sand grains and thousands of eggs, cemented together with mucus. These egg cases are common on sand and mud in bays and lagoons, especially in the summer months.

116. Southern Moon Snail, *Polinices reclusianus*. Similar to Lewis's Moon Snail (no.115), but smaller, not over 7 cm (2¾ in.). Shell globose, heavy; exterior smooth, light brown or gray, often with irregular reddish blotches. The umbilicus is covered, except for a small opening, by a smooth callus pad of shell material. Fairly common in the lower parts of the middle tide zone, especially in sandy locations.

117. Dove Shell, *Erato columbella*. Length usually about 7 mm (¼ in.). Shell pear-shaped, with short spire and a narrow aperture with minute teeth along the edges. The general color is red-brown or gray, the surface smooth; there is no periostracum. Common in the low tide zone and downward into deeper water. Although human collectors do not often come across live shells, gulls apparently know better where to find them, for their droppings often contain large numbers of Dove Shells.

There are many other species of tiny shells along our coast, and one of the best ways to find them is to sit down on a beach of coarse sand and sift handfuls of the sand through a tea strainer. The Dove Shell and the Coffee-Bean shells (nos. 118 and 119) are presented here as three examples of this near-microfauna.

118. Little Coffee Bean, *Trivia californiana*. Length to 11 mm (7/16 in.), color gray-purple. It has 10 to 12 white cross ridges that are interrupted along the center line by a shallow pale-colored groove. Common in the low tide zone, especially among the fronds of the seaweed *Eisenia*.

119. Large Coffee Bean, *Trivia solandri*. Length to 19 mm (3/4 in.). Larger and paler in color than the Little Coffee Bean, whose habitat it shares. The cross ridges terminate at the mid-line groove in small knobs; the groove itself is deeper and wider. Common from Palos Verdes (near Los Angeles) south-ward, often found in association with the Little Coffee Bean. Both kinds are most likely to be found as dead shells.

120. Chestnut Cowry, *Cypraea spadicea*. Length rarely to 10 cm (4 in.) or even more, but most specimens are under 5 cm (2 in.). Color white beneath, fading to purplish brown on the sides and rich chestnut brown on top, usually with darker spots and blotches. The mantle, when extruded, is sandy in color, with flecks of brown and black. The shell is nearly circular in cross section. Common in the low tide zone in protected crevices and ledges; more common offshore, especially among the kelp beds.

The cowries are a group of snails with shells whose bright colors and glossy surfaces have made them attractive to humans since earliest times. They have been used for money in several civilizations, a use that produced, according to some authorities, the Chinese word "cash" (oddly enough, unrelated to the English word "cash"). The Chinese cash is a perforated coin that was strung on cords. This method of stringing is said to have originated among people who used strings of cowry shells as a medium of exchange, and the word "cash" is an onomatopoeic representation of the sound made when a string of shells is shaken to signify a readiness to bargain.

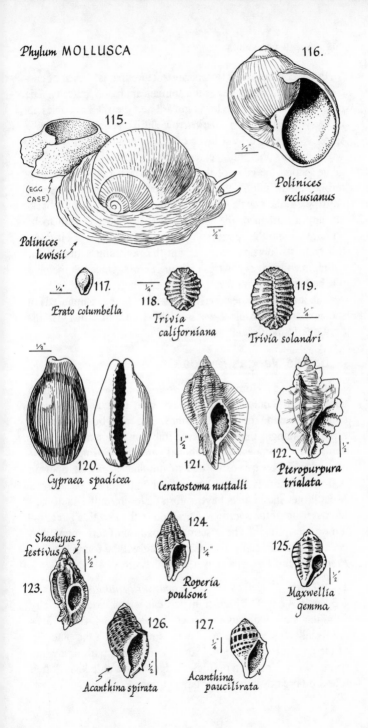

Phylum MOLLUSCA

115.

116.

(EGG CASE)

Polinices lewisii

Polinices reclusianus

117. Erato columbella

118. Trivia californiana

119. Trivia solandri

120. Cypraea spadicea

121. Ceratostoma nuttalli

122. Pteropurpura trialata

123. Shaskyus festivus

124. Roperia poulsoni

125. Maxwellia gemma

126. Acanthina spirata

127. Acanthina paucilirata

Infant cowries show the spiral structure that is typical of gastropods, but this changes as the animals approach maturity. The outer lip of the aperture turns inward and the shell becomes almost symmetrical along the narrow slitlike aperture, while the spire is obliterated by a layer of glossy enamel. This enamel, which covers the entire exterior of the shell, is secreted by glands along the edge of the mantle. When a cowry is undisturbed, the mantle is extended and reflexed so as to cover the entire shell, the mantle edges meeting at the midline of the back. On any disturbance, the mantle slides around the shell to be withdrawn into the aperture. The deposition of new shell material from the outside coupled with the polishing action of the sliding mantle gives cowries their high gloss. Once the shell has reached its final adult form, it stops growing.

The majority of the cowries, of which there are hundreds of species, live in tropical waters. The Chestnut Cowry is the only one found in Southern California.

Subclass Neogastropoda

121. Nuttall's Hornmouth, *Ceratostoma nuttalli*. Length about 5 cm (2 in.). Gray or brown with irregular markings, sometimes in the form of pale bands. The main body whorl has three flat flanges that vary considerably in size extending outward at right angles. The siphonal canal (extending from the end of the aperture to the end of the shell) may be open in young individuals but is generally completely closed over. Most larger individuals have a horn or tooth on the shell near the outer lip of the aperture. Common in the low tide zone, often on pier pilings. The systematic position of this animal has been a subject of some discussion, and it will be found listed as *Pterorytis* and *Purpura* as well as *Ceratostoma*.

122. Three-Winged Murex, *Pteropurpura trialata*. Length to 4.5 cm (1³/4 in.). Three thin vertical vanes extend radially from the shell, with smooth spaces between them; these vanes are usually frilled or fluted. There is no tooth on the outer lip of the aperture. Color light brown, sometimes with fine white spiral bands. Common on rocky ledges at low tide level; often found on breakwaters and at bay entrances.

123. Festive Murex, *Shaskyus festivus*. Length to 4 cm (1½ in.). Spire high; siphonal canal closed over to form a tube from the aperture to the tip. Frilled radial ridges are recurved at their outer edges, with rounded ridges between. Color pale brown with fine spiral lines of darker brown. Fairly common south of San Pedro in both rocky and muddy areas; most likely to be seen on pier pilings beneath overhanging seaweeds.

124. Poulson's Dwarf Triton, *Roperia poulsoni*. Length usually about 3 cm (1¼ in.). Shell heavy, spire fairly high. There are about nine vertical ridges crossed by spiral sets of fine brown lines with white bands between. Three or four small teeth on the outer edge of the aperture; interior white. Common from the middle tide zone down among rocks and on pier pilings. This is a carnivorous animal that feeds on mussels and other molluscs.

125. Gem Murex, *Maxwellia gemma*. Length to about 4.5 cm (1¾ in.), but usually smaller. A short and chunky shell, with six vertical ridges with sharp valleys between. The spire has several deep, irregular pits. Color white with brown or gray spiral cross stripes. Aperture small, nearly round. Common in the extreme low tide zone, and may be found higher up, especially in association with the Scaly Tube Snail (no. 106).

126. Angular Unicorn Shell, *Acanthina spirata*. Length occasionally to 4 cm (1½ in.). A sharp angle at the shoulder gives the spire a turreted appearance. Color gray or brown, often with a greenish tinge, with numerous fine broken dark lines running spirally. Aperture blue-white with a prominent spine on the outer lip. (This spine is often broken off or worn down, especially in specimens living in the upper parts of its tidal range.) Common in the middle tide zone in rocky places. At times, especially in winter, it is extremely abundant.

The spine is said to be used in opening barnacles, but this use has been observed and reported on by only one researcher, and there is some doubt about the accuracy of the observation. This snail does indeed consume small barnacles as well as periwinkles, but usually does so by laboriously boring through their shells with its radula.

127. Checkered Unicorn Shell, *Acanthina paucilirata*. Length to 2.5 cm (1 in.), but usually smaller. Fatter than the Angular Unicorn Shell (no. 126), with a lower spire. Color white or gray with irregular rows of square dark markings. The smooth inner part of the lip is usually tinged with purple, and there is usually a prominent spine on the outer edge of the aperture. Common south of Los Angeles, although never quite as abundant as the Angular Unicorn Shell.

128. Rock Thais, *Nucella emarginata*. Diameter to 3 cm (1¹/₈ in.). Usually globose in shape, although an occasional individual is rather long and narrow. Aperture large, round, with a thin outer lip; interior red-brown or purple. Shell sculptured with strong spiral ridges, often alternately wide and narrow. Found on exposed rocks in upper and middle tide zones. Not common in our area; more abundant farther north.

129. Kellett's Whelk, *Kellettia kellettii*. Length to 15 cm (6 in.) or more. Usually beige or straw colored, often overgrown with algae, bryozoans, or other organisms. Shell heavy; aperture white and glossy. Surface marked with very fine spiral grooves crossing rounded vertical ridges. This shell grows slowly and lives long: MacGinitie and MacGinitie (1968) report that a 3-in. individual is probably seven or eight years old. *Kellettia* is common at depths of more than 9 m (30 ft.) and is often encountered by scuba divers at the bottom of the kelp beds. Dead shells are often washed ashore.

130. Livid Macron, *Macron lividus*. Length occasionally to 2.5 cm (1 in.). A pale brown shell covered with a thick, dark brown, textile-like periostracum, which is often worn away in spots. The aperture is white, the columella polished. Common under rocks in the low tide zone from Santa Barbara to central Baja California.

131. Channeled Dog Whelk, *Nassarius fossatus*. Length occasionally to 5 cm (2 in.). Color yellow-gray to orange-brown, columella covered with a glossy callus of bright orange in mature individuals. Outer lip has a jagged edge. Common all along the California coast; especially abundant in mudflats. Like all of the dog whelks (which are also called "basket shells"), the Channeled Dog Whelk is a scavenger and locates its food by smell.

132. Ida's Mitre, *Mitra idae.* Length (rarely) to 6.5 cm (2¹/₂ in.). The shell is brown, but in fresh, unworn specimens is covered with a jet black periostracum marked with fine spiral threads. The soft parts are white, as is the narrow aperture. Occasionally found under rocks at the lowest tide level. This is a handsome little shell, although its somber coloring contrasts with the bright orange of some of the tropical mitre shells.

133. Purple Olive Snail, *Olivella biplicata.* Length to 3 cm (1¹/₄ in.). Color usually blue-purple or blue-gray, although a few are almost pure white. The surface is glossy and the columella is white, with two prominent folds. Abundant in areas of sand and rock in bays and protected areas of the outer coast; one of our most abundant shells. It often crawls just under the surface of the sand, leaving a furrow like that of a mole. Most individuals are active at night, remaining buried and motionless during the day. Many dead shells have a tiny, precise hole near the end drilled by the radula of an octopus (no. 154 or 155). The Purple Olive Snail is also eaten by several carnivorous snails, starfishes (such as the Ochre Starfish, no. 233), and gulls. The Purple Olives themselves are omnivorous, feeding on seaweed or dead animals. Empty Purple Olive shells are in great demand among small hermit crabs (such as no. 199) seeking a new home.

134. California Cone Shell, *Conus californicus.* Length to 4 cm (1¹/₂ in.). Shell yellow-brown, occasionally with a single, wide, indistinct darker spiral band; in life the shell is covered with a velvety dark brown or bluish periostracum. Common on rocky and sandy shores at the low tide level.

This shell is quite drab compared to some of its tropical relatives; the cone shells in general are most decorative. All of them are carnivorous and have a beautifully designed mechanism for planting poisoned darts in the flesh of their prey or their attackers. Some species are extremely dangerous to handle and have been known to kill humans. The California Cone Shell, however (the only one found in this state), has never been implicated in a human sting.

Subclass Opisthobranchia

135. Barrel Snail, *Rictaxis punctocaelatus*. Length about 12 mm (½ in.). Color white with three dark or light brown spiral bands. It lives mainly in subtidal areas, but is occasionally found in the littoral, around rocks partly buried in sand on protected outer coasts. Dead shells are found more often than living ones. An attractive little shell.

136. Bay Sea Hare, *Navanax inermis*. Length to 15 cm (6 in.). No shell. Body elongate, usually black with many bright yellow dots and dashes and vivid blue lines, especially along the edges of the body flaps. Abundant in quiet bays, and small specimens are common in protected pools on the outer coast. It is a carnivore, and bubble snails (nos. 137 and 138) are among its preferred foods. It tracks them down by their slime trails and swallows them whole; picking up a feeding specimen is like picking up a bag of marbles. The shells are defecated whole after the soft parts have been digested.

Bay Sea Hare eggs are laid in tangled skeins of yellow strings that may be found throughout the year.

137. Cloudy Bubble Snail, *Bulla gouldiana*. Length about 5 cm (2 in.). Shell globose, fragile. Color pinkish gray, with cloudy markings bordered on their left edges with white. Very common at low tide level in the quiet waters of our fast-vanishing lagoons and estuaries. When this snail is active its mantle almost completely covers the shell; when disturbed, it withdraws as far as it can, but the body is too large to be entirely hidden.

Like the Bay Sea Hare (no. 136) and the White Bubble Snail (no. 138), this animal lays yellow strings of eggs in tangles that are a familiar sight along bay shores.

138. White Bubble Snail, *Haminoea vesicula*. Length usually less than 2 cm (¾ in.). The shell is very fragile and usually colored white or yellow-brown. Similar to the Cloudy Bubble Snail (no. 137), but lighter colored and usually only half as long. Occasionally abundant in the low tide zone, especially on mudflats.

139. Brown Sea Hare, *Aplysia californica*. Length to 40 cm (15¾ in.). This mottled brown or reddish sea hare is a com-

Phylum MOLLUSCA

128. *Nucella emarginata* | ¼"

129.

Kellettia kellettii | 1"

Macron lividus
130. | ½"

131.
Nassarius fossatus | ½"

132. *Mitra idae* | ½

133. *Olivella biplicata* | ½

134. *Conus californicus* | ½

135. *Rictaxis punctocaelatus* | ⅛"

136. *Navanax inermis* | 1"

137. *Bulla gouldiana* | ½

138. *Flaminoea vesicula* | ½

NOTE: NO. 140 IS
SIMILAR, BUT
LARGER—and
BLACK.

139. *Aplysia californica* | 1"

mon sight in the middle tide zone and lower, especially in rocky areas where the receding tide leaves pools of water. The larger individuals are found in the low tide zone. The Brown Sea Hare is a strict vegetarian, browsing on various kinds of seaweed including kelp and Eelgrass, and has a complicated multi-stomached digestive system that can cope with such food. When disturbed, this animal discharges a deep purple ink that has earned it the name "inkfish"—which it shares with the Opalescent Squid (no. 152) and several other creatures.

Brown Sea Hares are hermaphroditic, each individual possessing a full complement of both female and male reproductive organs. They cannot fertilize their own eggs, however, and each one must copulate with another individual, operating as either male or female—or, when several individuals are involved, both at once. The eggs are laid in long strings like yellow spaghetti, which are formed into balls as big as grapefruit. The number of eggs contained in one of these masses is staggering; MacGinitie and MacGinitie (1968) have estimated that a large Brown Sea Hare may produce as many as half a billion eggs in a single year. Some authorities have felt this estimate to be excessive, but it is safe to say that a single mass can contain at least a million eggs. The larvae hatch in 10 to 12 days, and during their free-swimming period the vast majority fall prey to various plankton feeders. If this slaughter did not occur, all the young would grow to full size and produce their billions of eggs in turn, and in a few years the combined mass of sea hares would be greater than that of the Earth itself—a prospect of doom beside which either fire or ice sounds almost pleasant.

140. Black Sea Hare, *Aplysia vaccaria*. Similar in shape to the Brown Sea Hare (no. 139), but with skin that is black and rough instead of reddish-brown and smooth. It is also much larger; some Black Sea Hares attain a length of 76 cm (30 in.) and a weight of almost 16 kg (30 lbs.), which may make it the world's largest gastropod. Found mainly in the kelp beds offshore, but occasionally seen in low-level tidepools.

Nudibranchs

The nudibranchs are a group of snails without shells, many of which are brightly colored. The term "nudibranch" (pronounced NUDE-ee-brank) means "exposed gills"; the gills, technically known as *cerata,* are exposed without the covering of a shell or even a flap of skin as in the sea hares. These cerata are arranged in several ways: in some species they are gathered in a treelike structure at the posterior of the back, while in others they form a fringe all along the sides of the body, or several pairs, or they are spread more or less evenly over the back.

Nudibranchs can be seen in the still waters of tidepools, often concealed under the lip of an overhanging edge. All are carnivorous, and some have very restricted diets; a few, for example, eat nothing but sponges, while others limit themselves to hydroids. In some, the digestive tract has long fingers extending into the cerata.

Only a very few of our many nudibranchs can be presented here.

141. Orchid Nudibranch, *Chromodoris macfarlandi.* Length about 3.5 cm (1³/₈ in.). The body color is a rich orchid purple with yellow margins, and there are three longitudinal stripes of orange-yellow. This is one of the sponge eaters and is fairly common in the low tide zone. T. D. A. Cockerell named it in honor of F. M. MacFarland.

142. Blue-and-Gold Nudibranch, *Hypselodoris californiensis.* Length to 6.5 cm (2¹/₂ in.). Color deep royal blue, with brilliant yellow-orange stripes and spots. The specific name *californiensis* is said to have been bestowed in honor of the University of California, whose official colors are blue and gold. Moderately common at the low tide level, where it feeds on encrusting sponges.

143. Red Sponge Nudibranch, *Rostanga pulchra.* Length to 3 cm (1³/₁₆ in.), but usually smaller. Color usually bright red, although there is some variation. It lives on (in the dual senses of habitat and sustenance) red encrusting sponges such as *Plocamia* (no. 7). Its long flat ribbons of eggs are also red. This animal provides an example of concealing coloration, for it is the same color of its sponge habitat. The concealing effect is lessened, however, by the nudibranch's habit of eating the sponge right down to the bare rock as it crawls along, leaving a distinct rock-colored line pointing directly to its present position.

144. Lemon Nudibranch, *Anisodoris nobilis.* Length to 10 cm (4 in.). Color orange-yellow or lemon yellow, with a sprinkling of black dots; skin coarsely granular. This is our largest nudibranch. Its body is much flatter—pancakelike— than those of most of our other nudibranchs. The term "lemon" is appropriate to three attributes of this animal: its color, its fruity smell, and its flatness. ("Lemon" is an old English word, from the French *limonde,* meaning "flatfish.")

The Lemon Nudibranch is found only rarely in the low tide zone in our area and is much more common in deeper water; in the San Diego area it is especially abundant around the lower ends of outer pier pilings.

145. Rose Nudibranch, *Hopkinsia rosacea.* Length to 2.5 cm (1 in.). Body a uniform rose color, covered with long flexible processes. These processes are not gills, as they at first appear to be; this animal is a member of the dorid group, and its gill cluster, almost hidden by the filaments, is at the posterior end. The generic name was bestowed by F. M. MacFarland in honor of Timothy Hopkins, through whose generosity the Hopkins Marine Laboratory was established at Pacific Grove, California.

The rose color is caused by a pigment called hopkinsiaxanthin; this name implies that the pigment is made by the nudibranch, but it appears more likely that it comes from a pink bryozoan, *Eurystomella,* which is its usual food. Everything about the Rose Nudibranch is of a rose color—its food, its body, and its spiral ribbons of eggs.

146. Purple Fan Nudibranch, *Flabellinopsis iodinea* (Pl. 36). Length to 4 cm (1½ in.). Body compressed (higher than wide) and of a beautiful deep purple color; the fringing cerata are purple at the base and brilliant orange at the tips. Abundant at unpredictable times in the middle and lower tide zones. It feeds primarily on hydroids. Like several other nudibranchs, this one often crawls along in tidepools upside down, suspended from the surface film of the water. If dislodged from its contact with the surface, it sinks toward the bottom; while

Phylum MOLLUSCA

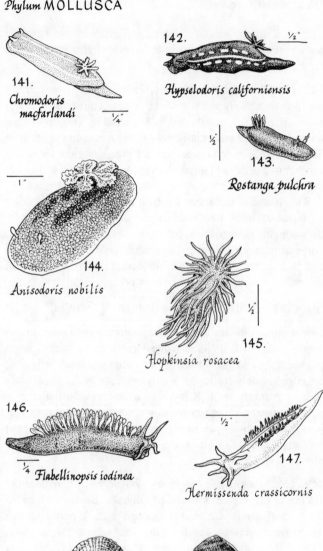

141.
*Chromodoris
macfarlandi*

¼"

142.

½"

Hypselodoris californiensis

½"

143.

Rostanga pulchra

1"

144.

Anisodoris nobilis

145.

½"

Hopkinsia rosacea

146.

¼" *Flabellinopsis iodinea*

½"

147.

Hermissenda crassicornis

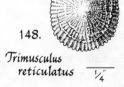

148.

*Trimusculus
reticulatus*

¼"

149.

¼"

Melampus olivaceus

sinking, it usually makes thrashing motions, curving its whole body first to one side and then to the other. This produces an erratic swimming progression.

147. Hermissenda, *Hermissenda crassicornis*. Length to 8 cm (3¹/₈ in.). Body usually white or pearly gray, with an orange stripe in the middle that is bordered by iridescent blue lines. The cerata are usually gray with an orange ring next to the white tip. These cerata form a fringe along the sides that consists of a series of paired clusters. Very common at times in the low tide area; probably our most abundant nudibranch.

This is one of the species known to eat hydroids and other cnidarians. These prey animals are supposedly protected by their stinging nematocysts, but the nudibranch is not deterred. Some nematocysts are even ingested without being discharged and pass into the outer tips of the cerata, where they furnish secondhand protection for their new host.

Subclass Pulmonata (Air-Breathing Snails)

148. Button Shell, *Trimusculus reticulatus*. Diameter to about 2 cm (³/₄ in.). Shell white, nearly round, with central pointed apex and a sculpture of fine radial and concentric ribs; the edge is finely scalloped. Fairly common at the middle tide level, but rarely seen. It hides in dark crevices, under protected overhangs, and (upside down) on the roofs of rock hollows. Like other pulmonate snails, it has no gills, but exchanges gas with water and air through mantle folds and the mantle cavity.

149. Salt Marsh Snail, *Melampus olivaceous*. Length about 1.5 cm (⁵/₈ in.); shell low-spired, globose. Brown with indistinct white bands just visible through a thick periostracum. There are several blunt teeth on the outer edge of the aperture. This shell is abundant in the high tide areas of quiet bay waters, often associated with the several species of pickleweed, genus *Salicornia*.

Class Scaphopoda (Tusk Shells)

These shells are all shaped like an elephant's tusk with openings at each end. A feeding individual is partially or completely buried in sand, with the small end angled upward. Water is both taken in and discharged through the opening in this small end, while the larger opening is filled by the large digging foot. ("Scaphopod" means "shovel-foot.") Just above the foot is a mouth surrounded by a cluster of slender tentacles with knobs on their tips. These tentacles wriggle through the sand picking up bits of food, which are conveyed by ciliary action to the mouth.

Tusk shells have been prized by the Indians on both coasts of North America, who often used them as currency. The great majority of the 200 or so species are confined to the tropics; only a few occur in Southern California, and they are not common.

150. Hexagonal Tusk Shell, *Dentalium neohexagonum*. Length to 4 cm (1½ in.). Color white. The shell is slightly curved, with six prominent longitudinal ribs and a hexagonal cross section. Moderately common offshore, but only dead shells are found in the intertidal zone.

151. Polished Tusk Shell, *Dentalium semipolitum*. Length 2.5 cm (1 in.). White, smooth, with a fairly sharp curve. Round in cross section. Very fine longitudinal ribs run down from the apex to about two-thirds the length of the shell. Dead shells are sometimes found in coarse sand.

Class Cephalopoda (Octopuses, Squids, and Their Relatives)

This class contains several kinds of animals that at first glance do not appear to be molluscs at all. Closer study clearly reveals their molluscan affinities, though their evolution has taken them a long way from the other molluscs. In many ways they are the most advanced members of the phylum.

Of all the cephalopods, only the Chambered Nautilus has an outer shell like the typical mollusc's. The argonauts also produce a type of shell, but this is actually an egg case, and the animal may leave it whenever it likes. But all have some sort of internal shell. In the deep-sea *Spirula,* this is coiled in a snail-like manner; in the octopuses, it is a pair of small stiffening structures; in the squids, it is a thin translucent structure extending the whole length of the mantle; and in the cuttlefishes (which do not live in our area), it is a thick, oval, chalklike organ that is widely used (under the name "cuttlebone") as a source of calcium for caged birds.

Other characteristics of the class include a distinct head with well-developed eyes that are not unlike our own in structure; a foot transformed into a set of appendages surrounding the mouth ("cephalopod" means "head-footed"); and a mouth with a radula and a chitinous parrotlike beak. The appendages nearly always have suction cups. Development is direct, the young emerging from the egg almost as miniature replicas of the adults, although body proportions, especially in the squids, may be quite different.

Order Decapoda

152. Opalescent Squid, *Loligo opalescens.* Length (including the eight arms but not the two long tentacles) to about 28 cm (11 in.). Squids dwell in the open sea and do not inhabit the intertidal zone. This one comes quite close to shore, however, and at night is often seen from the ends of lighted fishing piers. Dead specimens as well as egg cases are frequently washed up on the shore. The surest way to see an Opalescent Squid is to to visit a good fish market, where it is often sold under the name "inkfish." This word, like "calamari" and just plain "squid," connotes a food that is very popular in most parts of the world.

The Opalescent Squid has eight arms and two extensible tentacles much longer than the arms. The arms and the clubbed tentacle tips have numerous suction cups, many of them armed with rings and teeth of hard material. (Equivalent armament is not found in the octopuses.) This animal rarely crawls on the bottom, but swims in midwater, partly by graceful undulations of the broad tail fin and partly by jet propulsion through the use of its directable siphon. It can move backward, forward, or sideways with equal and bewildering rapidity; trying to capture any squid in a long-handled dip net as it swims in the circle of a spotlight shining from a boat is an experience in frustration.

The skin of this squid contains various types of pigment

Phylum MOLLUSCA

Dentalium neohexagonum ½" 151.
150. *Dentalium semipolitum* ½"

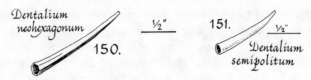

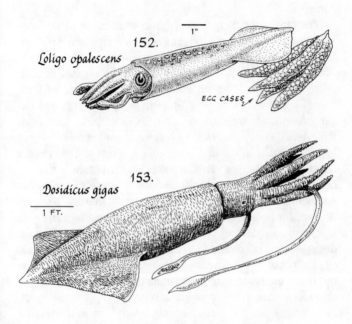

152. 1"
Loligo opalescens

EGG CASES

153.
Dosidicus gigas
1 FT.

(**155** NOT ILLUSTRATED)

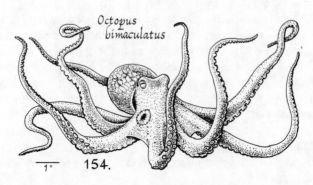

Octopus bimaculatus

1" 154.

cells, some of which, called *chromatophores,* can expand and contract, causing the most amazing play of colors over the skin. The color is never the same from one moment to the next: waves, bands, and spots appear and disappear or wash along the length of the body. Another type of pigment cell, the iridophore, remains constant and produces the scattered areas of brilliant blue-green opalescence that give this species its name.

The Opalescent Squid lays eggs in white cigar-shaped capsules about 15 cm (6 in.) long, often joined together at one end in bananalike bunches. Each separate case holds from 180 to 300 eggs. The whole case looks as if it were made of stiff-jelled tapioca pudding. In the winter great schools of these squids come within sight of shore to lay their eggs, and one can often locate them by spotting flocks of gulls (especially Ring-billed Gulls) that gather to eat the spent bodies of the egg layers, as many of the squids die after spawning. The eggs are attached to rocks, seaweeds, or other objects, often in tremendous numbers. A fisherman friend of mine once had to recruit another boat to help him retrieve a shark net that had been left in place for several days; the squids had attached so many eggs to it that a single boat could not lift it. And John McGowan, diving in the underwater La Jolla Canyon in 1954, found squid eggs attached to the canyon walls in masses measuring 12.2 m (40 ft.) in diameter. One would think that such great masses of organic matter would provide a bonanza for hordes of the ever-hungry sea dwellers, but only a very few creatures, including several kinds of annelid worms, seem able to make use of squid eggs.

Squids are active predators, capturing and eating many kinds of crustaceans, small fishes, and other creatures. Stomach analyses by Gordon Fields and others have shown that they also eat each other, especially where many squids are found in a restricted area. Squids are in turn eaten by sea lions and large fishes and are widely used by humans as both food and fish bait.

153. Humboldt Squid, *Dosidicus gigas.* Length of body (excluding the tentacles) up to 1.5 m (5 ft.). This is a very common pelagic (open sea) species from mid-Mexico southward but is not common here. It never lives in the intertidal zone, but an occasional specimen washes ashore—usually after floating dead at the surface for some time and pretty much damaged by gulls and crabs. In southern waters off Peru and Chile (in the Humboldt Current), this squid reaches a length of 3.5 m (almost 12 ft.).

There are other species of giant squid in the sea, and their dimensions are awesome. One in the genus *Architeuthis* that was stranded on a New Zealand shore in 1888 measured just over 17 m (57 ft.), including tentacles.

Order Octopoda (Octopuses)

154. Two-Spotted Octopus, *Octopus bimaculatus*. Armspread to 1 m (3 ft.), but most specimens are smaller. Color usually some combination of gray, gray-brown, red-brown, yellow-brown, and black. Color changes are swift and complete, apparently made according to the animal's mood rather than in an effort to fade into the background. Common in rocky areas of the low tide zone.

The eight arms are liberally studded on their inner surfaces with muscular suction cups, which are used entirely for grasping. Contrary to a widespread belief (propagated in the purplest of prose by Victor Hugo), neither they nor any other organs are used to suck the blood of the octopus's victims. The octopus subdues its prey by holding and biting it. The bite of many species, including this one, is poisonous, and crabs and other creatures are quickly anesthetized by it. The Two-Spotted Octopus envelops crabs in the umbrellalike web between its arms and releases its poison into the water that is also held there; this water passes over the crab's gills and anesthetizes it without the need to bite.

Some kinds of octopus bite quite readily in defense, but this one does not. My colleagues and I have handled thousands of individuals in the Aquarium-Museum at the Scripps Institution of Oceanography, and none of us has ever received a nip. There was a case of one bite—not serious—at the Steinhart Aquarium in San Francisco.

Another method of feeding involves the use of the radula to

bore through the shell of an abalone or other mollusc. After the toxin has taken effect, the shellfish is eaten by the octopus.

The dangers of contact with an octopus have been exaggerated. In general, a human is far stronger than even the largest octopus, which the Marshall Islanders demonstrate by making a game of catching and killing 12-footers with their bare hands and teeth. The largest known specimen had an armspread of 8.5 m (28 ft.); captured off the coast of Alaska, this was a long, skinny species and did not weigh more than the 12-footers from the Marshalls.

Properly prepared, the octopus is quite a delicacy, and this is partly responsible for its dwindling numbers in our area. Its would-be captors often poison the water in tidepools and surge channels by using copper sulfate or strong laundry bleaches to drive the hiding octopuses into the open. This is both cruel and illegal.

Octopuses are well known for their ink sacs, which can produce an obscuring cloud in the water. Ink expelled from the Two-Spotted Octopus usually hangs in the water for a few moments as a discrete blob, which probably serves as a decoy to attract a predator's attention rather than as a smoke screen. It also has a chemical function, temporarily destroying the sense of smell in the Moray (no. 250), the Two-Spotted Octopus's chief enemy, which hunts by smell.

Crawling on the bottom with graceful fluid loopings of its eight arms is the usual mode of progression for this octopus. In moments of stress, however, it will hold its arms together in a streamlined shape and squirt water forcefully out of its respiratory funnel, jetting itself rapidly with tentacles trailing.

There has been much discussion as to the proper plural for the word "octopus," and you are invited to take your choice. One authority has gone so far as to say that "the plural 'octopi' betrays an ignorance of three languages!" This is because it is a Greek word with a Latin plural, when the plural should be, according to this authority, in either Greek ("octopodes") or English ("octopuses"). Others prefer "octopi," but maintain that the proper pronunciation is "oc-TOPE-ee." Because it has become such a common word in English, most people are satisfied with the English construction of the added "es," or with simply using "octopus" as both singular and plural, as with "sheep."

155. Mudflat Octopus, *Octopus bimaculoides* (not illustrated). Common in muddy, protected waters at low tide levels. This species is identical in all external features to the Two-Spotted Octopus and may not be distinguishable in the field. The Mudflat Octopus lays eggs that are several times larger than those of the Two-Spotted Octopus (no. 154), the size of small seedless grapes rather than the size of grains of rice. There are other hidden differences as well, one important one being that each species harbors its own unique collection of mesozoan parasites.

Phylum Sipuncula
(Peanut Worms)

Sipunculan worms were first mentioned in scientific literature some 400 years ago, and ever since there has been some uncertainty as to their correct taxonomic position. Today most zoologists agree that they constitute a separate phylum.

Sipunculans live in a great variety of habitats from the intertidal zone to abyssal depths and from the arctic to the tropics. Most of the approximately 300 species, however, live in shallow coastal waters, and all are marine.

At the anterior end of the sipunculan body there is a retractable ring of branched, treelike tentacles. On retraction, these tentacles are turned outside in, as it were, and together with the forward third of the body are folded into the larger posterior portion. In this retracted position, some species resemble the kernel of a peanut. The shape and arrangement of the tentacles, the position of the mouth (inside the tentacle ring or outside), and the number of retracting muscle bands provide major features for classification. There are probably a dozen or more species in our area, but two of these will serve to illustrate the major characteristics of the group.

156. White Peanut Worm, *Sipunculus nudus*. Length occasionally to 25 cm (10 in.), but 7 to 10 cm (3 to 4 in.) is much more common. Shiny, iridescent white in color, with a surface composed of small rectangular bumps arranged in regular ranks and files. Found in quiet waters with sandy bottoms at low tide levels; most abundant in subtidal areas. It feeds by swallowing copious quantities of the sand that adheres to its sticky tentacles; any edible matter among the sand grains is digested, while the sand itself is passed through. In this manner, *Sipunculus* plays an important earthwormlike role in the conditioning of sandy bays and estuarine beaches. This is a widely distributed species in coastal waters of both the Old World and the New.

157. Tan Peanut Worm, *Themiste pyroides*. Length 7 to 10 cm (3 to 4 in.), although 20-cm giants have been reported in northern California. Color usually pale tan or straw. Body covered with numerous small tubercles that impart a feltlike texture. Often found under small rocks imbedded in the sand of exposed beaches at middle and low tide levels. When placed in a jar of fresh sea water, the peanut worm will usually expose its finely wrought tentacles.

Phylum Echiura
(Spoonworms)

There are about 130 species of spoonworms, all of them marine, with the majority confined to shallow coastal waters—although there is a record of one taken at a depth of 9,000 m (29,529 ft.). Only one of the several species in Southern California is considered here.

158. Innkeeper, *Urechis caupo*. Length between 20 and 46 cm (8 to 18 in.). Flesh-colored. Found in mudflats all along the California coast. It was at one time plentiful in Newport Bay.

The Innkeeper constructs a permanent U-shaped burrow in the mud, with the two ends, less than a meter apart, opening into the water. The animal is nearly as wide as the tunnel and keeps the water flowing through by causing constrictions to move down its body in a rhythmic peristalsis, or succession of muscular waves. At feeding time, the Innkeeper moves forward toward the headstock (where the water comes in) and attaches a ring of mucus to the tunnel walls. It then backs down, spinning a slime net as it goes. This ends up as a mucus cone, the big end fastened to the walls of the tunnel, the small end near the mouth of the Innkeeper; thus, all the water pumped through the burrow has to pass through this fine net. When the net is filled with small particulate matter and pumping gets difficult, the Innkeeper moves forward again—this time eating the net and its contents as it goes. Only the smaller particles are actually swallowed. Larger pieces are cast aside, where they provide the basic food for the clams, annelid worms, crabs, and fishes that share the Innkeeper's quarters and give it its name.

Phylum Annelida
(Annelid Worms)

The common earthworm is probably the most familiar member of this phylum. It contains about 9,000 species, divided into the classes Polychaeta (bristle worms), Oligochaeta (earthworms), and Hirudinea (leeches). There were formerly two small additional classes, the Archiannelida and the Myzostomida, but closer study has revealed them to be highly modified members of the class Polychaeta. Each class has representatives in the sea, but the polychaetes are by far the most numerous and are the only ones considered here. This book's coverage of the annelids is extremely sketchy—there are close to 700 species found in California coastal waters.

The word "Annelida" is taken from a root meaning "ringed," in reference to the ringlike body segments. In general, each segment of the annelid body has a complete set of organs and looks like the two segments before and behind it.

Each body segment is equipped with two bundles of bristles ("Polychaeta" means "many bristles") protruding from the footlike organs knows as *parapodia*. In most swimming polychaetes, and in some sedentary ones as well, a part of the parapodium is extended to form a paddle supported by stiff bristles set at right angles to the body.

Polychaetes have adapted to every sort of marine climate in every part of the world, from the shallows to the greatest abyssal depths. Some are scavengers, some predators, some vegetarians, and some filter feeders—in short, the group as a whole has taken advantage of every sort of food source offered by the sea. They are eaten in turn by a great many species, including, in some parts of the world, humans.

As with so many marine invertebrates, the annelids are not easily identified in the field. Laboratory analyses are rather simple, mainly involving examination of the head and tail regions and removal of some parapodia for magnified examination, but are nevertheless beyond the scope of this work. Accordingly, only a few of the more obvious kinds are presented here.

Class Polychaeta (Bristle Worms)

159. Scale Worm, *Halosydna johnsoni*. Length about 12 mm (1/2 in.), occasionally longer. Color pale brown with white centers in the scales, which lie in two longitudinal rows of overlapping plates. Found in a variety of habitats, most often at the middle tide level on rocky shores. Some individuals live a free life wandering among the rocks and crevices, while others seek a more sedentary existence as uninvited residents in the burrows of larger creatures. The sedentary ones seem to be larger and more brightly colored.

This species carries its fertilized eggs cemented to the body underneath the shielding scales. The young move away in the form of larvae called trochophores; these soon sink to the bottom, where they grow into the adult stage.

160. Pile Worm, *Neanthes succinea* (not illustrated). Length to 46 cm (18 in.), although the average size is much smaller. This animal can live under a wide variety of conditions. It not only lives in many sorts of marine habitats all along the Pacific coast, but is also at home in the Salton Sea and even in the waters of Oakland's Lake Merritt. The Salton Sea population is the result of deliberate importation; it forms an important part of the food chain involving the Orange-Mouth Corvina, a popular sportfish that was also deliberately introduced.

The Pile Worm makes excellent fish bait and is sold for this purpose in bait shops. It is much like the Clam Worm (no. 161) in looks and habits.

161. Clam Worm, *Neanthes brandti*. Length to 1 m (39 in.); a 1.8-m (6-ft.) specimen has been reported from Catalina

Phyla SIPUNCULA and ECHIURA

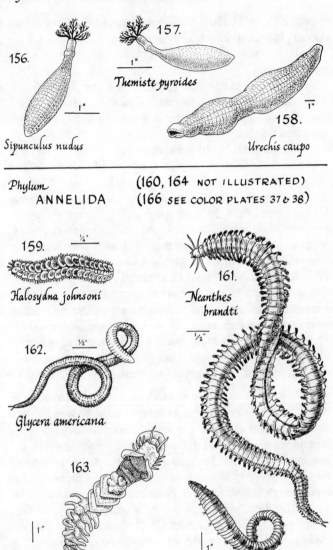

156.

Sipunculus nudus

157.

Themiste pyroides

158.

Urechis caupo

Phylum ANNELIDA

(160, 164 NOT ILLUSTRATED)
(166 SEE COLOR PLATES 37 & 38)

159.

Halosydna johnsoni

161.

Neanthes brandti

162.

Glycera americana

163.

Chaetopterus variopedatus

165.

Arenicola brasiliensis

Island. Most individuals are a great deal smaller, but even a 45-cm (18-in.) specimen is a magnificent creature, a far cry from the image brought to mind by the metaphorical use of the word "worm."

The color is olive or blue-green, often strikingly iridescent. Like many polychaetes, this one is a predator, eating all manner of small creatures; it also eats the sea lettuce *Ulva,* one of the green algae.

The breeding habits of this species and its relatives are quite spectacular. Both sexes undergo a number of changes in their body structures during breeding season. Early naturalists did not recognize the breeding and nonbreeding forms as different phases in the life of the same species. They named the breeding form *Heteronereis*—a word now used to designate the sexually active stage, but not a genus. The male heteronereis, at some signal given by the moon phase and the tide, joins his fellows as they emerge from their sheltered places. They swim to the surface and thrash and writhe there furiously, shedding sperm into the water. The females then join this eerie ballet while releasing their eggs. At the conclusion, males and females are completely spent and sink in death to the bottom.

The Clam Worm is found in many marine habitats, but in our area is most numerous among mussels (nos. 52 and 53).

162. Bloodworm, *Glycera americana.* Length to 20 to 30 cm (8 to 12 in.). Body rather smooth, tapered at both ends, with small parapodia. The color is reddish, and the body fluids resemble blood. The head contains a large infolding proboscis that can be everted and extended to a length equal to one-third the total body length. This proboscis is used for digging in the mud and gathering food. It is armed with four teeth, with which the Bloodworm can deliver a sharp nip to a human hand. A mild venom is associated with such a bite, and the resulting irritation may persist for several hours. In digging, the proboscis is thrust down into the sand and expanded as an anchor; when it is withdrawn, the body is pulled down into the substrate. Two or three thrusts will move the worm completely out of sight.

Found in mud and sandy mud on protected shores, this worm is popular as fish bait. What you buy in a bait shop, however, may be a closely related species, the Atlantic Blood-worm, *Glycera dibranchiata,* from the East Coast, where its capture and shipping constitute a minor industry.

163. Parchment Tube Worm, *Chaetopterus variopedatus.* Length occasionally to 38 cm (15 in.). The two words of the scientific name mean, respectively, "bristle-wing" and "various kinds of feet"—two appropriate terms, as will be shown in a moment. The vernacular name is also apt, referring to the worm's practice of secreting a parchmentlike lining for its U-shaped burrow. The ends of this burrow are slightly narrowed, and the lining projects a little above the surface of the substrate.

Near the center of the animal, three pairs of parapodia are expanded into rounded wings, or fans, which are long enough to brush against the walls of the tunnel. Rhythmic movements of these fans propel water through the tunnel at a rate of about 1 quart per hour (about 1 liter in 57 minutes) of work. A thimble-shaped mucus net is formed and held by a long pair of parapodia near the anterior end, and it streams backward with the current, trapping bits of food as the water passes. New net material is constantly produced at the small end, but the net does not increase in length, for the larger end is continually gathered in and rolled up into a tidy ball by specialized appendages. When this ball attains the size of a BB shot, which takes 18 to 22 minutes (depending on the amount of food in the water), the fans stop waving and the pellet of net and food is passed up to the mouth by the same appendages to be swallowed. Then the process starts over again.

This worm is famous for its regenerative powers. Segment no. 14 (the first of the three fan-bearing segments) seems to be the key. If the worm loses its body anterior to that segment, it regenerates a new head end; loss of the body behind that point results in regeneration of a new posterior end. And segment 14, isolated from the rest of the worm, will grow a new head end (always with exactly 13 segments) *and* a new tail end!

Chaetopterus is brilliantly luminescent, and even the mucous slime produced on various parts of the body has a glow of its own. The light is produced by a protein that is quite unrelated to the luciferin-luciferase complex that is so frequently related to marine bioluminescence. It is not known how the worm, in the lonely confines of its burrow, benefits by producing light; it may simply be a means of getting rid of waste material.

The species is fairly common in California's muddy bays and is found in similar European localities as well.

164. Red Worm, *Euzonus mucronata* (not illustrated). Length 5 to 10 cm (2 to 4 in.); color bright dark red; body smooth, with segments that are not easily discerned and minute parapodia. Burrowing just under the sand on exposed beaches, the Red Worm forms large colonies that move up and down the beach so as to remain a few feet above the present tide level. Such a colony may have a population of about 3,000 worms to each cubic foot of sand.

Red Worms feed by swallowing sand, digesting the minute bits of edible material on and between the grains, and passing the cleaned sand through the digestive tract. They are very active in their feeding, and in their vast numbers have a profound effect on the nature of the beach; it has been calculated that on a typical Red Worm beach, every grain of sand to a depth of 30 cm (1 ft.) is processed two or three times every year. So the next time you enjoy the clean sand of a La Jolla beach, you can breathe a small sigh of gratitude to the effective digestive tracts of the Red Worms.

In the winter, colonies of Red Worms may be located by watching for a peppering of small holes in the sand surface; these may have been made by Willets, Whimbrels, curlews, and other shorebirds that find the Red Worms delectable.

165. Lugworm, *Arenicola brasiliensis*. Length to 20 cm (8 in.), color greenish. Like the Red Worm, this one lives in the sand (or sometimes in sandy mud), but in much smaller numbers; two individuals per cubic foot of sand constitute the maximum population density. A widespread species, it is found on both coasts of North and South America and throughout the Pacific islands.

The Lugworm has an eversible proboscis covered with a sticky material. When this is everted and pushed against the sand, some sand sticks to it and is taken into the throat when the proboscis is retracted. This extension-retraction cycle is repeated every 5 seconds or so, with a few minutes' rest after each 7 to 15 thrusts, and a one-hour break once during each work day, which is normally from 5 to 7 hours. The indigestible material passed through the digestive tract is not ejected immediately, but stored in the posterior part of the body; once every 20 minutes or so, the Lugworm backs up to the surface and deposits it in a characteristic coiled casting.

The Lugworm's gills consist of 11 pairs of tufts on segments 7 through 17 in the middle part of the body, and they are quite efficient at extracting oxygen. The water in the Lugworm's habitat is often deficient in this vital element, and it can get along with less oxygen than most animals require.

166. Sand-Castle Worm, *Phragmatopoma californica* (Pls. 37 and 38). Length to about 7.5 cm (3 in.). Color dark brown with a crown of lavender tentacles. The worm itself is almost never seen, but the sand castles it builds are common on rocky beaches at middle and low tide levels. These constructions are made of sand grains cemented together, and in the aggregate look something like a honeycomb. The colony may cover an area as much as 2 m (more than 6 ft.) on a side, usually on vertical rock faces.

At low tide, when the colony is visible to the beach visitor, each worm closes the entrance to its tube with a dark operculum composed of a number of specialized setae. At high tide the lavender tentacles are extended into the water, where they collect food particles and sand grains; the food is swallowed, while the sand grains are sorted out, and the best ones used to keep the tube in repair.

Phylum Arthropoda
("Joint-Limbed" Animals)

This is the most successful group of animals on Earth. In number of species, number of individuals, adaptation to a wide variety of environments, geographical distribution, and so on, no other phylum comes close to this one. At least 80 percent of all known animals are arthropods.

The remarkable adaptive plasticity of this group has led to

confusing relationships, and there is some disagreement as to the placement of the higher categories; indeed, it has been argued that the group should be divided into several phyla. Nevertheless, all show variations on a basic plan that is both simple and efficient. They all have jointed appendages ("arthropod" means "joint-foot") with a wide range of functional specializations that provide basic criteria for classification. The entire body is covered with a continuous cuticle of a rather rigid substance known as *chitin*. This is formed in most cases into plates or rings, with freedom of movement assured by connecting links of tough, flexible, chitinous membranes. The whole structure provides an armor called an *exoskeleton,* and it is to this that the internal muscles are attached. Growth in arthropods requires the periodic shedding of the entire chitinous exoskeleton, with all increase in size occurring in the brief interval between the shedding of the old skin and the hardening of the new.

Most authorities recognize six or seven classes of arthropods, but only two of these will be considered here: Crustacea and Pycnogonida. The Merostoma (horseshoe crabs) are not found in American Pacific waters, while the Arachnida (true spiders) and Myriapoda (centipedes and millipedes) are only sparsely, if at all, represented in the marine environment. Insecta, by far the greatest class of all, is well represented on the seashore but is not included in this book. The interested reader is referred to Powell and Hogue (1979) for treatment of beach-dwelling genera such as *Coelopa, Condylostylus, Ephydra, Telmatogeton, Thinopinus, Tropisternus,* and many others. There is also some fine material on shore insects in Morris, Abbott, and Haderlie (1980).

Subphylum Mandibulata

Class Crustacea

The crustaceans constitute by far the most numerous group of marine arthropods, with at least 30,000 species. This book follows the plan of dividing the class into a number of subclasses, although some authorities place the crustaceans as a superclass, with the consequent elevation of our subclasses to classes.

The Crustacea are mainly aquatic in habit and have the usual arthropod characteristics. A head with five pairs of appendages is also a typical crustacean feature, as is a medial simple eye plus a pair of lateral compound eyes. The sexes are separate, and most of the young go through several complex larval stages that often provide clues to the relationships among species or higher categories. Adults may be very different from one another, but their larvae may be so similar as to demonstrate kinship.

Crustaceans have a long and rich paleontological history, and a number of quite primitive forms have survived to live side by side with more highly evolved forms. As we learn more about them, the group's diversity becomes more apparent, and two distinct subclasses have been discovered in recent years.

Subclass Cirripedia (Barnacles)

For a long time barnacles were classed with the molluscs, and it was not until 1830 that a British army surgeon recognized their affinity with the crustaceans by observing their larval development. A young barnacle leaves the egg as a microscopic *nauplius larva,* then becomes a *cypris larva;* in the latter form, it swims and drifts until it finds a suitable place to settle. It thereupon attaches its head to its chosen substrate, secretes a characteristic barnacle shell, and assumes the adult form.

Once settled down, the barnacle can do no more moving about. The population is spread by means of both the free-swimming larvae and the fact that many kinds of barnacles attach themselves to moving objects. Some kinds live on the bottoms of ships, for example, and others live only attached to turtles or whales. One kind can live nowhere but on another barnacle species that is itself attached to a whale! If the larva does not find the right set of conditions, it will die, and the odds against the survival of a newborn individual are staggering.

The name "cirripedia" means "feather-feet," and it is by

means of its feathery feet that the barnacle feeds. The feet are extended into the water, spread wide, then drawn back with a characteristic sweeping motion, retracted into the shell, and divested of adhering food particles. This led Thomas Henry Huxley to describe the barnacle as "a crustacean fixed by its head and kicking food into its mouth."

There are four orders of cirripeds, of which the order Thoracica contains by far the most species. The order Rhizocephala has only a few parasitic forms, one of which will be considered here; the Acrothoracica and Ascothoracica contain a few boring forms (that is, forms that bore holes in shells and other objects) and will not be presented.

167. Blue Goose Barnacle, *Lepas pacifica*. Length 4 to 7 cm (1½ to 2¾ in.). This species is closely related to *Lepas anatifera*, one of the chief foulers of ships' bottoms, which is rarely cast ashore in Southern California. The Blue Goose Barnacle, however, is common on our beaches, sometimes in large clumps attached to a floating box or hatch cover; it also attaches itself to small bits of wood, floating glass bottles, loose net floats, and many other objects, including the backs of Northern Elephant Seals, *Mirounga angustirostra*. It is a beautiful creature, its clean white shells edged with bright red and blue; the bluish interior body parts can usually be dimly seen through the thin shells.

Goose barnacles get their name from an old belief, held by at least one naturalist of some authority (John Gerard, who lived from 1545 to 1612), that geese hatched from them. Even the word "barnacle" probably referred to the goose (medieval Latin *bernaca*) before it came to mean the crustacean. Some present-day naturalists try to make sense of the common name by speaking of the gooseneck barnacle, in reference to its flexible stalk, but I prefer goose barnacle, which calls to mind the charming old tall tale.

168. Floating Goose Barnacle, *Lepas fascicularis*. Length 2.5 to 5 cm (1 to 2 in.). Similar to the Blue Goose Barnacle (no. 167), but smaller and with paper-thin shells. This is another high-seas dweller that comes ashore only through fatal misadventure. Very young specimens attach themselves to almost any kind of small floating object, such as a feather, tar globule, and so on. As they grow they begin secreting a raft of tiny, frothy bubbles. This eventually envelops the original floating object, and the barnacle is left with a raft of its own devising.

169. Leaf Barnacle, *Pollicipes polymerus* (Pls. 39 and 40). Total length to 10 cm (4 in.). This is another of the goose barnacles, with a long, fleshy neck attached at the lower end to the substrate and on the upper end bearing the complex arrangement of shell plates. Extremely abundant on rocks and pier pilings in the middle tide zone, usually associated with the California Mussel (no. 52.)

This species is hermaphroditic, but a given individual does not fertilize its own eggs. Breeding may occur from three to seven times in a year, with each individual producing between 100,000 and 240,000 larvae. The mortality among these nauplius larvae is tremendous, but once an individual settles down on a suitable substrate, preferably among other Leaf Barnacles, it has a long life expectancy and probably takes 20 years to reach its full size.

This is the only stalked barnacle in our area that has adapted to life in the intertidal zone.

170. Thatched Barnacle, *Tetraclita rubescens* (Pl. 41). Diameter to 4 cm (1½ in.). Shape conical, sometimes slightly higher than wide. This is one of the acorn barnacles, with an outer surface that is uniformly roughened by deep vertical grooves and ridges. Color dark brick-red. Common on rocks and pier pilings in the lower middle and low tide zones.

Acorn barnacles belong to the suborder Balanomorpha. Most of them are symmetrical when viewed from above (usually round) and volcano-shaped in profile. At the apex of the cone is an orifice that can be tightly closed by means of four movable opercular shell plates. When the barnacle is feeding, which can be done only under water, these plates are opened and the feathery cirri sweep the water for food. There is no flexible stalk, the base of the shell itself being firmly anchored to the substrate. This attachment is firm, and the shell remains fixed for a long time even after its occupant dies; such shells often have sharp edges, and human intertidal rock-clamberers must take care not to lacerate their hands and feet on them.

171. Brown Buckshot Barnacle, *Chthamalus fissus* (Pl. 42). Diameter less than 7 mm (¼ in.), color usually light brown. This and the White Buckshot Barnacle (no. 172) are not easy to separate in the field, the color difference not being constant. The best way is to observe the arrangement of the plates, as shown in the drawing. Both species are found attached to almost any sort of solid object—including the shells of snails, mussels, and crabs—throughout the intertidal zone. They reach their greatest numbers far up in the splash zone, where the uppermost members are kept wet less than half their lives. There they are truly abundant, often literally covering the rocks in a layer only one barnacle deep; up to 70,000 individuals per square meter have been counted in these aggregations.

A second species of Brown Buckshot Barnacle, *Chthamalus dalli,* is found in the same sort of habitat; its identification as separate from *C. fissus* requires laboratory dissection, and no effort to distinguish between them is made here. Your Brown Buckshot Barnacles are sure to be one or the other!

172. White Buckshot Barnacle, *Balanus glandula* (Pl. 42). Very similar to the Brown Buckshot Barnacle (no. 171), but often larger, sometimes up to 2 cm (¾ in.). Color usually white. Aggregations are not usually quite as dense as those of the Brown Buckshot Barnacle. The two kinds often occur together.

173. Little Pink Barnacle, *Balanus amphitrite* (Pl. 42). Diameter to 2 cm (¾ in.). Color gray with red or purple stripes on the outside plates that become narrower toward the apex. Fairly common in the low tide zone of protected waters, and occasionally found in association with mussel beds on the landward sides of exposed rocks on the open coast.

This species is frequent on ships' bottoms and is widely distributed in the warm seas of the world. It has even been intro-

Phylum ARTHROPODA

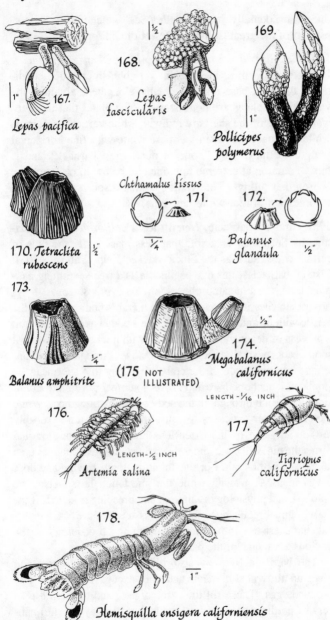

167.
Lepas pacifica

168.
Lepas
fascicularis

169.
Pollicipes
polymerus

170. Tetraclita
rubescens

Chthamalus fissus
171.

172.
Balanus
glandula

173.

Balanus amphitrite

174.
Megabalanus
californicus

(175 NOT
ILLUSTRATED)

176.
Artemia salina
LENGTH-½ INCH

177.
Tigriopus
californicus
LENGTH-¹⁄₁₆ INCH

178.

Hemisquilla ensigera californiensis

duced, accidentally, into the Salton Sea, which lies in the lowest part of the great Colorado Desert of California.

174. Red-Striped Acorn Barnacle, *Megabalanus californicus*. Diameter to 5 cm (2 in.), height variable; in crowded conditions, the hard base may be greatly elongated, although the well-defined plates are not distorted. The plates that taper toward the top of the shell are red with white vertical markings, while the spaces between them are white with fine horizontal sculptured lines. This is one of our largest barnacles and is fairly common at extreme low tide and below in rocky places and on pier pilings. The feeding animal displays patriotically colored cirri of red, white, and blue.

175. Parasitic Barnacle, *Heterosaccus californicus* (not illustrated). Seen only as a soft shapeless mass under the tails of certain crabs, such as the Shield-Backed Kelp Crab (no. 205). Like all barnacles, this one begins life as a free-swimming nauplius larva, then metamorphoses into the cypris stage. As a cypris, it attaches itself to a bristle on a crab's body, piercing the bristle with its antennae. The barnacle's body has by then begun a process of degeneration, shrinking within its own skin, and it soon becomes small enough to flow down through its own antennae into the inside of the crab. Migrating to a spot near the stomach, it anchors there and grows a number of rootlike extensions that reach throughout the body of its unwilling host. While the crab's outer cuticle is soft just after its next (and probably last) moult, one of the extensions pushes to the outside and forms the tumorlike sac under the crab's tail. Great changes then take place in the crab. For one thing, it stops growing and does not shed its skin again while the infestation lasts. Also, the crab's sexual physiology is altered, and breeding is halted. If the crab is a male, it changes shape and assumes many of the external characteristics of the female—including a broader tail, to the obvious advantage of the parasite.

The barnacle lives by absorbing food from its host and gives up all typical barnacle activities except for the ability to produce eggs. These fill the external sac, and through a process of parthenogenesis (without fertilization by a male) nauplius larvae are set free to begin the cycle all over again.

Heterosaccus has a life span of only three or four years, and on its death the host crab may return to normal; this is not usual, however, as most crabs die during the ordeal.

Subclass Branchiopoda (Fairy Shrimps and Their Relatives)

Most branchiopods dwell in fresh water, typically making their homes in ephemeral puddles and ponds. The adults die when the water dries up, but not before they have deposited fertilized eggs that are capable of withstanding years of drought, if necessary. The new generation begins with the next rain. The group as a whole has developed a remarkable ability to survive in situations that are hostile to most forms of life. The fossil record shows that they appeared sometime in the upper Cambrian period, about 500 million years ago.

Order Anacostraca

176. Brine Shrimp, *Artemia salina*. Length to 13 mm ($\frac{1}{2}$ in.). Brine Shrimp can live in water of extremely high salinity, and today thrive best in the brine pools of factories that extract table salt from sea water. The shallow pools at the salt factory at the southern end of San Diego Harbor (near the Mexican border), for example, are swarming with Brine Shrimp. These little creatures are popular as food for aquarium fish, and, years ago, aquarists were allowed to visit the evaporating ponds in order to collect a supply. Today, however, the general public is denied access, and the harvesting is done by licensed operators as part of a well-developed commercial operation. Brine Shrimp, both alive and frozen, are available at aquarium-supply shops, as are their eggs, which hatch into nauplius larvae as soon as they are placed in water.

Subclass Copepoda

In the open sea, the copepods are extremely important in the energy cycle, forming one of the primary links between the energy-capturing phytoplankton and the larger animals. Herring enthusiasts have spoken of the copepod *Calanus finmarchicus* as the world's most important invertebrate, since its numbers have a direct influence upon the numbers of herring.

The numbers of copepods in the sea are staggering, and if there were as many flies per cubic foot of air as there are copepods per cubic foot of water, our lives would hardly be worth living. The term "copepod" means "oar-footed."

Order Harpacticoidea

177. Tidepool Copepod, *Tigriopus californicus*. Length about 1.6 mm ($^1/_{16}$ in.). Color red. Common in small pools in the upper splash zone. One must look very closely to see these tiny creatures; watch for little red specks dancing about. Very few animals are capable of withstanding the extremes of temperature and salinity that are the lot of this copepod; it can survive a salt content six times that of sea water, and a water temperature of close to 40° C (102° F).

Subclass Malacostraca

Order Stomatopoda (Mantis Shrimps)

178. Mantis Shrimp, *Hemisquilla ensigera californiensis*. Length to 30 cm ($11^7/_8$ in.). Not often seen in the intertidal zone, but occasionally left stranded in pools on mudflats. Sometimes taken on hook and line, at which times it always creates a stir of excitement among the shore fishermen in the bays. It is truly an impressive animal. The eyes are mounted on movable stalks and are never still. The body is tan, usually with red-brown areas along the sides of the thorax. The walking legs and some of the head appendages are blue, while the large flat tail has two paddle-shaped appendages that are brilliant blue, fringed with bright red. The raptorial appendages—a pair of "legs" that resemble the claws of a praying mantis, only upside down—are yellow. These appendages are both strong and sharp and can inflict severe wounds if the Mantis Shrimp is not handled with the greatest respect.

This is a burrowing form, living just below low tide level and down to depths of 90 m (295 ft.).

Order Amphipoda (Beach Hoppers, Skeleton Shrimps, and Their Relatives)

These are the most numerous crustaceans in the intertidal zone. Most are active at night, but to see them in daylight, all you have to do is pick up and shake out a bit of kelp or other seaweed and watch the beach hoppers hop. They are often called "sand fleas" but are not related to the true fleas, and they don't bite. Their bodies are laterally *compressed*—that is, flattened from side to side, so that they look thin when seen from directly above but have a high profile.

More than 150 amphipod species are known to occur in Southern California, and about 5,500 worldwide. As detailed study of various microhabitats proceeds, new ones are constantly being discovered. They are usually divided into three suborders: Gammaridea (beach hoppers) and Caprellidea (skeleton shrimp) are represented in our area, while the third order, Hyperidea, has only a few forms, all of them pelagic, and will not be considered here.

Suborder Gammaridea (Beach Hoppers)

179. Large Beach Hopper, *Orchestoidea corniculata*. Body length to 2.5 cm (1 in.). Color brownish white, second antennae orange-red, not long enough to reach the middle of the body when folded back. Two shadowy gray spots on the sides. Abundant on beaches of coarse sand, usually staying above the reach of the highest waves at any given moment. During the day, Large Beach Hoppers burrow in the sand like miniature pocket gophers, leaving little mounds of sand at the mouth of the burrow. They are very active at night, and at times the beam of a flashlight will make the upper beach appear almost alive with them.

Many other beach hoppers inhabit our area, but this one is usually the most obvious. *Orchestoidea californiana* is a little larger, with proportionately longer antennae. It is found only north of Laguna and prefers beaches with gentle slopes and fine sand.

180. Seaweed Hopper, *Elasmopus rapax*. Body length to about 6.5 mm (¼ in.), color sandy brown. Abundant among clusters of red algae and other seaweeds in tidepools and at low tide level; also abundant under rocks, and often found in beds of the California Mussel (no. 52). In the latter habitat it performs an important scavenging role in the complex food chain of the mussel bed.

Suborder Caprellidea (Skeleton Shrimps)

181. Kelp Skeleton Shrimp, *Caprella equilibra*. Length to 2.5 cm (1 in.). Abundant on the fronds of kelp and other sea-weeds, and also (with several other species) among hydroid colonies. Caprellids fasten themselves to their substrate by their prehensile hind legs and stand upright, making continuous fore and aft bowing motions. They feed on anything that comes within their reach, and are so adaptable in this respect that food is probably not a factor that limits their numbers.

Order Isopoda

With about 4,000 species, this is an important group in the sea. Unlike the amphipods, which are compressed in shape, the isopods are *depressed*—that is, flattened from top to bottom and presenting a low profile. The term "isopod," meaning "similar feet," refers to the lack of pronounced differences among the appendages; the legs are usually simply adapted for crawling or running, and there are no large pinching claws. Some marine isopods are strong swimmers, some are burrowers, and some are parasitic, but most are crawlers and weak swimmers. The majority are marine, but some are land dwellers; the most familiar of these are those banes of the gardener's life, the pill bugs and sow bugs.

Like amphipods, isopods carry their eggs in a brood pouch on the underside of the body. The young go through their larval stages while still in this pouch and emerge as miniature replicas of the adults.

182. Swimming Isopod, *Cirolana harfordi*. Length to 2 cm (³/₄ in.). Color gray, yellowish, or brown, with or without a pattern of darker blotches and spots. Abundant in tidepools, under rocks, among mussels, seaweeds, and so on throughout the intertidal zone. This little isopod's scavenging activities are important in the cycle of intertidal life. Museum preparators have often placed skeletons of fishes and other animals in mesh cages, put the cages into a tidepool, and waited for these isopods to clean away all the meat, leaving a clean skeleton. *Cirolana* is equally at home crawling on the bottom or swimming in the quiet waters of a tidepool, looking like a fat little blimp.

183. Bigtail Isopod, *Exosphaeroma amplicauda*. Length to 8 mm ($5/16$ in.), wider at the hind end with comparatively huge "fins" (uropods) at the sides. Tan in color. Found among stones in the low tide zone and at the same level in protected bays.

184. Rock Louse, *Ligia occidentalis*. Length to 4 cm ($1^1/2$ in.). Color variable, usually somewhat matching the rock on which it lives. The color changes with the time of day, being paler by night. The agile Rock Louse scurries about on the rocks in the upper high tide and splash zones, preferring near-vertical rock faces with lots of crevices to hide in. It is especially active at night, although some individuals may be seen at almost any hour. Abundant.

185. Seaweed Isopod, *ldotea resecata*. Length to 4 cm ($1^1/2$ in.). Found on kelp and, in Central and Northern California, on Eelgrass as well. The body color always matches the background—yellow-brown on kelp stipes and fronds, green on Eelgrass. It always orients itself along the long axis of the seaweed. Found fairly often on the beach among masses of cast-up Giant Kelp, *Macrocystis pyrifera*.

186. Flat-Tailed Isopod, *Idotea urotoma*. Length to 2 cm ($3/4$ in.), color usually brown, although variable. This is a slow-moving form and is fairly common under rocks in the middle and lower tide zones.

187. Sea Urchin Isopod, *Colidotea rostrata*. Length 13 mm ($1/2$ in.), color purple-red. Common on the spines of Purple and Red Sea Urchins (nos. 235 and 236). Doing no harm to its host, the Sea Urchin Isopod is simply taking advantage of an effective refuge.

Order Decapoda (Shrimps, Lobsters, Crabs, and Their Relatives)

Most decapods have ten feet (that's what "decapod" means), which may include a pair of large pinching claws. This is a diverse order, with close to 9,000 species ranging through practically every imaginable aquatic or semiterrestrial habitat. A number of groups are recognized, although there is disagreement as to whether these groups should be called suborders, sections, superfamilies, tribes, or series. Here we follow a convenient but perhaps outmoded system that divides the decapods into two suborders—Natantia, the swimmers, and Reptantia, the crawlers; the Reptantia, in turn, are here divided into tribes as shown below.

Suborder Natantia (Swimming Decapods)

188. Snapping Shrimp, *Alpheus clamator.* Length of body about 3.7 cm (1³/₈ in.), length of large claw to 2 cm (³/₄ in.). Color dark brown and black. Common among rocks at extreme low tide. A microscopically smooth disk on the back of the thumb of the large claw meets a similar disk on the main part of the hand when the thumb is bent back to an angle of 90 degrees. These two disks adhere in a way that resists the closing motion of the thumb until the effort reaches a certain level, at which time the disks part with a loud crack. This sound, together with the forceful stream of water that is ejected from between the thumb and the palm, serves to frighten away potential enemies as well as to stun small nearby creatures that can then be eaten. It may be that the snapping is also done just for fun or to keep in practice, for the clamor produced by a bed of these shrimps sounds like the continuous crackling of a forest fire. You can hear it along any shallow water rocky reef by putting your ears under water.

There are several kinds of Snapping Shrimps (also known as Pistol Shrimps), and one or another of these can be found in any suitable habitat in temperate waters everywhere. At least three species of two genera are found in our area, but all are quite similar in appearance and habits.

189. Abalone Shrimp, *Betaeus harfordi.* Length to 2 cm (³/₄ in.), color glossy brown, although some are black and some are blue. Found living under the edge of the shell of living abalone, usually one shrimp to one abalone, of a size to match that of the host: the larger the abalone, the larger the shrimp. Occasionally seen among seaweed or in other habitats, but the abalone is its usual home. Very common.

190. Striped Rock Shrimp, *Lysmata californica.* Length to 6.5 cm (2¹/₂ in.). Color translucent white or cream, with bold

Phylum ARTHROPODA

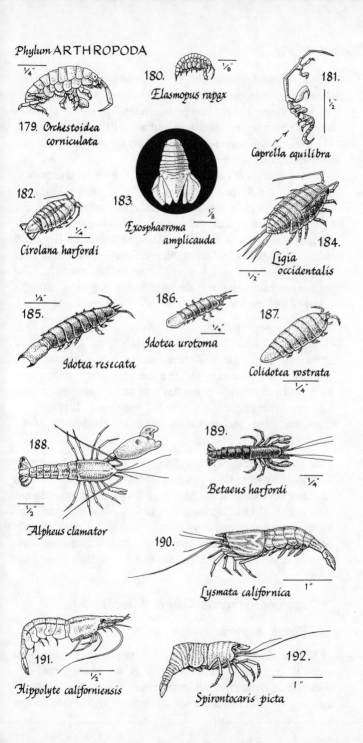

179. *Orchestoidea corniculata*

180. *Elasmopus rapax*

181. *Caprella equilibra*

182. *Cirolana harfordi*

183. *Exosphaeroma amplicauda*

184. *Ligia occidentalis*

185. *Idotea resecata*

186. *Idotea urotoma*

187. *Colidotea rostrata*

188. *Alpheus clamator*

189. *Betaeus harfordi*

190. *Lysmata californica*

191. *Hippolyte californiensis*

192. *Spirontocaris picta*

red longitudinal stripes. This is a graceful and delicate animal, abundant in tidepools. It is especially active at night. A number of Striped Rock Shrimp dancing on tiptoe across submerged rocks is a pleasant aspect of night life in the tidepools. They are easily located at such times by the ruby reflection of their eyes in a flashlight beam.

Every species has a role to play in the life of a community, and one of the Striped Rock Shrimp's jobs is to be a cleaner. This activity was first observed and written about by the late Conrad Limbaugh and some of his scuba-diving colleagues. Large fishes such as the Moray (no. 250) and the Garibaldi (no. 253) regularly let these (and other) shrimps clamber over them to pick off parasites and other edible morsels. The shrimp can even crawl into the mouth of the larger animal with (most of the time) impunity.

191. Grass Shrimp, *Hippolyte californiensis.* Length to 4 cm (1 1/2 in.), but usually less; color bright green. Very abundant in beds of the Eelgrass, *Zostera marina,* which grows at the low tide level in quiet bays. The shrimp exactly matches the Eelgrass in color, and during daylight hours it remains immobile on a blade of the plant, oriented lengthwise. It is active at night, and great numbers can be seen crawling about on barely submerged beds of Eelgrass.

192. Broken-Back Shrimp, *Spirontocaris picta.* Length to 3.2 cm (1 1/4 in.). Color usually greenish, transparent, with red-brown vertical or oblique bands. Abundant in tidepools and under rocks and among seaweeds in the low tide zone. The spirontocarid shrimps, most of which have the characteristic bent back, make up a large group of which at least a dozen species occur in Southern California; specific identification is not easy.

Suborder Reptantia (Crawling Decapods)

Tribe Macrura

193. Blue Mud Shrimp, *Upogebia pugettensis.* Length to about 10 cm (4 in.). Color blue-gray. A burrowing form fairly common in quiet, muddy waters from the middle tide zone downward. Its burrows are semipermanent and often a foot or more beneath the surface of the mud; each burrow houses one pair of Blue Mud Shrimps. The diameter of the burrow is just wide enough to permit passage of one animal, but there are numerous turnaround expansions provided. Fanlike motions of the flat tail appendages create a current of water through the burrow, and hairs on the first two pairs of legs strain out edible particles. There are usually several commensal animals sharing the burrow and the bounty of current-borne food particles.

North of Santa Barbara, this animal grows larger than its southern counterpart.

194. California Ghost Shrimp, *Callianassa affinis*. Length to 6.5 cm (2½ in.), with a large claw very nearly the same length as the body. Color white, with blotches of orange-pink. This too is a burrowing form, often making its tunnels beneath a stone, letting the stone serve as the roof of the gallery. Its vertical range extends well up into the middle tide zone.

Each burrow houses a pair of California Ghost Shrimps and a pair of fish—Blind Gobies (no. 260), which are found in almost no other habitat. Few if any other commensals share the burrow.

The various appendages of the California Ghost Shrimp and Blue Mud Shrimp (no. 193) are admirably suited to digging, each pair of legs carrying out a specific job like an efficient assembly line. Loads of mud and sand are clutched between the forelegs, carried to the mouth of the burrow, and dumped outside.

This is the smallest of the several kinds of ghost shrimps that are found in our area. All are quite similar in habits and form, and all are sought after as fish bait. California fish and game regulations forbid the possession of more than 50 individuals of all ghost shrimps and mud shrimps combined.

195. California Spiny Lobster, *Panulirus interruptus*. Length rarely to 76 cm (30 in.), weight may reach a maximum of almost 13.6 k (30 lbs.). Such giants are increasingly rare, however; the legal minimum size is 3¼ inches, measuring only the thorax, which is about two-fifths of the total length. Specimens found in tidepools are almost always far below legal size. Color dark brick red.

Unlike the Northern or Maine Lobster (*Homarus ameri-*

canus), this species has no large pinching claws, although the female does have small pincers on the last pair of walking legs; these are used to care for her eggs, which she carries attached to the swimmerets on the underside of the tail. They are also used to transfer sperm cells to the eggs from the packet affixed to her chest during mating.

The lack of claws does not denote helplessness, as anyone knows who has grabbed a large spiny lobster with bare hands. The long antennae are thickly set with sandpapery spines, and when these are sawed across a wrist, the would-be captor is likely to let go in a hurry. There are sharp spines on the body, too, and the saw teeth on the under margins are especially dangerous; don't let the animal curl its tail on your fingers! Most skin divers wear good strong gloves when out to capture California Spiny Lobsters. The law prohibits the use of spears, and diving sports fishermen have to use only their hands.

Other Spiny Lobster laws include a strictly observed closed season. Be sure to familiarize yourself with these before attempting any lobster catching.

The California Spiny Lobster (or langosta, as it is often called) is an offshore form, but small specimens temporarily caught in intertidal pools are common. Also, shed exoskeletons are frequently washed up on the beach.

Tribe Anomura (Sand Crabs, Hermit Crabs, and Their Relatives)

196. Sand Crab, *Emerita analoga*. Length to 3.5 cm (1⅝ in.). Extremely abundant in restricted localities. This plump little crab is somewhat longer than it is wide, about the size and shape of a jumbo olive. Its color is pale bluish or yellowish white.

Colonies of Sand Crabs inhabit surf-swept sandy beaches, moving up and down as necessary to remain in the area being washed by each wave. While under water in the wave wash, each individual usually emerges from the sand and swims to a new spot, then, as the wave recedes, burrows quickly tail first into the sand, leaving only the V-shaped antennae showing. The point of the V points up the beach, away from the water. These antennae entrap food particles as the receding wave

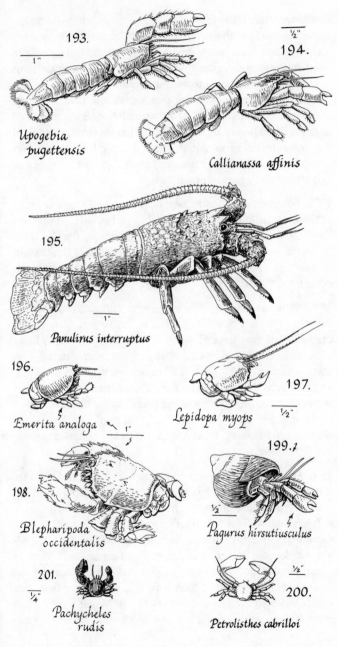

Phylum ARTHROPODA

193.
1"

194.
½"

Upogebia
pugettensis

Callianassa affinis

195.
1"

Panulirus interruptus

196.
Emerita analoga
1"

197.
Lepidopa myops
½"

198.
Blepharipoda
occidentalis

199.
Pagurus hirsutiusculus
½

201.
¼"
Pachycheles
rudis

200.
Petrolisthes cabrilloi
½"

flows over them, and there is just time to withdraw them, remove the food, and swim to a new spot before the next wave arrives. The whole colony moves along the beach in response to whatever longshore currents are flowing at the moment; this is generally a movement toward the south.

Sand Crabs make excellent fish bait. Some surf fishermen claim better results with soft-shelled individuals captured just after the shedding of the old skin and before the hardening of the new. In late spring, summer, and early fall, many *ovigerous* (egg-bearing) females can be seen carrying masses of bright orange eggs under their tails.

197. Porcelain Sand Crab, *Lepidopa myops*. Length to about 2.5 cm (1 in.). Color iridescent blue-white. The Porcelain Sand Crab can be distinguished from the Sand Crab (no. 196) by its much longer antennae, the squarish shape of the front of its carapace, and its pinching claws. Never very abundant, it is occasionally seen in Sand Crab beds.

198. Spiny Sand Crab, *Blepharipoda occidentalis*. Length to 7.5 cm (3 in.). Color ivory. This is the largest of our sand crabs. It has two large flat claws, each fringed with a hairy border. The front and sides of the carapace are armed with many sharp spines. It lives in association with Sand Crab (no. 196) colonies, but remains on the seaward fringe of the colony. Adults are scavengers, depending primarily on the dead bodies of Sand Crabs as a source of food. South of San Pedro, the shed skins of Spiny Sand Crabs are quite common among beach flotsam.

199. Hermit Crab, *Pagurus hirsutiusculus*. Hermit Crabs are familiar to anyone who has ever gazed into a tidepool. All are well armored on the forward part of the body but have large, soft abdomens. This construction would be a disadvantage in the hungry intertidal world, except that the Hermit Crab always hides its vulnerable abdomen in an empty snail shell or other suitably hollow object, leaving only the armored front quarters exposed. The abdomen even has a natural twist that corresponds to the spiral direction of most snail shells. As a Hermit Crab grows, it must move continually from one shell to another, always seeking a good fit; its life consists largely of an endless search for more stately mansions.

A Hermit Crab will make a home out of almost any sort of hollow object. Some adopt straight worm shells, and I knew one that lived happily in a pretty blue pill bottle! Whatever the shape of the house, the soft abdomen is protected while the armored wrists and claws provide a shield at the open entrance.

There are many species of hermit crabs, but *Pagurus hirsutiusculus* is typical of the group. Those in our intertidal zone are usually no more than 2.5 cm (1 in.) long, although they grow four times that size in Northern California waters and in deeper waters here. The antennae are gray or brown, banded with white; there are no bands on the red-brown walking legs. Small individuals are frequently found in the shells of Purple Olive Snails (no. 133), middle-sized ones in Angular and Checkered Unicorn Shells (nos. 126 and 127), and larger ones in shells the size of the Black Turban (no. 101). This is one of our most abundant crustaceans.

200. Flat Porcelain Crab, *Petrolisthes cabrilloi*. Diameter of body about 13 mm (½ in.). Color variable, usually yellow-brown with lighter spots. Often there are marks of blue and red on the edges of the large flat claws. This crab looks as if it had been cut out of paper, giving it a flatness appropriate to its under-rock habitat. In the middle and low tide zones, turning over almost any rock will reveal scores of little Flat Porcelain Crabs scurrying for shelter.

201. Thick-Clawed Porcelain Crab, *Pachycheles rudis*. Diameter of the dark brown body to about 1.5 cm (⅝ in.); the large pinching claw (which may be either the left or the right) is almost as big as the body. Common in protected locations—among mussels, in empty barnacle shells, in kelp holdfasts, Eelgrass roots, and so on. This is a slow-moving little animal and, when dragged into the open, may easily be captured. At such times, however, it is likely to resort to autotomy, breaking off the large claw—which will subsequently grow back.

202. Red Crab or Squat Lobster, *Pleuroncodes planipes*. Length to 13 cm (5 in.), color bright red. This is not an intertidal species, but every few years hordes of them are swept ashore to die. Their usual home is the open sea southwest of San Diego, where at times they cover acres of the sea surface. Quirks of winds and currents are probably responsible for their infrequent incursions ashore. Red Crabs are a favorite food of several kinds of tuna, and fishermen call them "tuna crabs."

Tribe Brachyura ("True" Crabs)

203. Elbow Crab, *Heterocrypta occidentalis.* Width of carapace at widest point about 3.2 cm (1¼ in.). Color sandy brown. Found occasionally in sandy areas, the Elbow Crab cannot be mistaken for any other local species. It is mainly a tropical form, with Southern California the extreme northern limit of its range.

204. Globose Kelp Crab, *Taliepus nuttalli.* Body length to 13 cm (5 in.), color purplish or brick red. The surface of the globular carapace usually has a dull matte texture. The claws may be very large, especially among the males. This crab is always associated with some of the large brown seaweeds, such as the Feather-Boa Kelp, *Egregia laevigata,* or (farther offshore) the Giant Kelp, *Macrocystis pyrifera.* In the intertidal zone, it is most likely to be seen among seaweeds in surge channels that are not drained at even the lowest tides.

205. Shield-Backed Kelp Crab, *Pugettia producta.* Body length to about 10 cm (4 in.), color glossy olive green, spotted beneath with bright red. Found in the same sorts of habitats as the Globose Kelp Crab (no. 204). These two kelp crabs are superficially similar, but the Shield-Backed Kelp Crab can be identified by its flattened, shield-shaped carapace and its glossy texture.

Small tangled skeins of kelp and Surfgrass are sometimes thrown onto the beach, and occasionally one of these will have a Shield-Backed Kelp Crab wound up in it. At least one naturalist considered the possibility that the crabs made these "nests" themselves, but this has not been borne out by further observation. Their involvement with the seaweed balls is accidental—and fatal.

Phylum ARTHROPODA

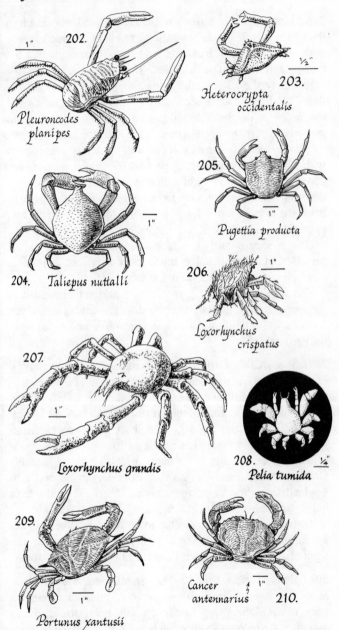

202. 1"
Pleuroncodes
planipes

203. ½"
Heterocrypta
occidentalis

205. 1"
Pugettia producta

204. Taliepus nuttalli 1"

206. 1"
Loxorhynchus
crispatus

207. 1"
Loxorhynchus grandis

208. ¼"
Pelia tumida

209. 1"
Portunus xantusii

Cancer 1"
antennarius 210.

206. Masking Crab, *Loxorhynchus crispatus*. Body length to 9 cm (3 1/2 in.), but usually smaller. The carapace is so covered with algae, bryozoa, hydroids, and other organisms that the crab's natural red color is hidden. This camouflage is applied deliberately, the crab carefully attaching it to little hooked bristles. The disguise always matches the environment; if moved to a new locality, the crab will gradually divest itself of its old garden and plant a new one made of local materials.

I once had a Masking Crab that was placed in an aquarium with a bunch of young Opaleye fish (*Girella nigricans,* no. 254), whose browsing habits quickly denuded the crab of its covering. With nothing else to cover its nakedness, the crab managed to pry loose a lot of flakes of aquarium cement and plant *them* on its back.

The species is fairly common at extreme low tide on the protected outer coast but is much more abundant at subtidal levels, especially on pier pilings in quiet waters.

Our locality has several species of masking crabs, most of them smaller than this one. All are slow and deliberate in their movements, as befits one who is trying to fade into a stationary background.

207. Sheep Crab, *Loxorhynchus grandis*. This is our largest crab, attaining a leg-spread of at least 96 cm (38 in.); the globular body is relatively small, rarely exceeding 18 cm (7 in.). Young individuals practice the art of masking and are similar to the Masking Crab (no. 206); the Sheep Crab may be distinguished by its down-bent *rostrum* (a narrow forward extension of the edge of the carapace at the midline), while the Masking Crab's rostrum is straight. As they grow larger, Sheep Crabs gradually stop their masking activities, and the adults have hardly any attached flora and fauna.

Only occasionally seen in the low tide zone, Sheep Crabs are most common below the lowest tide. They are a familiar sight to divers working at the bottom of the offshore kelp beds.

208. Dwarf Crab, *Pelia tumida*. Small; carapace length to about 15 mm (5/8 in.). Color variable, often matching the background. Often seen in cast-up kelp holdfasts, in which case they are colored a yellowish tan. Common in the low tide zone, but hard to find. They are slow-moving and usually partly covered with sponges or other organisms. The walking legs are broad and flat.

209. Swimming Crab, *Portunus xantusii.* Width of carapace to about 7 cm (2³/₄ in.). Color blue-gray or brown. This crab is easy to identify, with its two strong lateral spines, its ridged, razor-sharp claws, and its paddle-shaped hind feet. It commonly swims about in protected bay waters, but takes refuge on the bottom when disturbed. This crab must be handled with caution; the sharp lateral spines make the usual thumb-and-finger hold difficult, and any awkwardness on the part of the handler can result in a severe cut from the claws.

210. Spot-Bellied Rock Crab, *Cancer antennarius.* Body width to about 11.5 cm (4¹/₂ in.); color dark red on top, yellow with bold red spots underneath. The carapace between the eyes is not extended forward. Often found half-buried in sand under rocks in the low tide zone. Most active at night.

Both this and the Red Rock Crab (no. 211) have young that are attractively striped and spotted, and these are common among rocks and seaweed.

211. Red Rock Crab, *Cancer productus.* Width of body to about 16 cm (6¹/₄ in.), color usually brick red. The front edge of the carapace between the eyes is scalloped with five small teeth of almost equal size and is extended forward slightly beyond the eyes. Found in the same sort of habitats as the Spot-Bellied Rock Crab (no. 210).

All of the crabs of the genus *Cancer* are edible. The most popular one is the Dungeness Crab, *Cancer magister,* which lives rarely, if ever, in our area, although dead ones on crushed ice are a common feature of local seafood markets. California game laws single it out, requiring a carapace breadth of at least 6¹/₂ inches, with a bag limit of 10 specimens. All other crabs are lumped together, with an aggregate bag limit of 35, and a minimum size of 4 in. "across the back at the widest point." In Southern California, only the Red Rock Crab (*Cancer productus*) and the Yellow Rock Crab (*Cancer anthonyi,* which as an adult does not occur intertidally) regularly attain the legal size.

The Yellow Rock Crab is taken commercially, and it too is a common feature of our fish markets.

212. Nine-Toothed Pebble Crab, *Cycloxanthops novemdentatus.* Carapace width to 9.4 cm (3³/₄ in.). Usually brown or reddish; the tips of the pinching claws are black. The front of the carapace on each side of the eyes has nine small teeth. Common in the southern parts of our area, usually among rocks at the middle and low tide levels.

213. Black-Fingered Crab, *Lophopanopeus bellus.* Width of carapace to 3.5 cm (1³/₈ in.), color extremely variable; probably the most common color in our area is creamy white, but many red ones are also found. Fingers of the pinching claws are always dark, usually black, with none of the dark color extending onto the hand. Common under rocks and in seaweed at low tide, in both protected waters and those of the outer coast.

214. Lumpy Crab, *Paraxanthias taylori.* Width of carapace to 2.5 cm (1 in.), usually smaller. Color uniform red-brown, lighter underneath; fingers of pinching claws often dark brown. Carapace and claws covered with coarse granulations. One of the best ways to find a Lumpy Crab is to look carefully at the underside of a rock you have just turned over; the crab hides in holes in the rock and will not move out unless deliberately prodded. It is also quite common in cast-up kelp holdfasts.

215. Burrowing Crab, *Malacoplax californiensis.* Carapace width to 2 cm (³/₄ in.), color pale brown; tips of pinching fingers black. The carapace is rounded fore and aft, so that the side profile is almost a half-circle, while the front or rear profile shows a straight line across the back. Common throughout the intertidal zone and below along muddy waterways, where it constructs its burrows. Turning over a discarded tire, a plank, or an old boat on the mudflats will nearly always expose several burrowing crabs.

216. Pea Crab, *Fabia subquadrata.* Diameter usually less than 1 cm (³/₈ in.). The translucent brown and gray carapace is almost as long as wide and smooth, with two blind-ended

Phylum ARTHROPODA

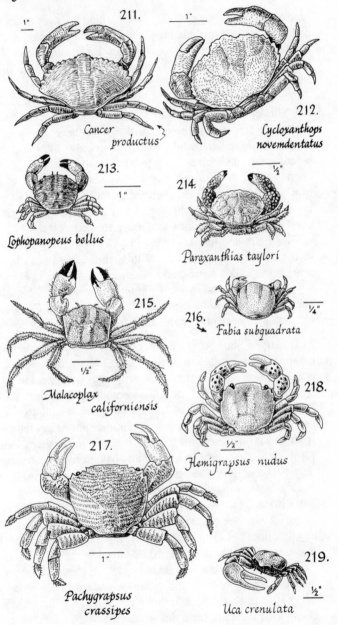

211. *Cancer productus*

212. *Cycloxanthops novemdentatus*

213. *Lophopanopeus bellus*

214. *Paraxanthias taylori*

215. *Malacoplax californiensis*

216. *Fabia subquadrata*

218. *Hemigrapsus nudus*

217. *Pachygrapsus crassipes*

219. *Uca crenulata*

grooves running longitudinally from behind the eyes to about half the length. This little crab is chosen here to represent the family Pinnotheridae, whose members habitually inhabit the tubes of annelid worms, the cloacae of sea cucumbers, or the gill-chambers of molluscs.

The Pea Crab favors the California Mussel (no. 52) and the Bay Mussel (no. 53), and in some areas 80 percent of the mussels have a crab living within their shells. There is usually only one crab to a mussel. Males and females leave their hosts at breeding time and return after mating. The mussel-crab association has been cited as an example of a commensal relationship in which neither member is harmed by the association, but recent studies have shown that the mussel is injured by the crab's constant picking at the gills to remove food particles.

The males and females of the Pea Crab are very different, as is the case with most crabs of this family. The male of this species was called *Pinnotheres concharum* until 1928, when it was shown to be the male of *Fabia subquadrata*. *Fabia* had been named first, so by the rules of the International Congress of Zoology, her name became the official one for both sexes.

217. Striped Shore Crab, *Pachygrapsus crassipes*. Width of carapace usually a little less than 5 cm (2 in.). Color variable, almost always showing transverse striping; the base color may be blackish, green, red, or some combination of these. The large claws are often red and are always marked with deep red or purple veining. This is our most familiar intertidal crab and is abundant on all sorts of beaches throughout Southern California. It is also found in Hawaii and has recently been introduced (probably accidentally) to Asia. It occurs sparingly in muddy bays, where it often hides along estuarine banks in holes made by the washing away of pickleweed roots, but is abundant on rocky outer shores. It seeks shelter during the day, but does not always get completely out of sight. A peek into any rocky crevice above the tide level of the moment will show a Striped Shore Crab in hiding, its red claws folded protectively across its face. If a crab is surprised in the open or backed up against a rock it can't get under, it will open its claws wide and raise them threateningly toward the pursuer.

These crabs are among the most effective of the intertidal scavengers, although stomach analyses have shown that carrion and trash do not constitute a high proportion of their diet; their chief food is algae. Feeding is most often done at night, when the crabs present an engaging appearance as they shovel it in with both claws alternately.

Like other female crabs, the female Striped Shore Crab carries her eggs under her recurved tail. The eggs are yellow-orange, and ovigerous (egg-bearing) females are quite common.

218. Purple Shore Crab, *Hemigrapsus nudus.* Carapace width to 5.5 cm (2³/₈ in.). Color variable, often purple or maroon, but never with the transverse stripes of the preceding species. Has large red spots on the large claws. The two sides of the carapace in this species are almost parallel, while in the Striped Shore Crab the sides converge slightly toward the rear. Both inhabit the same sort of environments, but this one is usually a little lower in the tide zone. It becomes more abundant toward the north, where it finally replaces *Pachygrapus.*

The Mud-Flat Crab, *Hemigrapsus oregonensis,* is rather similar. It largely replaces the Purple Shore Crab in lagoons and quiet bays.

219. Fiddler Crab, *Uca crenulata.* Carapace width about 2 cm (³/₄ in.), color uniform glossy brown. The female has two pinching claws of equal size; in the males, one or another of the claws is of grotesque size, actually longer than the body is wide. The large claw is used in courtship and fighting other males of the same species, and there is some evidence that its movements constitute an elaborate set of communicative signals. If the large claw is lost in a fight or an accident, the small claw will become the larger one at the next moulting, at which time a small one will appear in place of the lost big one.

Fiddler crabs live in muddy-sandy bays, where they make semipermanent burrows in the high tide zone. These burrows may be identified by a pile of mud and sand pellets around the opening, often taking the form of a short chimney. Burrows may be as much as 1.2 m (4 ft.) deep, usually in sites above the reach of all but the highest tides. Wherever they are found, fiddler crabs are likely to occur in great numbers, but, like all inhabitants of California's estuarine waters, they are in grave danger of extinction as the environment is destroyed.

Subphylum Chelicerata
Class Pycnogonida (Sea Spiders)

Sea spiders resemble land spiders superficially, but nothing on Earth is really similar. They have a small body and eight long legs; internal organs branch out into these hollow legs. There is no excretory system and no respiratory system; the circulatory system is simple, and assimilation is accomplished through a unique method of intracellular digestion. Certain cells lining the gut become engorged with food then break loose and float around inside the body, allowing other mucosal cells to absorb their loads of food.

Some deep-sea pycnogonids attain a leg-spread of nearly 30 cm (1 ft.), but the shore species are much smaller and quite inconspicuous. There are no vernacular names for most of these specific forms, and I have not tried to invent any.

220. Sea Spider, *Ammothella biunguiculata.* Leg-spread to about 1 cm (3/8 in.). Common under stones at the low tide level; also found among several kinds of hydroids. This light brown species was first described in Italy in 1881 and has since been shown to have a cosmopolitan distribution, with specimens recorded in Hawaii, Japan, Australia, and North America.

221. Sea Spider, *Anaplodactylus erectus.* Leg-spread to 1 cm (3/8 in.). Common among clusters of the Oaten Pipe Hydroid (no. 15), especially in the area of Balboa and Laguna Beach. The adults eat the hydroids, and their young burrow into the hydroids' digestive tracts to spend their larval days as parasites. The adult is a translucent straw color.

222. Sea Spider, *Ammothea hilgendorfi.* Leg-spread about 7 mm (1/4 in.). Color light yellow-brown, often with indistinct reddish bands and splotches on the legs. Fairly common at the low tide level on rocky shores, almost always associated with hydroids such as the Ostrich Plume Hydroid (no. 21). Like

Anaplodactylus erectus (no. 221), the young are parasitic on the insides of the hosts' bodies.

Phylum Echinodermata
(Spiny-Skinned Animals)

This phylum includes the starfishes, brittle stars, sea urchins, sea lilies, and sea cucumbers. All of its 6,000 members are marine.

Several characteristics separate this phylum from all others. One is the *water-vascular system,* an arrangement of tubes and bulbs carrying water throughout the body and hydraulically operating the tube feet, which are variously used in locomotion, sensory reception, and food gathering. Another feature is an endoskeleton of overlapping, intertwined, or separated small hard parts, each composed of a single crystal of calcite imbedded in the flesh; of microscopic size, these *ossicles* come in many strange shapes and are important in echinoderm classification. Still another unique echinoderm feature is the presence of *pedicellariae,* very small organs with a protective function, sometimes built like tiny pliers, sometimes like the three-jawed "orange-peel" power machines used to handle large stones in building marine ripraps. The pedicellariae are located on the external skin and act as a deterrent to the larvae of barnacles and other creatures looking for a permanent place to settle down.

The basic plan of echinoderm anatomy is one of secondary pentamerous radial symmetry. This means that, although the larvae start life in bilaterally symmetrical form (with a mirror-image half on each side of an imaginary longitudinal midline), the adults of most species attain a radial symmetry (around a common center point), which in this phylum is based on a plan of five. The rich fossil record of the group shows that this plan was characteristic of a number of extinct classes as well as of the four surviving classes.

There are several systems for dividing up the phylum. This book follows that of H. B. Fell (1963), which recognizes four classes: Asterozoa, which is divided into two subclasses, Ophiuroidea (brittle stars) and Asteroidea (starfishes); Echinoidea (sea urchins and sand dollars); Holothuroidea (sea cucumbers); and Crinoidea (sea lilies, which in our area are all subtidal and are therefore not treated here).

Class Asterozoa

Subclass Ophiuroidea (Brittle Stars)

Also known as serpent stars. In this subclass the central portion of the animal is a round, relatively flat disk, on which the five slender arms are sharply set off. The arms themselves are flexible and in many species are fringed. Little pockets (called *bursae*) in the disk between the arms serve as brood pouches for the young and also form part of the respiratory system. Ophiuroids feed upon detritus, bacteria, and larger bits of food, all of which is swallowed; their stomachs, unlike those of most asteroids, cannot be everted. (See the Ochre Starfish, no. 233, for a description of feeding through an everted stomach.)

The term "brittle star" refers to the autotomous habits of many species, which react to alarm by breaking off some of their arms. In some cases even the broken off arms may continue the process, breaking into smaller and smaller pieces.

There are many kinds of brittle stars, some of them occurring in tremendous numbers; they may constitute the most abundant group of echinoderms. Most live in the deep sea. Of those that are found in our area, only a few have been selected as typical.

223. Holdfast Brittle Star, *Amphipholis squamata*. Diameter of disk to 5 mm (³/₁₆ in.), leg-spread up to 40 mm (1⁹/₁₆ in.). The disk is pale gray, often with a lavender tinge. This is our most often seen brittle star, and the same is true in other localities; the species has almost worldwide distribution. It lives on rocky shores in the middle and low tide zones and below. To be sure of seeing one, you need only find a kelp holdfast freshly washed up on the beach and break it apart.

224. Spiny Brittle Star, *Ophiothryx spiculata*. Disk diameter to about 19 mm (³/₄ in.), arm length four to eight times the disk diameter. Disk and arms are very thickly set with spines; the arms are unusually flexible and autotomy is common. The color is very variable and often striking, with dark orange-

Phylum ARTHROPODA

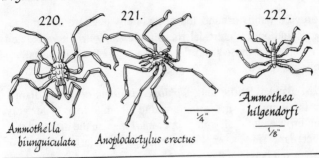

220.

Ammothella
biunguiculata

221.

Anoplodactylus erectus

¼"

222.

Ammothea
hilgendorfi

⅛"

Phylum ECHINODERMATA

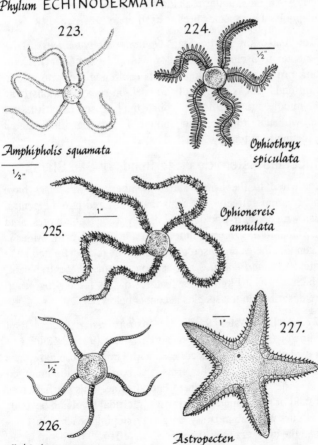

223.

Amphipholis squamata

½"

224.

½"

Ophiothryx
spiculata

225.

1"

Ophionereis
annulata

226.

½

Ophioderma panamense

227.

1"

Astropecten
armatus

bordered bands around the arms. Individuals found in tide-pools and under intertidal rocks often show bright variegated colors, while those from deeper water offshore are usually a solid, deep red.

225. Banded Brittle Star, *Ophionereis annulata.* Disk diameter to 19 mm ($^3/_4$ in.), arm-spread to 10 cm (4 in.). Color gray and brown, with salt-and-pepper markings on the disk and distinct dark rings completely encircling the arms. The disk bulges out between the arms. Common in low tide zones south of Los Angeles, under rocks in sand, among seaweeds, and in tidepools. This species breaks itself apart rather readily.

226. Snakeskin Brittle Star, *Ophioderma panamense.* Disk diameter to 3 cm ($1^3/_{16}$ in.), spread to 18 cm (7 in.). Color dark brown with faint light bands encircling the arms. Common under rocks, especially in rock-on-rock situations from the middle tide zone down. This is the largest local brittle star and will submit to a certain amount of gentle handling without resorting to autotomy.

Subclass Asteroidea (Starfishes or Sea Stars)

Compared to the brittle stars, members of this class have thick, comparatively stiff arms that are faired into the central disk with no sharp line of demarcation. Tube feet are present in an *ambulacral groove* on the underside of each arm. Water is taken into the water-vascular system through a perforated plate called the *madreporite,* situated on top of the central disk, which acts as a filter. Other features of this fascinating group are described in the species accounts below.

227. Shallow-Water Sand Star, *Astropecten armatus.* Total diameter (including arms) to about 20 cm (9 in.). Color is a grayed rose. The back is covered with granular rosetted spines called *paxillae,* and the arms are bordered with enlarged plates, each with a prominent lateral spine. This starfish lives in sand or sandy mud at the lowest intertidal level and beyond. It occurs most abundantly on gently sloping beaches just beyond the breakers in water 3.5 to 7 m (10 to 20 ft.) deep. It can crawl equally well on the surface of the sand or just under it and is almost never seen completely exposed. Its food consists of organisms like the Purple Olive Snail (no. 133), which it swallows whole; the empty shells are discarded through the mouth. Its tube feet are pointed rather than ending in suction cups like those of the rock-clinging starfishes—an obvious adaptation to locomotion in loose sand.

228. Variable Starfish, *Linckia columbiae.* Longest arm usually not more than 2.5 cm (1 in.) long. Lives among rocks and tidepools in the low tide zone. Color maroon, usually with gray mottling. All starfishes are good at regenerating lost parts, but this one is perhaps the champion. If it loses an arm, it immediately sets about growing a new one. Meanwhile, the lost arm may itself start to grow another starfish and will be a complete animal in a few months. This new starfish is, of course, quite asymmetrical, with one very large arm (the old one) and four new buds. As if to even things up, the large arm will break off, leaving a stump more nearly equal to the other arms—and the cast-off arm will start the whole process again. This will continue four or five times until the original arm is down to about 13 mm (1/2 in.) long; after that, it stays put. Even with all this effort, a real radial symmetry is never obtained, and all specimens are more or less lopsided. Individuals with four, six, or seven arms are not uncommon.

229. Leather Star, *Dermasterias imbricata.* Total leg-spread to about 18 cm (7 in.). The color is usually blue-gray with mottlings of red or orange. The surface of the leathery skin is smooth and slippery. This is an abundant intertidal species north of our area, but here it is rare. Just offshore, however, it is occasionally met with, especially in connection with kelp beds. It is very rare in Southern California intertidal areas, but a few have been found in low-lying tidepools where sea anemones (the Leather Star's favorite food) abound. Anemones are pulled from their substrate and swallowed whole.

230. Webbed Starfish, *Patiria miniata* (Pl. 44). Also known as the Bat Star. Diameter about 15 cm (6 in.). Readily recognized by its flat profile, rough scaly skin, and bright colors. These colors range from almost white through yellow, orange, red, and purple-brown; some individuals are of a solid color, while others have irregular spots and mottlings. It is an omnivorous scavenger, feeding on whatever it can find by extruding its stomach and digesting parts of large objects that it cannot swallow.

The Webbed Starfish, found at middle and low tide levels in both rocky and muddy areas, has been one of the dominant features of the kelp bed bottom fauna and is seen by divers on the walls of submarine canyons to depths of at least 42 m (140 ft.). It was formerly abundant in San Diego's Mission Bay in the Eelgrass beds, but the virtual disappearance of Eelgrass through "improvements" to Mission Bay has almost eliminated the animal from this habitat. It is now sparingly found on the coast under rocks, and only small ones live above the lowest tide mark. In the early 1980s, this and several other kinds of starfishes suffered a sharp decline in numbers, becoming practically extinct in some areas. The decline was particularly sharp between 1981 and 1983, when Southern California waters were much warmer than usual. It is thought that a bacterium, not yet identified, may be responsible; whatever the etiology, the species may well be in danger.

This starfish is long-lived in captivity. About 20 individuals were placed in a tank at the Scripps Institution of Oceanography sometime before 1936, and most of these were still going strong in 1952, when they were removed to the new public aquarium. At that time the identity of the group became confused with newly caught specimens, but a life span of at least 30 years is likely.

231. Blood Star, *Henricia leviuscula*. Diameter to about 11.5 cm (4½ in.), but usually smaller. The arms are slender, and there is a very small central disk. The surface is marked with a network of tiny spines, and there are no pedicellariae. The color is usually some shade of red, often quite brilliant. It is found in the low tide zone, frequently on the sides of rocks in surge channels.

232. Soft Starfish, *Astrometis sertulifera*. Diameter to about 15 cm (6 in.). Common at low tide levels in rocky areas, often under rocks. The Soft Starfish may be identified by its limp-

Phylum ECHINODERMATA

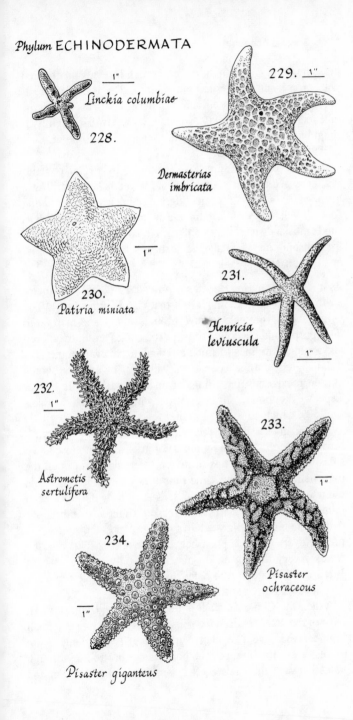

228. Linckia columbiae

229. Dermasterias imbricata

230. Patiria miniata

231. Henricia leviuscula

232. Astrometis sertulifera

233. Pisaster ochraceous

234. Pisaster giganteus

ness, flexibility, and slightly slimy rough brown skin covered with prominent orange and blue spines. The undersurface is bright orange. This is an active starfish and uses its yellow tube feet to move toward the shadows with surprising agility. If roughly handled it may autotomize, snapping off one or more of its five tapering arms.

Each of the larger spines is surrounded by a ridge containing large pedicellariae, quite visible to the naked eye. These are useful not only in protecting the animal but in obtaining food as well. They can catch large swimming creatures such as sand crabs and small fishes and pass them around to the mouth for consumption. The starfish also eats barnacles, molluscs, and other sessile organisms.

233. Ochre Starfish, *Pisaster ochraceous* (Pl. 45). Diameter to 45 cm (18 in.), although half that size is more usual. The color ranges from pale yellow through orange and maroon to deep purple and chocolate brown. The spines are light colored and arranged in lines forming a reticulate pattern; on the central disk, they outline a pentagon. Abundant on exposed shores and on rocks and pier pilings at middle and low tide levels. Especially common in association with California Mussels (no. 52), which constitute its chief food.

Like many starfishes, this one feeds without actually swallowing its food. In eating a mussel it grasps the mollusc's two sides with the suction tips of its tube feet and tries to pull the two shells apart. At the same time it turns its stomach inside out and holds it against the mussel's shell near the ligamental joining. Eventually the mussel relaxes slightly, or perhaps a part of the hinge is digested away; at any rate, the stomach is further everted and slipped between the shells. The stomach forms a very thin sheet; an opening of only 0.1 mm (about $^4/_{1000}$ in.) will allow it to enter the mussel and digest and absorb its unprotected soft flesh.

When the Ochre Starfish is under water and undisturbed, most of the body between the spines is covered with very small filaments that give it a velvety appearance. These filaments are extrusions of the lining of the body cavity protruding through holes between the calcareous plates of the endoskeleton and are used for respiration. These "skin gills" have cilia on both surfaces, which move body fluids along one side and sea water along the other. Oxygen is simply absorbed through the membrane into the body fluids. Many asteroids respire in this manner.

Another common asteroid feature is the possession of light-sensitive organs at the tips of the arms. These are easily visible in this species. These eyes cannot focus on an image, but can distinguish between dark and light.

The Ochre Starfish is often obvious to the casual beach visitor, and it has no means of escape. It therefore frequently falls prey to people who wrench it free of its substrate and carry it away from the shore, only to be discarded. This not only is a very bad ecological practice but is now against California law as well.

234. Knobby Starfish, *Pisaster giganteus* (Pl. 46). Diameter to 46 cm (18 in.). The Knobby Starfish is very much like the Ochre Starfish (no. 233), but differs in having larger white spines with knobbed ends; these spines are scattered at random in no discernable pattern, and never trace the form of a pentagon on the central disk. Each white spine is surrounded by a bright blue aureole.

Close examination will reveal that the blue base around the white spines is in turn surrounded by a ring of brown fuzz. This is a concentration of pedicellariae, which will show their plierlike shape and action under the magnification of a good hand lens. Their function is to protect against fouling organisms, although some starfishes have no pedicellariae and still somehow remain unfouled.

Class Echinoidea (Sea Urchins and Sand Dollars)

Members of this class are armless and have compact globular or disk-shaped bodies composed of stiff calcareous plates covered with spines. In the globose sea urchins these spines are usually long and prominent, while in the flat sand dollars they are short and velvety. The calcareous plates form a shell, usually called a *test,* that is often elaborately and decoratively perforated to provide openings for tube feet and respiratory filaments. These tests, dried and bleached, are popular items at seaside souvenir counters.

The echinoids have a complex set of five jaws, which together form a structure known as *Aristotle's lantern* (although the term probably originally referred to the entire test). These jaws come together at their pointed inner ends and form an efficient tool for eating or, in some species, boring. As far as is known, Aristotle's lantern is not used for defense. Other defense mechanisms, however, are available, and some sea urchins with venomous barbed spines and venomous biting pedicellariae are dangerous. Our local species are quite innocent in this respect, although there is a report (probably erroneous) of the poisonous *Diadema mexicanus* in San Diego's Mission Bay.

235. Purple Sea Urchin, *Strongylocentrotus purpuratus* (Pl. 47). Diameter of test to 6.5 cm (2 1/2 in.), occasionally larger. Spines numerous, and when compared to the following species, rather short and blunt. Color usually bright blue-purple. This is our most abundant intertidal sea urchin, found all along the rocky outer coasts of California and northern Mexico. It regularly makes shallow burrows in solid rock or concrete, and most individuals in open surf-swept areas will be buried to at least half the height of the test. This burrowing is accomplished by the action of the five jaws and by motions of the test and spines while the animal clings to the substrate with its tube feet; these motions may result from efforts to resist rotation by whirling surges. Spines and jaws are quickly worn away by this abrasive contact, but they are being constantly renewed, while the rock is not. Vertical burrows become quite deep over a long period of time, and as an urchin at the bottom of such a shaft continues to grow and to abrade the rock with its spines it forms a chamber larger than the shaft, and the animal is imprisoned for life.

Purple Sea Urchins are often seen on the outer sides of natural stone or concrete breakwaters. Their presence on steel casings of concrete pilings can result in holes right through the steel. The urchin keeps the surface with which it is in contact free of protective rust and growths, setting up a more favorable environment for quick erosion.

The food of the Purple Sea Urchin is primarily seaweed,

which it masticates with its five-toothed jaws. The sea urchin population is very large at the bottom of the kelp beds, and the animals have a strong influence on the extent and health of the seaweed forests. Several years ago the kelp beds of most of Southern California were devastated by a succession of unusually warm winters. This left millions of hungry Purple and Red (no. 236) Sea Urchins, and they promptly gobbled up any young plants that chanced to appear; thus the re-establishment of the kelp bed was prevented, or at least delayed. In the normal course of events the sea urchins would soon have died back of starvation, but now sewage outfalls have made our coastal waters richer in organic materials, and the urchins are able to absorb enough food to keep them alive but undernourished. In several experimental tracts the sea urchins were removed by divers, and the kelp came back right away. In other locations, equilibrium was established without human help, but it took far longer than expected, and some localities have never fully recovered.

Young Purple Sea Urchins are green, which has led to their being confused with a green Northern California form, *Strongylocentrotus droebachensis*.

236. Red Sea Urchin, *Strongylocentrotus franciscanus*. Diameter of test to 13 cm (5 in.) or more; spines long, tapering to a point. Color red-purple. Occasional among rocks at low tide levels; more abundant offshore and, intertidally, to the north.

The gonads of certain sea urchins, which are eaten raw, are the "frutta del mare" of Italian markets, and this species is popular among many Californians. The males' are yellow and sour, while the females' are reddish and sweet, and one devout fisherman has praised the Deity for His thoughtfulness in providing these two flavors to be used appropriately during the course of a meal as an alternative to the white and red wines that poor people cannot afford.

Like most sea urchins, this one has two chief means of defense—the long, sharp spines and, scattered at their bases, the pedicellariae. If you touch one of these sea urchins under water with a sharp object like a pencil, the spines will bend so that their tips converge toward the object, preventing further encroachment. Touching with a blunt object, however, will result in the opposite reaction, the spines bending away and allowing the object to get next to the test, where the venom-bearing pedicellariae can take over.

The Red Sea Urchin does not show the burrowing tendencies of the Purple Sea Urchin and is far less abundant in the intertidal zone.

237. Sand Dollar, *Dendraster excentricus.* Test flat on the bottom, slightly rounded on top; diameter to 3.6 cm (3 in.). In living specimens the test is densely covered with tiny spines, usually of a light lavender or greenish color, giving a texture like coarse velvet. The beach visitor, however, is more likely to find the bleached bare test with its characteristic off-center flower design. This design is formed by the small openings that accommodate the tube feet.

In the intertidal zone sand dollars are confined to low-level sand flats in protected bays. On the open coast they live only out beyond the breakers at depths of 6 to 15 m (20 to 50 ft.), where they often occur in sufficient numbers to pave large areas of the sandy sea floor, with 625 or more individuals to each square meter. When active, they stand on edge, with the lower third or half of the test buried in the sand. Food particles are trapped in the sticky mucus among the spines or caught by the pedicellariae; they are then passed along the treelike ("dendritic") food channels that converge on the mouth, which is on the flat lower surface.

The jaw parts (Aristotle's lantern) are flattened, and each of the five segments resembles a white dove with its wings partly spread. Commercial purveyors of marine curios have latched onto this and made up what they call "legends" about it. I have not been able, however, to find any of these legends in the oral tradition.

Many of these sand dollars support a single small acorn barnacle, *Balanus pacificus,* near the rim of the upper surface.

Class Holothuroidea (Sea Cucumbers)

Most sea cucumbers are elongate, often appropriately cucumber-shaped. They are soft and flexible, the skeleton composed of separated calcareous plates and spines; as in so

Phylum ECHINODERMATA

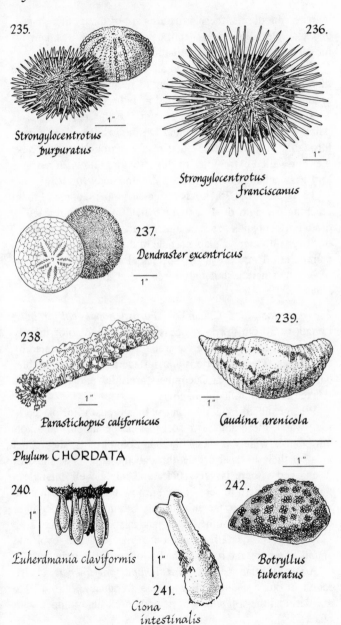

235.

236.

Strongylocentrotus
purpuratus

Strongylocentrotus
franciscanus

237.
Dendraster excentricus

238.

239.

Parastichopus californicus

Caudina arenicola

Phylum CHORDATA

240.

242.

Euherdmania claviformis

241.
Ciona
intestinalis

Botryllus
tuberatus

many echinoderms, these structures are of distinctive shapes, and accurate holothurian identification often requires their removal and microscopic examination.

Tube feet are not present in all holothurians. In some, the tube feet have evolved into a ring of multibranched tentacles around the mouth, which are used in gathering food.

Respiration is by a method unique to this class: water is pumped in and out of the anus. On the inside, water travels through a "branchial tree" that reaches throughout the body; the thin-walled extremities of this structure allow for respiratory gas exchange between sea water and body fluids.

There are about 700 kinds of sea cucumbers, some of them reaching a length of 2 m (over 6 ft.). In the South Pacific, dried muscle bands of sea cucumbers are made into "trepang" or "bêche-de-mer," a staple article of diet, folk medicine, and commerce. There are many species along the Pacific Coast of North America, but only three are at all common in our area.

238. Common Sea Cucumber, *Parastichopus californicus.* Length to 30 cm (12 in.), occasionally more. Color usually orange-umber, the surface covered with warts surmounted by soft spines. The proportions and surface texture are variable: harassed Common Sea Cucumbers are thick and firm, while relaxed ones are thin and flabby.

When handled roughly, attacked by a predator, or placed in stale water, these animals resort to a desperate sort of autotomy that is widely practiced among holothurians: they expel most of their internal organs through the anus. The mass of discharged viscera is very sticky and might well entangle a predator; it's hard to see, however, how this reaction to stale water is of benefit to the animal. The Common Sea Cucumber can grow a new set of the lost organs in six or eight weeks.

This species is fairly common at the low tide level and abundant among the rocks at the bottom of the kelp beds.

A very similar species, *Parastichopus parvimensis,* is also found in our area, though with less frequency. It is a little smaller, and the soft spines of its body are usually tipped with black.

239. Sweet Potato Sea Cucumber, *Caudina arenicola*.
Length to 23 cm (9 in.); sometimes more. The term "sweet
potato" accurately describes the size and shape of this animal.
It is smooth all over, with little wrinkles where it bends, and
has no tube feet. The color is brownish or reddish purple, with
darker red blotches.

The Sweet Potato Sea Cucumber lives in sandy or muddy
areas, apparently choosing a habitat that is just barely capable
of supporting life, and survives only because of several special
adaptations. One of these is its ability to process enormous
quantities of sand or mud, passing it through the digestive system to extract whatever nourishment is there. Another is its
highly efficient circulatory system, which is able to extract a
viable supply of oxygen where other sea cucumbers would be
asphyxiated. The respiratory oxygen-gathering pigment is
concentrated in blood cells, as in the so-called higher animals;
the Sweet Potato Sea Cucumber is one of the very few invertebrates with this characteristic.

Phylum Chordata

This is the phylum to which we humans belong, and thus it is
usually placed, as here, at the apex of the phylogenetic tree, as
if all evolution had been aimed at producing chordates. In
truth, however, it is a group that has made effective use of a
few pretty primitive arrangements, and some authorities place
it below the molluscs.

Three basic characteristics separate the chordates from
other phyla: (1) a stiffening axial rod called the *notochord;* (2)
a dorsal nerve tube that becomes the spinal chord and brain
in the "higher" forms; and (3) pharyngeal gill openings.
Of these, only the second is always present throughout the
lives of all chordates; the other two features are present, in
many of the 45,000 or so chordate species, only in embryonic
stages.

Many schemes for breaking down this phylum into classes
and orders have been tried, and some authorities prefer several
phyla instead of the classes shown here. It might be useful to
show one approach to subdividing the phylum, even though

many of the subheads (those marked with an asterisk in the list below) are not considered in this book:

Phylum Chordata
  Subphylum Tunicata
      Class Ascidiacea (Ascidians or Sea Squirts)
      Class Thaliacea (Salps)
    *Class Larvacea (*Oikopleura* and its relatives)
  Subphylum Cephalochorda (Lancelets)
  Subphylum Gnathostoma (Craniates, with brain and skull)
      Class Chondrichthyes (Sharks and Rays)
      Class Osteichthyes (Bony Fishes)
    *Class Amphibia (Frogs, Toads, and Salamanders)
    *Class Reptilia (Turtles, Crocodiles, Lizards, and Snakes)
    *Class Aves (Birds)
    *Class Mammalia (Mammals)

Subphylum Tunicata

This is often listed as a separate phylum. One of the features that makes its members unique is their blood flow, which operates on an alternating current; it flows in one direction for a while, then the heart stops, takes a short rest, and starts again, propelling the blood in the opposite direction.

Class Ascidiacea (Sea Squirts)

Sea squirts start life as rather advanced larvae, somewhat resembling microscopic tadpoles. When the time comes to settle down, they lose most of the features that identify them as chordates. It is tempting to speak of this process as a degenerative one, but this is a loaded term; after all, the sea squirts are a very successful group. They have been on Earth for a long time, have evolved a multitude of species, have filled a great many marine niches, and are beautifully suited to their environment. Only a selected few are presented here. For a more nearly complete treatment, see Morris, Abbott, and Haderlie (1980), pp. 177–226.

240. Club-Shaped Ascidian, *Euherdmania claviformis*. Each tubular individual member (zooid) is 2 to 6 cm (³/₄ to 2³/₈ in.)

in length, united with its fellows only at the base. Grows in colorless clusters or lines at extreme low tide; often found on the undersides of overhanging rock ledges.

Vanadium is a very scarce element in sea water, but this tunicate is somehow able to concentrate it in its blood cells.

241. Yellow-Green Sea Squirt, *Ciona intestinalis.* Length to 13 cm (5 in.), color translucent yellow-green. This animal requires relatively clean and quiet waters, and where these conditions obtain, it is extremely abundant. The bottoms of floats and mooring buoys and the sides of pilings may be covered with dense layers of them. This sea squirt is often covered with debris near the point of attachment to the substrate, but the two siphons are always kept clean. It is a widespread species, familiar in temperate harbors the world over.

Like the Club-Shaped Ascidian (no. 240), this one is a vanadium concentrator, and it has been seriously proposed that the cultivation and harvesting of *Ciona* for its vanadium would be commercially feasible.

242. Encrusting Compound Ascidian, *Botryllus tuberatus.* Forms a thin crust over rocks and other substrates, preferring quiet bay waters. The color ranges from light red to maroon, and from a distance a colony resembles a piece of beef liver. The individual zooids are of pinhead size and of a pale yellow color; they are arranged in elliptical patterns.

243. Long-Stalked Sea Squirt, *Styela montereyensis.* Length to 25 cm (10 in.), color usually red-brown with maroon veining; the siphon tips may be reddish-orange. One of the siphons is curved downward. The body has a number of longitudinal ridges with depressed wrinkles between. The outer covering, or *tunic,* is tough and opaque. Lives in the low tide zone and below attached to rocks, pier pilings, or kelp. The specimens in quiet bays tend to be larger than those of the outer coast.

In quiet bays, especially in the southern parts of our area, there is another tunicate species that is quite similar. This is *Styela clava,* an introduced species from Japan. It is stouter, and its siphons are parallel.

Class Thaliacea (Salps)

These are free-swimming inhabitants of the open sea that are frequently found washed up on the shore. Most of them are quite transparent, and the typical shape is like a barrel open at both ends. The inner organs are visible, although they too are so transparent as to be hard to locate. The only opacity is in the visceral organs, which are often brightly colored and form a small mass near the posterior opening. Salps breed by a complicated alternation of generation, with the sexual generation swimming in long chains or wheels of connected individuals, while the more familiar asexual generation (illustrated here) is solitary.

There are many species of salps, and their distribution has been correlated with certain water masses. Their presence in a net haul may thus give information to the physical oceanographer as well as to the biologist.

The specimens found ashore at almost any time of the year are nearly always damaged and fragmented, often appearing only as pieces of tough, clear jelly.

244. Common Salp, *Thetys vagina.* Length to about 19 cm (7½ in.). Two prominent tail-like appendages on opposite sides of the posterior opening. Like other salps, this one takes in water through the front opening, processes it for food particles, and ejects it from the aft opening, providing a gentle jet propulsion. (The word *vagina,* by the way, is Latin for "sheath or scabbard.")

Subphylum Cephalochorda
(Lancelets)

Here again is a group that is often described as a separate phylum. It has only a few species of one basic sort of animal, which inhabits shallow waters and sandy shores in most temperate parts of the world.

245. California Lancelet or Amphioxus, *Branchiostoma californiense.* Length to about 7.5 cm (3 in.). Translucent, flesh-colored. Not often seen unless looked for systematically. Its usual home is in the intertidal sand on beaches surrounding bay inlets, where it burrows to a depth two or three times

Phylum CHORDATA

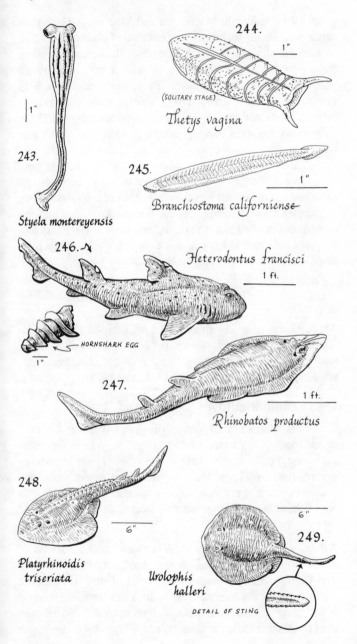

244.
1"
(SOLITARY STAGE)
Thetys vagina

243.
1"
Styela montereyensis

245.
1"
Branchiostoma californiense

246.
Heterodontus francisci
1 ft.

HORNSHARK EGG
1"

247.
1 ft.
Rhinobatos productus

248.
6"
*Platyrhinoidis
triseriata*

*Urolophis
halleri*
249.
6"

DETAIL OF STING

greater than its length. MacGinitie and MacGinitie (1968) describe a collecting technique that consists of pushing the blade of a shovel straight down into the sand, then sharply jerking the handle back; this compresses the sand in front of the lower part of the blade, which causes any nearby lancelets to leap into the air. Unless grabbed very quickly, they will wriggle their way into the sand again. Another method that is all too easy to try involves looking carefully inside beer cans discarded on the sandy beach.

The name "Amphioxus," which means "pointed at both ends," was the official name of the genus many years ago. At that time it was thought that the cephalochords were similar to a direct ancestor of the vertebrates. We now know that they are an offshoot, a blind alley; nevertheless, there is a salutary lesson for us all in the old song that says: "It's a long way from amphioxus, but we all came from there!"

Subphylum Gnathostoma
(Craniate Animals)

This group is often classified as the phylum Vertebrata. It includes both the cartilaginous and the bony fishes; only a few of each type are mentioned here. For a more complete treatment, see Fitch and Lavenberg (1968, 1971, and 1975).

Class Chondrichthyes (Sharks and Rays)

This class, characterized by a cartilaginous skeleton, does not include any animals that spend their entire lives in the intertidal zone, but its members can be seen there by the human observer. Beach-walkers, for example, often come across the body of a shark or ray that has been caught and discarded by a surf fisherman, and tidepools may occasionally trap some of these as the tide goes out.

246. California Horn Shark, *Heterodontus francisci*. Also called Bullhead Shark. Length to 1.2 m (4 ft.), color brown. The California Horn Shark is common in kelp beds but does not often visit the intertidal zone. Its peculiar spiral-flanged eggs, however, are sometimes washed ashore. Laid in pairs about two weeks after mating, these glossy brown eggs hatch after about eight or nine months. The young do not go through a visible larval stage, but emerge as slender miniatures of their parents. Like the majority of sharks, this one is harmless, although its clam-cracking jaws could painfully squeeze a finger or toe foolishly placed in its mouth.

The unusual shape of the egg has always aroused curiosity, but no good reason for it is known. Some say that if the egg is laid in midwater it will spin as it sinks, causing it to become entwined in seaweed and so kept from sinking into the bottom sediments. Others hold that the spiral flanges hold the main body of the egg up off the substrate, allowing water to circulate around it. We know that the shape, whatever its purpose, is successful, for California Horn Sharks are numerous. On the other hand, their success may not be due to the egg shape at all, since other species produce eggs that lack all those spirals and flanges, and they do all right too. Perhaps the best explanation, and the least teleological one, is that the female's egg-producing organs are constructed so as to produce eggs of this shape; there may be no adaptive value at all.

247. Shovelnose Guitarfish, *Rhinobatos productus.* Length to 1.2 cm (4 ft.). Although frequently called a Shovelnose Shark by fishermen, this is not a shark, but a ray. It is quite harmless, having no stinger and not being prone to bite, but it looks fearsome; I have heard several visitors swear, after watching a large shovelnose being hauled in by a surf fisherman, that they would never again enter the water. The color is sandy brown, with translucent cartilage forming the pointed nose. This is an *ovoviviparous* species, the female retaining the eggs in her body until the fully formed young are born. The trauma of being caught on a hook sometimes starts the birth process, and 15 or 20 babies may be born from a dying mother. At times, especially in the fall, the Shovelnose Guitarfish is extremely abundant, lying almost wing-to-wing on the sandy bottom just beyond the breakers.

248. Thornback Guitarfish, *Platyrhinoidis triseriata.* Similar to the Shovelnose Guitarfish (no. 247), but smaller—not more than 61 cm (2 ft.), with a rounded nose that is not translucent and three rows of prominent sawtooth spines down the back and onto the tail.

249. Round Stingray, *Urolophis halleri*. Length to 38 cm (15 in.). Color brown usually marbled and speckled with black, darker brown, and gold. Tail a little longer than the round body. This is the "stingaree" that brings the most grief to Southern California bathers, and public lifeguards treat scores of stings every year. The sting is inflicted with a bonelike venomous barb at the outer end of the flexible tail. Stings, most of which are on the top or sides of the foot, are incurred when a bather steps on a stingray, which thereupon lashes its tail in self-defense.

If you should be so unfortunate as to be stung, try to find a big pan of hot water and soak the injured member in it; the pain, which can be extreme, will then go away as by magic. The wound will need debriding, and you should arrange to visit a physician right away; while making the arrangements, and while en route to the doctor's office, keep the foot immersed in hot water.

Prevention is preferable to the cure. Most of the stings happen when bathers are jumping up and down in the waves to keep the cold water from encroaching on their midriffs, and they come down on top of the poor stingrays. It's better to grit your teeth, let the cold water rise around you, and keep your feet solidly on the bottom. Advancing with a shuffling motion will (usually) scare the rays up ahead of you.

The Round Stingray is most abundant on gently sloping sandy beaches in the late summer and early fall—just the time and place for the best bathing. There are three other species of stingrays in our area, but they usually stay farther offshore and are rarely implicated in human injuries.

Class Osteichthyes (Bony Fishes)

250. Moray, *Gymnothorax mordax*. Length (rarely) to 1.5 m (5 ft.). Usually below the lowest tide, but occasionally found among rocks at times of minus tides. Younger specimens of 30 cm (1 ft.) or so in length are most common in such situations.

These youngsters are usually yellow in color, while the adults are dark olive green. They are quite adept at wriggling among rocks to find a new hiding place when rousted out of the old one.

Morays are not creatures to be trifled with, but their aggressiveness has been exaggerated. Most Moray bites are incurred when a foolhardy lobster diver investigates a rocky crevice and finds a home-defending Moray instead of a spiny lobster. Such a bite can be serious and will probably require sutures, but is not venomous. Nor will a Moray doggedly hang onto its victim until the victim is drowned.

This is a long-lived species. Two individuals named Moray and Miranda lived for 27 years in the Aquarium-Museum at the Scripps Institution of Oceanography. Legend ascribes an even longer life to the Moray. Specimens were supposedly kept by ancient Roman emperors for several human generations. They were said to have been fed mainly on recalcitrant Christians—a diet that modern researchers have not attempted to emulate.

251. Killifish, *Fundulus parvipinnis*. Length to 10 cm (4 in.), but usually about one-quarter of that. Color olive-brown, paler below. Abundant in the shallow waters of sloughs and estuaries. The Killifish is a representative of a numerous and widespread genus, various species of which are to be found in practically every part of North America. Most of them live in fresh or brackish water, and some are brightly colored. This species makes a hardy and attractive resident in the home seawater aquarium.

252. Grunion, *Leuresthes tenuis*. Length to 20 cm (8 in.). Green above, silvery below, with a broad longitudinal band of iridescent deep blue along each side. It closely resembles the Topsmelt (both are in the silversides family, Atherinidae), except that its dorsal fin is placed farther back, more than halfway from the gill covers to the tail.

The breeding habits of the Grunion are so unusual as to cause many visitors to reject a proposed Grunion hunt in the belief that they will be subjected to a "snipe-hunt" practical joke. Grunion really do exist, however, and they really do "run" on the beach at predictable times, when they may be picked up with bare hands.

California Grunion runs are always at night, usually on the second, third, and fourth nights after a full or new Moon, beginning each night about half an hour after the highest tide and continuing for two or three hours. The run may begin an hour or so later than this and may not occur at all in some particular location. Predictions show the time period within which a run will occur, but there is no way of predicting exactly where it will happen. If Grunion appear on the first night at a given locality, it is fairly certain that they will run more heavily in the same place on the two succeeding nights.

Grunion lay and fertilize their eggs during these runs. The female rides in on a wave, and while the sand is stirred up, wriggles backward down into it until only her head and the front third of her body are exposed. She remains this way as the wave recedes. The male does not bury himself, but curves horizontally on top of the sand around the female. As she deposits eggs in a little sand pocket created by her wriggling, he deposits sperm at the surface, which trickles down to the eggs. Both fish catch a subsequent wave back to the sea.

The whole process constitutes a marvelous adaptation to the tide conditions on the Pacific Coast. If the eggs were laid before the high tide, they would be washed away in the rising waters. If they were laid at the highest tide several days before the new or full moon, the maximum high tide would increase during the next few days and wash the eggs away. As it is, the eggs are not reached by water again until the next series of spring tides, about two weeks later. By that time they are ready to hatch as soon as the water touches them, and the larval Grunion swim merrily out to sea. If the first spring tide after the laying is not high enough, the eggs can wait without harm for an additional two, four, six, or even eight weeks. Grunion runs occur only in the late spring and summer, and at those times the highest spring tides come in the darkness of the wee hours of morning. If this were not the case, the spawning Grunion on the beach would surely fall prey to marauding gulls—although a related species in the Gulf of California,

Phylum CHORDATA

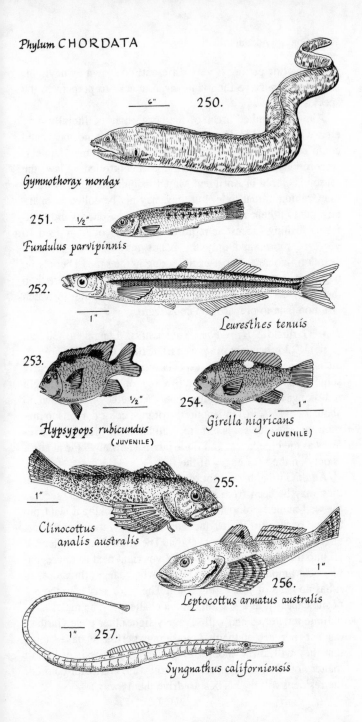

250.
6"

Gymnothorax mordax

251.
½"

Fundulus parvipinnis

252.
1"

Leuresthes tenuis

253.
½"

Hypsypops rubicundus
(JUVENILE)

254.
1"

Girella nigricans
(JUVENILE)

255.
1"

Clinocottus analis australis

256.
1"

Leptocottus armatus australis

257.
1"

Syngnathus californiensis

where the tide picture is very different, do spawn by daylight, and enough survive the avian aerial attacks to perpetuate the species.

Although limited areas of the beach may be literally covered with spawning Grunion, the population is not large and could easily be reduced by too many greedy human hunters. Accordingly, the capture of Grunion is controlled by law: the season is closed in April and May. It is quite all right to watch the Grunion at that time, but they may not be collected or interrupted in their activities. During open season, a valid California Fishing License is required for every collector aged 16 years or more, and only the hands may be used to catch Grunion—no nets, traps, or holes dug in the sand. There is no bag limit, but conscientious collectors will take no more than they may eat at the next meal. It's really more fun to watch Grunion than to prepare and cook them.

253. Garibaldi, *Hypsypops rubicundus*. Length to 30 cm (1 ft.). Color brilliant orange-scarlet. Baby Garibaldis are frequently seen in tidepools, especially in the spring and early summer. They are about 2 cm (3/4 in.) long at first and bright red-orange with brilliant blue spots. When they have grown to about 7 cm (2 3/4 in.) in length, the orange color darkens to maroon, but the blue spots remain. Still later, the orange color returns as the blue fades, and if the adults show any blue at all, it is only on the very edges of the fins.

Adult Garibaldis are not often found in intertidal pools, but they may be seen from several good vantage points, such as the well-named Goldfish Point at La Jolla. Looking down from the top of the cliff there, one may see numerous flashes of orange as the Garibaldis move about. The color does not blend at all into the background. This fish lives right next to impregnable rocks among which it can retreat when danger threatens, so it has no need of concealing color. The color serves in the opposite capacity, as a warning and a challenge. The males have definite territories and will savagely fight other male Garibaldis that encroach on them. Aquarium experiments have shown that they will attack model fishes carved of wood; it doesn't matter how they are shaped, but if they are Garibaldi-colored, the resident will try his best to drive them away.

Garibaldis of all ages are fully protected by law. The attractive young are sometimes caught for the home aquarium, but this is strictly illegal.

Giuseppe Garibaldi (1807–1882), the patron patriot of unified Italy, and his followers wore a scarlet shirt as a uniform. The fish may have been named directly for him or at second hand for the popular loose-fitting garment worn by children and emancipated, corsetless women in the 1880s; the style was to have this comfortable shirt-waist in bright red, and it was called a "garibaldi."

254. Opaleye, *Girella nigricans*. Adult length to 38 cm (15 in.); tidepool inhabitants usually less than 5 cm (2 in.). Color light green-gray to dark blue-gray, lighter below, with a single (rarely double) white spot on each side at the juncture of the back and the dorsal fin. The eye is, as one might expect from the common name, opalescent blue.

Adult Opaleyes are abundant just offshore among kelp beds or along rocky reefs. Their eggs drift freely out to sea, and the young are born well away from shore. The young are quite different from the grownups, being silvery and slender. As they grow, they gradually make their way toward shore, at last seeking the haven of a tidepool. Once there they quickly metamorphose into small editions of the adult in form and color. They remain tidepool residents until they reach a length of 5 to 10 cm (2 to 4 in.), at which time they return to the offshore waters.

The juveniles are active little fish and may be seen darting about in almost any tidepool at any level. They are especially noticeable when skittering through a stretch of tidepool that is shallower than their bodies. Opaleyes are hardy in the seawater aquarium, although their pugnacious habits make them dangerous tankmates for prized fishes of other kinds.

Another common name for this fish is Opaleye Perch, which is all right as long as we remember that it is not related to the perches, but is our only local representative of the family Girellidae.

255. Tidepool Wooly Sculpin, *Clinocottus analis australis*. Length to 18 cm (7 in.), usually much smaller. Color variable, ranging from pale greenish white to dark olive brown, always with a complicated pattern of darker and lighter colors in spots and bands. Liberally covered with hairlike cirri.

This species spends all its life in tidepools, where it is abundant. It is passive and active by turns, nearly always staying on the bottom of its tidepool, using its fins like legs for crawling and "perching," or swimming in short bursts to a new location.

This little fish is not related to the larger California Scorpionfish (*Scorpaena guttata*), which is often caught by pier fishermen who call it a Sculpin—a name probably derived from the Italian *scorpione*. The Scorpionfish is a potent stinger, but the Tidepool Sculpin is completely harmless. Like the Opaleye, it adapts well to captivity, and it makes a gentle and attractive member of a community tank.

256. Southern Staghorn Sculpin, *Leptocottus armatus australis*. Length to 30 cm (1 ft.), although 13 cm (5 in.) is more usual. Color dark brown, sometimes with a tinge of olive above; lighter below. Pectoral fins yellow with several dusky crossbars. Skin smooth. Abundant in estuaries. The Southern Staghorn Sculpin has a spine with a sharp cutting edge on the rear margin of the gill cover. This can be extended at right angles to the head, making the fish a difficult mouthful for any but the largest predators and presenting a minor hazard for the human who picks it up. There is no venom connected with this spine, so any little cuts it makes are nothing more than a nuisance.

257. Kelp Pipefish, *Syngnathus californiensis*. Length to 46 cm (18 in.) or occasionally more. There are several kinds of pipefishes in our area, but this one will serve to represent them all. All live offshore, and only dead ones are to be found on the beach.

The pipefishes belong to the family Syngnathidae, which also includes the seahorses, and their breeding habits are similar. The males have an elongate brood pouch in which the female deposits her eggs; later, the male appears to give birth to the tiny young.

One species of seahorse, *Hippocampus ingens,* has been found in our area. It is the largest of the many species of seahorses, being up to 30 cm (12 in.) long, but is by no means common; there are only a few records of its occurrence in Southern California during the last 50 years.

258. Mudsucker, *Gillichthys mirabilis*. Length to 20 cm (8 in.). Color olive, marbled with brown and black. Skin very smooth and slick. Abundant in bays in estuaries, but declining in numbers as its environment shrinks. It is a popular bait fish and may be purchased alive at many bait stores; an increasing percentage of these specimens are imported from Mexico. It is quite hardy and will live for several days packed in damp seaweed.

The Mudsucker has a huge mouth with parasol-like side flaps; the whole thing unfurls to a diameter twice that of the body. Opening the mouth in this way has nothing to do with eating. It is connected with courtship and is practiced especially by two males fighting over a waiting female. The combatants open their mouths to the fullest then push them against each other as if kissing. They push back and forth until one appears to get tired and goes away. It is an interesting duel to watch, as neither of the participants is ever hurt.

259. Arrow Goby, *Clevelandia ios*. Length to 5 cm (2 in.). Color light brown with minute reddish and black spots and a small blue-black patch on the gill cover. This little fish is present in great numbers in puddles and channels on mudflats. When frightened, it dives into holes and crevices or simply into the soft mud itself. G. E. MacGinitie once collected 425 individuals in a muddy pool only 91 cm by 2.13 m in extent and 20 cm deep (3 by 7 ft. by 8 in.). As he points out, any animal living in such concentrations must be an important ecological factor in the community (MacGinitie and MacGinitie, 1968).

260. Blind Goby, *Typhlogobius californiensis*. Length to 6.5 cm (2½ in.), color flesh pink, usually a little darker on the puffy cheeks. There are no eyes. This little fish lives in the burrows of the California Ghost Shrimp (no. 194). The pink color is the result of a network of blood vessels just below the skin, an adaptation to the oxygen-deficient environment of the burrow. Oxygen is absorbed directly through the skin into the blood, complementing the work of the gills.

Blind Gobies eat bits of seaweed and other detritus. They do not compete for food with their hosts, for the California Ghost Shrimp eats only particles of much smaller size.

Blind Gobies are nearly always found in pairs, one pair to one burrow. They appear to mate for life, although if one dies, the remaining one will accept a new spouse. If an intruder of the same species happens into a burrow where an unbroken pair is living, it will be vigorously repulsed by both partners.

In spite of her small size, the female lays as many as 15,000 eggs at one time. The young have two perfectly formed eyes, but these cease to be functional and are covered over in six months or so, at which time the Blind Goby finds a mate and settles down in a burrow.

261. California Clingfish, *Gobiesox rhessodon*. Length to 6.5 cm (2½ in.); color usually olive, although it varies with the surroundings. There are often three pale crossbands. The head is broad and flat with a prominent spine on the gill cover. All of the clingfishes (of which we have several species) have an adhesive suction disk on the underside of the body, with which they cling firmly to seaweeds or rocks. The forward part of this organ is formed by the pelvic fins, while the aft portion is a fold of skin.

The California Clingfish is commonly found on the undersides of rocks in the low tide zone and doesn't seem to mind being upside down most of the time. Other local clingfishes are smaller than this one, although it is possible that one more than twice as large, *Gobiesox meandricus,* may occasionally wander to our waters from its usual home in Northern California.

262. Tidepool Ocellated Klipfish, *Gibbonsia elegans elegans*. Length to 13 cm (5 in.). This klipfish matches its background color; among brown seaweeds it is usually of a reddish color, with eight or so vertical darker bands. The prominent eyelike spot, usually blue-black with an orange border, just above and behind the gill cover is a diagnostic feature. There is a similar but usually less conspicuous spot nearer the

Phylum CHORDATA

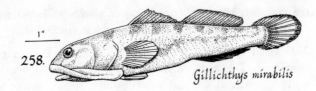

258.

Gillichthys mirabilis

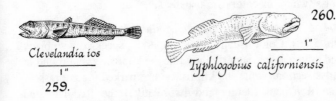

Clevelandia ios

259.

260.

Typhlogobius californiensis

TOP VIEW

BOTTOM VIEW

Gobiesox rhessodon

261.

262.

Gibbonsia elegans elegans

263.

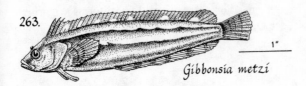

Gibbonsia metzi

264.

Hypsoblennius gilberti

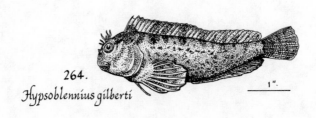

tail. This is a shy little fish, hiding in clumps of kelp (especially *Egregia*) and Surfgrass in the low tide zone.

263. Weed Klipfish, *Gibbonsia metzi.* Similar in size and shape to the Tidepool Ocellated Klipfish (no. 262), but without the eye spots; also, this fish is usually either solid brown or has longitudinal rather than vertical lines. Most common in Surfgrass, where its colors are usually silver and green.

264. Rockpool Blenny, *Hypsoblennius gilberti.* Length to 13 cm (5 in.). Color usually brown, liberally speckled with black and other colors. Superficially like the klipfishes, but round in cross section, while the klipfishes are markedly compressed. The Rockpool Blenny and its relative, the Red-Throated Blenny, *Hypsoblennius gentilis,* are common in the lower tide zone. They usually hide among seaweeds when the tide is out. Both make excellent aquarium fishes.

Class Aves (Birds)

Many birds can be seen in the intertidal zone, and they constitute a group that is important to seashore ecology. For treatment of these wonderful creatures, see Cogswell (1977).

Class Mammalia (Mammals)

While not permanent residents of the intertidal zone, several kinds of mammals—whales, dolphins, and seals—are often visible from there. For a treatment of California's marine mammals, see Orr (1972).

Glossary

algae (sing., alga): "Plants" of the kingdom Protoctista, containing chlorophyll and ranging in size from microscopic unicellular organisms to the giant kelps. Unlike members of the kingdom Plantae, algae do not have well-developed vascular structures and lack differentiated root, stem, and leaf organs.

alternation of generation: A reproductive process in which the sexual form produces an asexual form, which in turn reproduces sexually. The result is a life history in which each individual is like its grandparents and grandchildren but different from its parent(s) and children.

ambulacral groove: A ciliated groove on the lower sides of the arms of starfish, or around the **test** of **echinoids,** containing the **tube feet** and other parts of the **water-vascular system.** In many forms it conducts food to the mouth.

anemone: Short for sea anemone, any of an abundant group of **cnidarians;** named for a fancied resemblance to the anemone or wind flower.

anterior: Toward the front or head end.

aperture: Among **gastropods,** the opening into the shell, through which the foot and/or **mantle** may be extended.

apex: The highest point of a shell.

Aristotle's lantern: Today, the five-jawed masticating organ of some **echinoderms**, especially the sea urchins and sand dollars. May formerly have referred to the entire **test.**

arthropod: Any member of the phylum Arthropoda.

ascidian: A member of the class Ascidiacea in the phylum Chordata. Also known as **tunicates,** the ascidians include sea squirts and compound colonial forms.

asexual generation: The nonsexual stage in the life history of an organism reproducing by **alternation of generation.** In asexual reproduction, each new individual has only one parent.

autotomy: Literally "self-cutting." The casting off of organs and structures that can later be regenerated.

autotrophic: Said of plants and bacteria producing their own nutritive substances through **chemosynthesis** or **photosynthesis.**

avicularium (pl., avicularia): A **zooid** in an ectoproct moss animal colony, shaped like a snapping bird beak, presumably used to keep the colony free of fouling organisms.

beak: In **bivalves,** the earliest-formed part of the shell, located at or near the **hinge.** Synonymous with **umbo.**

benthic: Living on the sea floor. Occasionally used to refer to abyssal depths, but this is incorrect; even shallow-water creatures may be benthic in habit.

bilateral symmetry: An arrangement in which the right and left halves of an organism are approximate mirror images of each other.

bioluminescence: Light produced by biological activity.

biota: The whole assemblage of living organisms in a given area.

bivalve: An organism with two **valves,** or shells. When used without any qualification, the term usually refers to a member of the class Pelecypoda (clams, mussels, and oysters).

breaker: A wave whose forward progress has been slowed by shallowing water, so that its **crest** topples and spills forward.

bryozoan: A collective term for the moss animals, formerly placed in the phylum Bryozoa but now put into two phyla—Entoprocta and Ectoprocta.

budding: A means of **asexual reproduction,** the offspring beginning as buds on the parent body.

bursa: A pocket (literally "purse") or cavity in the body of an organism.

byssus: A plasticlike thread produced by some **bivalves** as a means of attachment to the **substrate.**

callus: In **gastropods,** a thickening of the shell, often covering the **umbilicus.**

calyx: In zoology, a cuplike structure. In many sessile **cnidarians,** the **polyp** is supported by a calyx.

carapace: A shield or shell covering all or part of an animal's back; in Crustacea, refers to the covering of the **cephalothorax.**

cephalothorax: Among **arthropods,** the head and thorax when these are fused, as in many **crustaceans.**

cerata: Fingerlike dorsal projections on the bodies of certain nudibranchs, functioning as gills.

chemosynthesis: An **autotrophic** method of producing organic compounds by oxidation of inorganic material without the aid of sunlight. Used in this manner, these inorganic materials provide both the necessary carbon and the energy for the process of conversion to organic matter.

chitin: An impervious, stable, horny substance secreted by **arthropods,** usually forming a firm **exoskeleton.**

chromatophore: A pigmented cell or group of cells that by expansion and contraction produces color changes in the bodies of animals such as squids and octopuses.

cilia: Microscopic hairlike structures whose coordinated rhythmic movement transports food, water, and other materials. Used for swimming by many small species. Functionally similar to **flagella,** but shorter and stiffer.

cirri: The featherlike appendages used by barnacles to net food from the water.

class: The major taxonomic category just below **phylum,** consisting of one or more **orders.**

clone: An organism identical to its immediate ancestor, produced by **fission** or other asexual means. Also, a community of such organisms, descended in this way from a single ancestor.

cnidarian: Any member of the phylum Cnidaria.

cobbles: Small smooth stones, larger than gravel, rounded by the action of water.

coelenterate: Any member of the phylum Cnidaria. (This phylum was formerly called Coelenterata.)

collar cells: Specialized cells whose **flagella** create the water currents flowing through sponges.

columella: The central pillar in most **gastropod** shells, around which the whorls are formed.

commensal: Said of two different organisms that live together, often sharing the same food, but have little effect—either harmful or beneficial—on each other.

community: The total group of organisms living within any given set of bounds.

compressed: Flattened from side to side; narrow from a frontal viewpoint, with a high lateral profile.

corbula: A case or receptacle in some hydroids (such as the Ostrich Plume Hydroid, no. 21) containing members of the **sexual generation.**

Coriolis force: A fictitious force invented to account for the fact that motion in a straight line looks curved when viewed from within a rotating system. The Coriolis force is responsible for a deflection of movement on the rotating Earth, and is important when considering the behavior of large masses such as ocean currents.

countershading: A basic principle of camouflage in which a three-dimensional object is made to look flat. The underside, away from the light source, is of a lighter color than the upper side and so does not appear darker even though it is in shadow.

crest: The highest point of an ocean wave.

crustacean: A member of the class Crustacea in the phylum Arthropoda. This class includes, among others, the barnacles, copepods, fairy shrimp, amphipods, isopods, shrimps, lobsters, and crabs.

current: Movement of water. May be intermittent and periodic, as in tidal currents, or practically permanent, as in the California Current.

cypris larva: The second larval stage of the barnacles, resembling members of the genus *Cypris* in the subclass Ostracoda—microscopic bivalved crustaceans not covered in this book.

decapod: Any member of the Decapoda, an order in the class Crustacea that includes shrimps, lobsters, and crabs.

depressed: Flattened top-to-bottom, pancakelike, presenting a low profile from every viewpoint.

detritus: Small loose particles of natural material. In the sense of a marine food source for detritus feeders, consists of dead and decaying organic matter plus bacteria, often forming a film on the sea floor in quiet waters.

diatom: A microscopic **alga** with a two-piece shell composed of silicates; a basic source (**primary producer**) of food for marine animals, which may eat these **autotrophic** organisms directly, or eat other creatures that have eaten diatoms, and so on.

dorsal fin: The foremost fin along the midline of a fish's back.

echinoderm: Any member of the phylum Echinodermata.

echinoid: A member of the class Echinoidea, which includes the sea urchins and sand dollars.

ecosystem: The interrelated flora, fauna, and physical environment of a community.

encrusting: Covering the **substrate** in a thin film that more or less follows the substrate's contours.

estuary: An area subject to incursion by both sea water and fresh water.

eukaryotes: Cells containing a nucleus with genetic material bound in discrete units.

eversible: Capable of being turned inside out.

excurrent: Flowing outward.

exoskeleton: An external supporting structure in some animals, often serving as armor as well as a site for muscle attachment. In **arthropods,** the exoskeleton is made of **chitin.**

family: The major **taxonomic category** just below **order,** containing at least one **genus.**

fauna: The animal components of any designated community.

fertilization, external: Fertilization of the egg after it is discharged from the female's body.

fertilization, internal: Fertilization of the egg while still within the female's body.

filter feeding: Straining food, by any of a number of methods, from the water.

fission: In biology, the producing of a **clone** by the longitudinal splitting of one body into two halves, each of which becomes a complete organism.

flagellum (pl., flagella): A whiplike organelle extending out from a cell, often used by unicellular forms for locomotion. Internal structure of flagella, recently studied with the electron microscope, constitutes one of the basic differences between **prokaryotes** and **eukaryotes.** Similar to **cilia** but longer.

flora: The **autotrophic** components of any designated community.

fluorescence: The property of emitting light upon bombardment by some form of radiation. When the radiation consists of light waves, the re-emitted light may be of a different wavelength and therefore of a different color.

food chain: The succession of **trophic levels** through which energy is transferred from its primary source to any subject organism.

food web: The combined **food chains** in a given community.

frond: Leaflike structure in the larger **algae,** such as the kelps.

gamete: A germ cell, male or female; two gametes of opposite sex unite to form a **zygote.**

gastropod: A member of the class Gastropoda, the snails and their relatives.

genus (pl., genera): The major **taxonomic category** just below **family,** containing one or more **species.** The generic name plus the specific name constitute the scientific name of an organism.

gill: An organ of respiration that takes up oxygen from the surrounding water, in contrast to a lung, which takes up oxygen from the air.

gill cover: External plate covering the gill in most bony fishes.

girdle: Among chitons, the leathery peripheral band holding the eight plates together.

grazer: An animal that secures its food by grazing or cropping **sessile** plants.

habitat: Any particular environment.

headland: A land promontory extending into the sea, usually marking the landward end of an underwater ridge.

heat capacity: Also called specific heat. A measure of the amount of heat required to raise the temperature of a given mass of a given substance. Water has a very high heat capacity.

hermaphrodite: An individual organism with both male and female organs.

heterotrophic: Unable to synthesize energy-bearing substances and therefore dependent on secondhand solar or chemical energy obtained from **autotrophic** organisms. All heterotrophic forms exist at the secondary **trophic level** or higher.

hinge: The thickened dorsal edge of **bivalve** shells where the pair joins together.

hinge ligament: A brown horny substance that holds together the two shells of **bivalves,** located just dorsal to the **hinge.**

holdfast: The part of a large seaweed attached to the **substrate;** often resembles the intertwined roots of vascular plants.

hydranth: An individual **polyp** in a hydroid colony, usually specialized for securing food.

hydrologic cycle: The process by which water evaporates and falls as rain, snow, or dew somewhere on Earth, then winds its way back to the sea to continue the cycle.

hydrotheca: A cuplike structure partially enclosing an individual **polyp** in a hydroid colony.

incurrent: Flowing inward.

intertidal zone: The shore lying between the lowest and highest tides.

kingdom: The highest **taxonomic category** in the classification of living things, containing a number of **phyla.** Formerly only two kingdoms, Plantae and Animalia, were recognized. Today, many biologists agree that five are necessary: Monera (bacteria, which are **prokaryotes** existing as single cells); Protoctista (**eukaryotes,** mostly unicellular but including the multicellular **algae**); Fungi (**eukaryotes** nourished by absorption); Plantae (primarily **autotrophic eukaryotes**); and Animalia (**heterotrophic eukaryotes**).

knot: A nautical term measuring velocity. A certain number of knots means that many nautical miles per hour. "Knots per hour" is tautological and incorrect.

larva: A juvenile form prior to its **metamorphosis** into the adult form. Many marine species go through a number of larval stages.

littoral: The part of the shore lying between the tides. Synonymous with **intertidal zone.**

longshore current: A current, often temporary, flowing close to the shore and parallel to it.

lophophore: A ciliated feeding structure, usually looped, coiled, or horseshoe-shaped, surrounding the mouth; typical of adults in at least four phyla—Entoprocta, Ectoprocta, Brachiopoda (not considered in this book), and Phoronida.

madreporite: A perforated plate through which water is filtered and admitted into the **water-vascular** system of **echinoderms.** Also called "sieve plate."

mantle: In molluscs, a soft flap enveloping the body and producing the shell.

mantle cavity: Space formed by the molluscan **mantle,** usually containing the **gills** and some other organs.

mean lower low water: The mean of all the lower low tides; selected as **tide zero** on the West Coast.

medusa: A free-swimming organism, usually umbrella-shaped and often transparent, with trailing snaky tentacles. May be a jellyfish or the sexual stage of some other **cnidarian.**

mesoglea: The noncellular jellylike substance between the two body layers of jellyfishes and other cnidarians.

metamorphosis: The changes in form, often marked and abrupt in marine animals, that occur in the transition from an embryo through the larval stages to the adult form.

minus tide: A low tide measured as being below **tide zero,** which on the West Coast is at **mean lower low water.**

monotypic: Describes a **taxon** with only one member in the next-lower category; a monotypic **family** has only one **genus,** a monotypic **genus** only one **species.**

muscle scar: A mark on the inside of a **bivalve** shell, showing where muscles were attached in life.

nacre: The mother-of-pearl inner layer of molluscan shells.

nauplius larva: The free-swimming first larval stage in many **crustaceans.**

neap tide: The tide during a period when the Sun and Moon are not in line with the Earth, resulting in a diminished **tidal range.** Occurs when the Moon is in its quarters.

nematocyst: A microscopic stinging structure typical of the phylum Cnidaria. Often called "stinging cells," although they are cells only in the old sense of any small compartment or bounded area.

neritic: Said of a non-**benthic** organism that lives in the relatively shallow waters overlying the continental shelves.

notochord: A stiffening structure lying between the nerve chord and the alimentary canal; typical of the phylum Chordata, although none of the higher chordates retain it past their embryonic stages.

omnivorous: Eating both plants and animals.

operculum: A "door" of shelly material fastened to the fleshy parts of many **gastropods** so as to close the aperture when the foot is withdrawn into the shell.

order: The major **taxonomic category** just below **class,** containing one or more **families.**

organic matter: Energy-containing compounds based on combinations of carbon, hydrogen, and oxygen; in nature, all organic substances exist in or are derived from living organisms.

osculum: A large **excurrent** opening in a sponge.

ossicle: Among vertebrates, a small bone such as those of the inner ear. In invertebrates, a small (often microscopic) stiffening structure made of various complex crystalline substances. Examples include the dermal plates of **echinoderms** and the spicules of sponges.

ostia (sing., ostium): The many small **incurrent** openings into the body of a sponge.

ovigerous: Carrying eggs.

oviparous: Egg-laying.

ovoviviparous: Nurturing the young internally by attachment to a yolk sac not attached to the mother; offspring are born as miniature adults.

parapodium: In polychaete worms, paired appendages on each body segment.

paxilla (pl., paxillae): A raised **ossicle** in the form of a vertical column crowned with numerous small spines; found on the upper surface of some starfish.

pectoral fin: A paired fin on each side of a fish just aft of the gill cover.

pedicellaria (pl., pedicellariae): A small pincerlike defensive or cleaning organ on many **echinoderms.** May be stalked or **sessile.**

pelagic: Pertaining to the non-**benthic** habitats of the open sea, beyond the continental shelf.

pelvic fin: The foremost fin on the bottom side of a fish, always paired.

periostracum: In molluscs, a thin horny covering of the shell's outer surface.

phosphorescence: Commonly used, but not recommended, to mean **bioluminescence.** Also refers to a glowing by absorbed light after the impinging light has ceased.

photosynthesis: The process of using the sun's energy, captured by a green pigment called chlorophyll, to power the linking of carbon dioxide and water so as to produce energy-bearing glucose.

phylogenetic order: An arrangement of **taxa** made in hope of showing evolutionary relationships.

phylum (pl., phyla): The major **taxonomic category** just below **kingdom,** containing one or more **classes.**

phytoplankton: The **autotrophic** elements of plankton.

plankton: The whole population of organisms, primarily very small in size, drifting more or less passively in the water.

planula: A small ciliated larva of many marine members of the phylum Cnidaria.

polyp: An individual of a moss animal or coral colony, or of the **asexual generation** of a hydroid; a sea **anemone.** Usually tubular in form, closed and attached at the base, open at the upper end with a mouth typically surrounded by tentacles.

predator: An animal that kills and feeds on other animals.

primary consumer: A direct consumer of **autotrophic** organisms (**primary producers**) and thereby a member of the secondary **trophic level.**

primary producer: An **autotrophic** organism producing energy-containing **organic matter** through **chemosynthesis** or **photosynthesis.** Existing at the primary **trophic level,** these producers pass energy on to the secondary and higher trophic levels.

proboscis: A tubular extension of the head or snout, often capable of withdrawing and extending through a process of inversion and eversion (see **eversible**). In **crustaceans,** may refer to certain of the mouth parts.

prokaryotes: Cells with no membrane-bound nucleus and no chromosomes. The evolution of the more complex eukaryotic cells (see **eukaryotes**) of the "higher" life forms has been explained as a symbiotic (see **symbiosis**) association of prokaryotes.

protandric hermaphrodite: An organism functioning first as a male then as a female. Some marine animals reverse sexes several times during a lifetime.

radial symmetry: Regular arrangement of similar parts around a central point or axis.

radula: A band or ribbon with file-like texture, typical of certain molluscs. Used for rasping or boring to obtain food.

red tide: A drastic increase in a population of microscopic **algae,** often dinoflagellates, imparting a distinct reddish color to the water. May have a strongly adverse local effect on fishes and other organisms.

red water: Formerly used for a dinoflagellate bloom (**red tide**) that colors the water but does not kill off local fishes and other creatures. A useful term worth reviving.

refraction: Change in the direction of wave travel as a wave front obliquely enters an area in which its velocity is altered. Light and sound waves are refracted as they pass through layers of differing density; ocean waves are refracted as their speed is affected by changing water depth.

ring canal: In **echinoderms,** a doughnut-shaped calcareous tube. Water, strained through the **madreporite,** passes through the **stone canal** into the ring canal, thence through radial branches to other parts of the organism.

rip current: A narrow, swift, seaward-flowing current at beaches.

riptide: In the vernacular, synonymous with **rip current.** Not a recommended term, as the phenomenon has nothing to do with the tide.

rostrum: A point on the **carapace** projecting forward between the eyes of some **crustaceans.**

scavenger: An animal that feeds on dead **organic matter.**

scuba: Self-Contained Underwater Breathing Apparatus; the diving device that has revolutionized the science of marine natural history by allowing direct observation of underwater communities.

sea: In nautical terms, the irregular wild waves produced at the site of a storm. (See **swell** and **surf.**)

secondary consumer: An organism that lives by eating **primary consumers,** as when a small fish eats **zooplankton.** A secondary consumer is at the third **trophic level** (primary producer to primary consumer to secondary consumer).

septum (pl., septa): A partition. In stony corals, the septa radiate from the center like the divisions between the sections of an orange.

sessile: Describes organisms permanently attached to a substrate, generally incapable of moving from one spot to another. In describing organs, it means attached without a stem.

sexual generation: In organisms reproducing by **alternation of generation,** the stage in the life cycle that produces male and female reproductive cells (**gametes**).

siphon: A tubular structure for taking in or discharging water; found in **molluscs** and **ascidians.**

siphonal canal: In some **gastropod** shells an extension of the aperture, providing a channel for the soft **siphon.** In some cases the canal is partially closed over to form a tube.

species: A population or group of populations within which breeding is carried on or is at least potentially possible. This population must be reproductively isolated from others. The specific name is perhaps the only **taxonomic category** representing something that actually exists in nature.

spring tide: The period of the greatest range between high tides and low tides; usually occurs twice each month, at full Moon and new Moon. Both the highest tides and the lowest tides usually occur on the same day.

stipe: The stemlike structure of a seaweed; not a true stem in the physiological sense.

stone canal: In **echinoderms,** a calcareous tube leading from the **madreporite** to the **ring canal,** from which radial tubes branch out. The upper part of the **water-vascular system.**

submarine canyon: A nearshore canyon in the sea floor, running at approximately right angles to the shoreline.

substrate: Any surface that plants or animals live on or are attached to. Sand, mud, rocks, pier pilings, seaweeds, animals, and so on all provide a substrate for some life form.

subtidal: Below the level of the lowest tide; always, therefore, under water.

surf: waves breaking against a shore; **breakers,** or an area in which they occur.

swell: A train of fairly regular waves sorted by their varying velocities as they depart a storm area and advancing until they break as **surf** on some shore.

swimmeret: An appendage on the lower side of a **decapod** crustacean abdomen, often the site of egg attachment. Technically, a "pleopod."

symbiosis: Describes two or more species living together without disadvantage to either. In some works the term implies positive benefit to at least one of the parties concerned, and this is the meaning favored by the present author.

taxon (pl., taxa): A group of organisms at any level in the hierarchy of **taxonomic categories;** any taxonomic unit, such as a particular genus, family, order, and so on.

taxonomic category: A classificatory category at any level in the hierarchy of classification. Includes all terms such as **kingdom, phylum, class, order, family, genus, species,** and all intercalary categories such as superfamily, subgenus, tribe, and so on.

taxonomy: The science of classifying living things.

teleological: Exhibiting a belief that everything exists for some purpose.

test: The hard outer covering of sea urchins and sand dollars, or the leathery jacket (**tunic**) of the **tunicates.**

tidal range: The vertical distance between high tide and low tide.

tide: The rhythmic rise and fall of sea level caused by the gravitational relationships among Earth, Sun, and Moon. May also refer to tidal currents, as when changing sea level causes water to run into or out of a harbor.

tide zero: An arbitrary tide level originally chosen as an aid to sailors; tide height is measured as so many feet and tenths of feet above or below zero. On the Pacific Coast, **mean lower low water** has been selected as the zero point.

tidepool: A spot in which sea water is trapped as the tide goes out. In the vernacular, often used to refer to the entire intertidal zone.

trace elements: Chemical elements occurring in minute amounts; in spite of their small quantity, some are essential to life.

trophic level: A rough measurement of position in a **food chain,** showing how far a given species is from the **autotrophic primary producers** that are the basis of all life. "This is the shark that ate the bass that ate the smelt that ate the copepods that ate the diatoms"; the shark is at the fifth **trophic level.**

trough: The lowest part of an ocean wave, between the **crests.**

tube feet: Organs of locomotion in most **echinoderms;** small flexible appendages operated partly by muscles and partly by hydraulic pressure.

tunic: The outer covering of the **tunicates.**

tunicate: A member of the subphylum Tunicata, which includes the classes Ascidiacea (sea squirts) and Thaliacea (salps).

umbilicus: A depression near the center of the body whorl on the lower side of a gastropod shell.

umbo (pl., umbones): In a clam shell, the projection (**beak**) of the shell above the **hinge.**

undertow: A fictitious steady current flowing seaward along the bottom on sloping beaches. No such steady flow actually exists; wave wash goes in both directions. (Not to be confused with **rip current.**)

upwelling: A process by which water is brought from lower layers to or near the surface; an upward-moving vertical current.

valve: A single section or plate forming part of an invertebrate's shell.

veliger: The planktonic second larval stage of **gastropods** and **bivalves;** usually has a shell.

ventral: Toward the lower part or under surface of an animal.

viviparous: Nurturing the embryo through placental attachment to the mother and bearing it alive.

water mass: A mass of water from a certain source, such as the melting of Antarctic ice; usually identified by its individual "T-S Curve," which is derived by plotting its temperature against its salinity at various depths.

water-vascular system: A system of tubes in the body of an **echinoderm.** Water is strained through the **madreporite,** enters a **stone canal** leading to the circular **ring canal** from which radial tubes branch out; from these, small lateral tubes extend to the **tube feet.**

wave height: The vertical distance from a **crest** to a **trough.**

wave length: The horizontal distance between two successive wave fronts, most easily measured from **crest** to crest.

wave period: The time required for a given wave to pass a stationary point.

zonation, intertidal: The distribution of intertidal flora and fauna in relation to tide level.

zooid: An individual member of a colony, not capable of existing as a separate organism.

zooplankton: The **heterotrophic** (animal) elements of the planktonic community.

zygote: A cell or nucleus produced by the union of a male and female gamete; a fertilized egg.

Selected References

Abbot, R. Tucker. 1974. *American Seashells*. New York: Van Nostrand Reinhold.

Allen, Richard K. 1976. *Common Intertidal Invertebrates of Southern California*. Rev. ed. Palo Alto, Calif.: Peek Publications.

Brusca, Gary J., and Richard C. Brusca. 1978. *A Naturalist's Seashore Guide*. Eureka, Calif.: Mad River Press. Covers the coast far to the north of us, but nonetheless useful and informative.

Brusca, Richard C. 1980. *Common Intertidal Invertebrates of the Gulf of California*. 2d ed. Tucson: University of Arizona Press. An excellent work with much information appropriate to our area.

California Coastal Commission. 1983. *California Coastal Access Guide*. 3d ed. Berkeley: University of California Press.

Carson, Rachel L. 1950. *The Sea Around Us*. New York: Oxford University Press.

Carefoot, Thomas. 1977. *Pacific Seashores*. Seattle: University of Washington Press. A guide to intertidal ecology emphasizing the Pacific Northwest.

Coe, W. R. 1940. Revision of the Nemertean Fauna of the Pacific Coasts of North, Central, and Northern South America. *Allan Hancock Pacific Expeditions*, First Series, vol. 2, pp. 247–323.

Cogswell, Howard L. 1977. *Water Birds of California*. Berkeley: University of California Press.

Cox, Keith W. 1962. *California Abalones, Family Haliotidae*. Fish Bulletin 118. Sacramento: California Department of Fish and Game.

Dawson, E. Yale, and Michael S. Foster. 1982. *Seashore Plants of California*. Berkeley: University of California Press.

Fell, H. B. 1963. The Phylogeny of Sea-Stars. *Transactions of the Royal Society of London*, Series B, vol. 246.

Fitch, John E. 1953. *Common Marine Bivalves of California*. Fish Bulletin 90. Sacramento: California Department of Fish and Game.

Fitch, John E., and Robert J. Lavenberg. 1968. *Deep-Water Teleostean Fishes of California*. Berkeley: University of California Press.

———. 1971. *Marine Food and Game Fishes of California*. Berkeley: University of California Press.

———. 1975. *Tidepool and Nearshore Fishes of California*. Berkeley: University of California Press.

Griggs, Gary, and Lauret Savoy (eds.). 1985. *Living with the California Coast*. Durham, N.C.: Duke University Press. The main thrust of this book is to point out the problems that arise when builders fail to reckon with the dynamic nature of our seacoast. In so doing, the editors and their authors present a useful detailed description of the entire shoreline.

Halstead, Bruce. 1965. *Poisonous and Venomous Marine Animals*. Washington, D.C.: U.S. Government Printing Office. In three big volumes.

Hand, Cadet H. 1954. The Sea Anemones of Central California. Part 1: The Corallimorpharian and Athenarian Anemones. *Wasmann Journal of Biology,* vol. 12, no. 3, pp. 345–375.

———. 1955. The Sea Anemones of Central California. Part 2: The Endomyarian and Mesomyarian Anemones. *Wasmann Journal of Biology*, vol. 13, no. 2, pp. 37–99.

———. 1955. The Sea Anemones of Central California. Part 3: The Acontiarian Anemones. *Wasmann Journal of Biology*, vol. 13, no. 3, pp. 189–251.

Hedgpeth, Joel W. 1941. *A Key to the Pycnogonida of the Pacific Coast of North America*. Transactions of the San Diego Society of Natural History, vol. 9, no. 26.

———. 1962. *Seashore Life of the San Francisco Bay Area and the Coast of Northern California*. Berkeley: University of California Press. Covers territory outside of our area but is full of useful general information; an exemplary little book.

Hopkins, Thomas S., and George F. Crozier. 1966. Observations of the Asteroid Echinoderm Fauna Occurring in the Shallow Water of Southern California. *Bulletin of the Southern California Academy of Science,* vol. 65, no. 3, pp. 129–145.

International Code of Botanical Nomenclature. 1983. Adopted by the International Botanical Congress, 1981. Boston: W. Junk.

International Code of Nomenclature of Bacteria. 1975. Published for the International Association of Microbiological Societies by the American Society for Microbiology.

International Code of Zoological Nomenclature. 1985. Adopted by the XXth General Assembly of the International Union of Biological Sciences. Berkeley: University of California Press.

Johnson, Myrtle E., and Harry James Snook. 1927. *Seashore Animals of the Pacific Coast*. Stanford, Calif.: Stanford University Press. A paperbound reprint of this pioneering work has been published by Dover.

Keen, A. Myra. 1971. *Seashells of Tropical West America*. Stanford, Calif.: Stanford University Press. Covers areas south of Southern California, but many species overlap. An admirable work in every way.

Keen, A. Myra, and Eugene Coan. *Marine Molluscan Genera of*

Western North America. Stanford, Calif.: Stanford University Press.

Keep, Josiah, and Joshua L. Baily, Jr. 1935. *West Coast Shells.* Stanford, Calif.: Stanford University Press.

Kozloff, Eugene N. 1973. *Seashore Life of Puget Sound, the Strait of Georgia, and the San Juan Archipelago.* Seattle: University of Washington Press. This is another book to enjoy and learn from, even though its coverage is outside of our immediate area.

Leighton, David L. 1961. Observations on the Effect of Diet on Shell Coloration in the Red Abalone, *Haliotus rufescens* Swainson. *Veliger,* vol. 4, pp. 29–32.

Margulis, Lynn, and Karlene V. Schwartz. 1982. *Five Kingdoms.* San Francisco: W. H. Freeman. Sets forth the sequence of phyla used in the present book.

McConnaughey, Bayard H., and Evelyn McConnaughey. *Pacific Coast.* 1985. New York: Alfred A. Knopf. One of the Audubon Society Nature Guides.

MacGinitie, G. E., and Nettie MacGinitie. 1968. *Natural History of Marine Animals.* 2d ed. New York: McGraw-Hill.

McLean, James H. 1978. *Marine Shells of Southern California.* Rev. ed. Los Angeles: Natural History Museum of Los Angeles County, Science Series 24. The best shell book for our area.

Meinkoth, Norman A. 1981. *The Audubon Society Field Guide to North American Seashore Creatures.* New York: Chanticleer Press (a Borzoi Book).

Morris, Percy. 1966. *A Field Guide to Shells of the Pacific Coast and Hawaii.* Cambridge: Houghton Mifflin. One of the Peterson Field Guide Series.

Morris, Robert H., Donald P. Abbott, and Eugene C. Haderlie. 1980. *Intertidal Invertebrates of California.* Stanford, Calif.: Stanford University Press. By far the most complete work available; extremely useful.

Miller, Daniel J., and Robert N. Lea. 1972. *Guide to the Coastal Marine Fishes of California.* Fish Bulletin 157. Sacramento: California Department of Fish and Game.

North, Wheeler J. 1976. *Underwater California.* Berkeley: University of California Press. Useful for anyone snorkeling or scuba diving in California coastal waters.

North, Wheeler J., and J. S. Pearce. 1970. Sea Urchin Population Explosion in Southern California Coastal Waters. *Science* 67: 209.

Orr, Robert T. 1972. *Marine Mammals of California.* Berkeley: University of California Press.

Pickford, G. E., and Bayard H. McConnaughey. 1949. The *Octopus bimaculatus* Problem; a Study in Sibling Species. *Bulletin of the Bingham Oceanogr. Coll.* 12: pp. 1–66. This is the important paper that first distinguished between *O. bimaculatus* and *O. bimaculoides.*

Powell, Jerry A., and Charles L. Hogue. 1979. *California Insects.* Berkeley: University of California Press.

Reish, Donald J. 1972. *Marine Life of Southern California.* Long Beach, Calif.: The Forty-Niner Shops (distributors), California State University, Long Beach.

Ricketts, Edward F., Jack Calvin, and Joel W. Hedgpeth. 1985. *Between Pacific Tides.* 5th ed. Revised by David W. Phillips. Stanford, Calif.: Stanford University Press. Still the vade mecum of Pacific seashore naturalists.

Smith, Ralph I., and James T. Carlton. 1975. *Light's Manual: Intertidal Invertebrates of the Central California Coast.* 3d ed. Berkeley: University of California Press. This is the third edition of the classic "Light, Smith, Pitelka, Abbott, and Weesner," first published in 1954. Indispensable.

Straughan, Dale, and Richard W. Klink. 1980. *A Taxonomic Listing of Common Invertebrate Species from Southern California.* Technical Reports of the Allan Hancock Foundation, no. 3.

Tidelines, Inc. Published annually. *Tide Calendar.* Write to P.O. Box 431, Encinitas, CA 92024. Convenient and attractive wall calendars showing the daily tidal curves, with highs, lows, moon phases, and times of sunrise and sunset all expressly set forth. Separate calendars published for several locations on Pacific and Atlantic coasts.

U. S. Department of Commerce, National Oceanic and Atmospheric Administration. Published annually. *Tide Tables, West Coast of North and South America.* Washington, D.C.: National Ocean Service.

Index

References to species numbers used in this book are printed in boldface type. References to color plates are preceded by "Pl." All other references, including those for species mentioned only in passing, are to page numbers.

Editor:	Sean Cotter
Designer:	Nancy Warner
Compositor:	QuadraType
Text:	10/12 Times Roman
Display:	Helvetica
Printer:	Consolidated Printers
Binder:	Consolidated Printers